In her new book, Jan Abram continues the impressive endeavour to explore, discuss and develop the work of D.W.Winnicott. This time her personal voice is stronger. By offering the reader an Ariadne thread, through her clinical innovation of the intrapsychic surviving and non surviving objects, she takes the reader on a journey through the complexity of Winnicott's work, and her own reflections of its clinical and theoretical implications. She includes an abundance of examples from her clinical work, and a continuous dialogue with other psychoanalytic writers. This makes Abram's contribution not only helpful to the understanding of Winnicott, but also to several of the most important discussions in contemporary psychoanalysis.

– **Sølvi Kristiansen,**
Training and Supervising Analyst; Past President,
The Norwegian Psychoanalytic Society

Jan Abram has made this marvellous achievement showing that DW Winnicott's two-person psychology is three-dimensional, following her inspiring meeting with André Green. To illustrate her psychoanalytic journey, she makes heuristic use of Japanese Ukiyo-e so that readers may enjoy viewing the transient and transitional object together while learning from the author, and in the end, shall realize the object has survived intrapsychically.

– **Osamu Kitayama,**
Training and Supervising Analyst & Past President
Japan Psychoanalytic Society

In *The Surviving Object,* Jan Abram, the foremost Winnicott scholar writing today, discusses the way Winnicott reinvents the meanings of words as he goes, and uses the unique language he creates to convey understandings that analytic writing has never previously held. In this new work, she presents her own clinical work, which is strongly rooted in Winnicott's thinking, but is uniquely her own. She speaks with her patients in a way that is sometimes calming, sometimes confrontational, sometimes stunningly insightful, but always profoundly personal and humane. This is an extraordinary book that must not be missed.

– **Thomas Ogden**,
author most recently of *Reclaiming Unlived Life*
and *Creative Readings: Essays on Seminal Analytic Works.*

The Surviving Object is a significant milestone in understanding the richness of Winnicott's contributions to psychoanalysis. Jan Abram, a leading exponent of Winnicott's work, traces the evolution of his central concepts, with the detailed grasp of them for which she is known. She also traces how her own understanding of them has developed over time and found expression in her clinical work. Winnicott's ideas are carried forward in the process, and their links to French psychoanalysis in particular are valuably explored. This book is both an extremely useful survey of Winnicott's thought and a creative elaboration of it.

– **Michael Parsons**,
author of Living Psychoanalysis: From Theory to Experience

The Surviving Object

In this book, Abram proposes and elaborates the dual concept of an intrapsychic surviving and non surviving object and examines how psychic *survival-of-the-object* places the early m/Other at the centre of the nascent psyche before innate factors are relevant.

Abram's clinical-theoretical elaborations advance several of Winnicott's key concepts. Moreover, the clinical illustrations show how her advances arise out of the transference–countertransference matrix of the analysing situation. Chapter by chapter, the reader witnesses the evolution of her proposals that not only enhance an appreciation of Winnicott's original clinical paradigm but also demonstrate how much more there is to glean from his texts, especially in the contemporary consulting room. *The Surviving Object* comprises eight chapters covering themes such as: the incommunicado self; violation of the self; the paradox of communication; terror at the roots of non survival; an implicit theory of desire; the fear of WOMAN underlying misogyny; the meaning of infantile sexuality; the 'father in the nursing mother's mind' as an 'integrate' in the nascent psyche; formlessness preceding integration; and a theory of madness.

The volume will appeal to psychoanalysts and psychoanalytically-informed psychotherapists of all levels who are inspired by clinical psychoanalysis and the study of human nature.

Jan Abram is a Training and Supervising Psychoanalyst of the British Psychoanalytical Society and Visiting Professor of the Psychoanalysis Unit, University College, London. She has published several books and articles, notably: *The Language of Winnicott* (1st edition 1996; 2nd edition 2007), which was judged Outstanding Academic Book of the Year (1997); *Donald Winnicott Today* (2013); and *The Clinical Paradigms of Melanie Klein and Donald Winnicott: comparisons and dialogues* (2018 with co-author R. D. Hinshelwood).

THE NEW LIBRARY OF PSYCHOANALYSIS
General Editor: Alessandra Lemma

The New Library of Psychoanalysis was launched in 1987 in association with the Institute of Psychoanalysis, London. It took over from the International Psychoanalytical Library which published many of the early translations of the works of Freud and the writings of most of the leading British and Continental psychoanalysts.

The purpose of the New Library of Psychoanalysis is to facilitate a greater and more widespread appreciation of psychoanalysis and to provide a forum for increasing mutual understanding between psychoanalysts and those working in other disciplines such as the social sciences, medicine, philosophy, history, linguistics, literature and the arts. It aims to represent different trends both in British psychoanalysis and in psychoanalysis generally. The New Library of Psychoanalysis is well placed to make available to the English-speaking world psychoanalytic writings from other European countries and to increase the interchange of ideas between British and American psychoanalysts. Through the *Teaching Series*, the New Library of Psychoanalysis now also publishes books that provide comprehensive, yet accessible, overviews of selected subject areas aimed at those studying psychoanalysis and related fields such as the social sciences, philosophy, literature and the arts.

The Institute, together with the British Psychoanalytical Society, runs a low-fee psychoanalytic clinic, organises lectures and scientific events concerned with psychoanalysis and publishes the *International Journal of Psychoanalysis*. It runs a training course in psychoanalysis which leads to membership of the International Psychoanalytical Association – the body which preserves internationally agreed standards of training, of professional entry, and of professional ethics and practice for psychoanalysis as initiated and developed by Sigmund Freud. Distinguished members of the Institute have included Michael Balint, Wilfred Bion, Ronald Fairbairn, Anna Freud, Ernest Jones, Melanie Klein, John Rickman and Donald Winnicott.

Previous general editors have included David Tuckett, who played a very active role in the establishment of the New Library. He was followed as general editor by Elizabeth Bott Spillius, who was in turn followed by Susan Budd and then by Dana Birksted-Breen. Current members of the Advisory Board include Giovanna Di Ceglie, Liz Allison, Anne Patterson, Josh Cohen and Daniel Pick.

Previous members of the Advisory Board include Christopher Bollas, Ronald Britton, Catalina Bronstein, Donald Campbell, Rosemary Davies, Sara Flanders, Stephen Grosz, John Keene, Eglé Laufer, Alessandra Lemma, Juliet Mitchell, Michael Parsons, Rosine Jozef Perelberg, Richard Rusbridger, Mary Target and David Taylor.

For a full list of all the titles in the New Library of Psychoanalysis main series as well as both the New Library of Psychoanalysis 'Teaching' and 'Beyond the Couch' subseries, please visit the Routledge website.

The Surviving Object

Psychoanalytic clinical essays on psychic
survival-of-the-object

Jan Abram

LONDON AND NEW YORK

First published 2022
by Routledge
2 Park Square, Milton Park, Abingdon, Oxon OX14 4RN

and by Routledge
605 Third Avenue, New York, NY 10158

Routledge is an imprint of the Taylor & Francis Group, an informa business

© 2022 Jan Abram

The right of Jan Abram to be identified as author of this work has been asserted by her in accordance with sections 77 and 78 of the Copyright, Designs and Patents Act 1988.

All rights reserved. No part of this book may be reprinted or reproduced or utilised in any form or by any electronic, mechanical, or other means, now known or hereafter invented, including photocopying and recording, or in any information storage or retrieval system, without permission in writing from the publishers.

Trademark notice: Product or corporate names may be trademarks or registered trademarks, and are used only for identification and explanation without intent to infringe.

British Library Cataloguing-in-Publication Data
A catalogue record for this book is available from the British Library

Library of Congress Cataloging-in-Publication Data

ISBN: 978-1-032-07523-5 (hbk)
ISBN: 978-1-032-07518-1 (pbk)
ISBN: 978-1-003-20750-4 (ebk)

DOI: 10.4324/9781003207504

Typeset in Bembo
by SPi Technologies India Pvt Ltd (Straive)

For my mother and the memory of my father

For John, our children and grandchildren

and the mothers of our grandchildren

Figure 1 The Surviving Object.
An Ukiyo-e woodblock 'Kindergarten - Carp Fish' by Yōshū Chikanobu (1838–1912) Owned by Kumon Institute of Education (see Preface).

Figure 2 The Non Surviving Object.
Gouache on paper L'Esprit de géométrie (originally Maternité) by René Magritte (1898–1967) © ADAGP, Paris and DACS, London 2020. (see Preface).

Contents

	List of figures	xv
	Author	xvi
	Acknowledgements	xviii
	Preface	xxiii
	Why Winnicott?	1
1	Squiggles, clowns and Catherine wheels: violation of the self and its vicissitudes (1996)	10
2	The surviving object (2003)	33
3	The non surviving object: some reflections on the roots of terror (2005)	59
4	The fear of WOMAN/analysis: reflections on desire, infantile sexuality and psychic *survival-of-the-object* (2010)	77
5	On Winnicott's clinical innovations in the analysis of adults (2012)	94
6	On Winnicott's area of formlessness: the pure female element and the capacity to feel real (2013)	112

Contents

7 The paternal integrate and its role in the analysing situation (2013)   132

8 Fear of madness in the context of nachträglichkeit and the negative therapeutic reaction (2018)   145

Appendix: the dating of 'Fear of Breakdown' and 'The Psychology of Madness' and why it matters (2018)   164

Afterword: psychic *survival-of-the-object* in the context of Covid-19 (2020)   173

Abram Bibliography   180

Index   183

Figures

Figure 1 The Surviving Object.
An Ukiyo-e woodblock 'Kindergarten - Carp Fish' by
Yōshū Chikanobu (1838–1912) Owned by Kumon Institute
of Education (see Preface)   x

Figure 2 The Non Surviving Object.
Gouache on paper L'Esprit de géométrie
(originally Maternité) by René Magritte (1898–1967)
© ADAGP, Paris and DACS, London 2020. (see Preface)   xi

Figure 3 Basic Split in Personality Abram elaboration (1996)
of Winnicott's Basic Split in Personality (1952) (Chapter 1)   14

Figure 4 Inter-Related Self – enrichment through
relationship Diagram (1996) by Jan Abram (Chapter 1)   18

Author

Jan Abram is a Training and Supervising Psychoanalyst of the British Psychoanalytical Society in private practice in London. She is Visiting Professor of the Psychoanalysis Unit, University College, London where she convenes courses for the MSc in Psychoanalytic Studies. She is a Visiting Lecturer, Adult Department, Tavistock Clinic, London. She is a member of the Paris Group, a research group of the EPF and of a Working Party of the International Psychoanalytic Association for 'The Specificity of Psychoanalytic Treatment Today'. She was chair of the group between 2016 and 2019. Between 2011 and 2013 she was Visiting Professor for the Centre for Psychoanalytic Studies, University of Essex. Later, in 2016 was Visiting Professor at Kyoto University, Kyoto, Japan, which was a three-month writing sabbatical. During this time, she lectured, taught and supervised and co-authored with R.D. Hinshelwood, *The Clinical Paradigms of Melanie Klein and Donald Winnicott: comparisons and dialogues* (Routledge, 2018). During this sabbatical she also prepared the synopsis for this book – *The Surviving Object*.

Her present administrative posts include Chair of the Archives Committee of the British Psychoanalytical Society (BPaS) and Progress Advisor for candidates following their analytic training. She teaches on several courses for the BPaS, and runs clinical seminars. She is Vice President for the European Psychoanalytic Federation (EPF) (2020–2024) for the Annual Conferences and was formerly Chair of the Scientific Committee (BPaS).

Jan Abram has published several books and articles (see Abram Bibliography in this book), notably: *The Language of Winnicott* (1st edition 1996; 2nd edition 2007), which was judged Outstanding Academic Book of the Year in 1997; *Donald Winnicott Today* (2013) – shortlisted for the Gradiva Award for edited volumes; *The Clinical Paradigms of Melanie Klein and Donald Winnicott: comparisons and dialogues* (2018 with co-author R. D. Hinshelwood). She is presently in the process of preparing an introductory book, *Donald Winnicott: A Contemporary Introduction* for Routledge, and another book with R.D. Hinshelwood, *The Clinical Paradigms of Donald Winnicott and Wilfred Bion: comparisons and dialogues*. With R.D. Hinshelwood she is Series Editor for **The Routledge Clinical Paradigms Dialogues Series**.

For more details go to:
janabram.com
https://psychoanalysis.org.uk/authors-and-theorists/janabram

Acknowledgements

All the chapters in this book were originally written for an invited talk or conference. The synopsis for this collection of (mostly) clinical papers was carried out during a three-month writing sabbatical in the summer of 2016 when I held the post of Visiting Professor at the University of Kyoto, Japan. I have several people to thank for giving me this precious opportunity. Vic Sedlak, who had been the Visiting Professor in 2012, generously encouraged me to apply for the post. Professor Kunihiro Matsuki and Professor Ken Okano gave me a warm welcome and it was a pleasure to work with them in workshops and conferences during this time. It was a privilege to participate in a workshop with Professor Osamu Kitayama on the Japanese concept of 'amae', where I was introduced to the Ukiyo-e by Yōshū Chikanobu that Professor Kitayama used to illustrate Winnicott's concepts on holding and object presenting. His stimulating work on transience and his links with psychoanalysis and Japanese culture introduced me to many concepts and ideas that will continue to occupy me for many years to come (see Preface). I am also grateful to him for allowing me to use the Chikanobu woodblock picture to depict my concept of the intrapsychic surviving object. This Ukiyo-e is owned by the Kumon Institute of Education, Tokyo and I am grateful to Mr Yoshizawa for giving me permission to use the woodblock to illustrate the theme of this book. I say a little more about the art of Ukiyo-e in the Preface.

Chapter 1, 'Squiggles, clowns and Catherine wheels: violation of the self and its vicissitudes' ([1996] 1998; 2003), was written for the Winnicott Centenary organised by the French Institute and The

Acknowledgements

Squiggle Foundation in 1996. In that year *The Language of Winnicott* was published and I took on the post of director of the Squiggle Foundation following Nina Farhi, who had encouraged me in my work on Winnicott for several years previously when she was director of Squiggle. I will always be indebted to Nina Farhi and the Saturday seminars at Squiggle which offered so many opportunities for in-depth discussions on Winnicott's work. This experience gave me a veritable facilitating environment from which to develop my ideas alongside my early experience in private practice. I am grateful to Juliet Mitchell, who agreed to discuss some of my developing ideas in my early attempt at writing a clinical paper. It was she who recognised that my notion of a 'surviving object' was new and something worth developing.

In 1997, Zeljko Loparic invited me to participate in a conference in Sao Paulo, Brazil, for a Winnicott Conference and later in 1998 he proposed publishing the paper in *Natureza Humana*, a journal dedicated to Winnicott's work, of which he was editor. I am grateful to Professor Loparic for permission to re-publish the paper for this collection. But I am also indebted to Zeljko Loparic for many of those stimulating conversations on Winnicott's paradigm more than two decades ago. Thanks to Zeljko Loparic, the inspiration for editing the volume *Donald Winnicott Today* came to fruition.

Chapter 2 was written at the invitation of Le Groupe d'étude et de recherches psychanalytiques pour le développement de l'enfant et du nourrisson (GERPEN) and presented in French as a keynote paper in 2003 at a conference organised to celebrate the French translation by Cléopatre Athanassiou-Popesco, of *The Language of Winnicott*. The paper was later published in French in the GERPEN journal and subsequently the *Journal de la psychanalyse d'enfant* by the invitation of Didier Houzel, the editor of that journal. My gratitude goes to GERPEN and the *Journal de la psychanalyse d'enfant* for permission to re-publish it for this collection. With many thanks also to Cléopatre Athanassiou-Popesco for the translation as well as to René Roussillon and André Green for their Discussion papers on The Surviving Object, which were published in French in the Le Compte Rendu of GERPEN Volume 55 (2004).

Chapter 3 was originally presented to the British Association of Psychotherapists in 2005 (now the British Psychoanalytic Association and the British Psychotherapy Foundation) by invitation from Jean Arundale who was Chair of the Scientific Committee at that time.

Acknowledgements

Subsequently, it was presented to the Trauma Unit of the Tavistock Clinic, London, through the invitation of Dr Jo Stubley in 2006. I am grateful to both Jean Arundale and Jo Stubley for their friendship and colleagueship over the years. Later, it was translated into French for publication in the *Journal de la psychanalyse de l'enfant* commissioned by Didier Houzel in 2007. My thanks to Didier Houzel for permission to re-publish it here for the first time in English.

Chapter 4 was written for the 23rd Annual Conference of the EPF on the theme of 'Passion, love and sexuality' in London, 2010. It was presented in English and originally entitled 'On desire and female sexuality: some tentative reflections' and published in the *Bulletin of the EPF* No. 64. Later, it was revised for a Scientific Meeting of the British Psychoanalytical Society and published in the Society's Bulletin in July 2016 with a new title, as seen in Chapter 4. A version of the paper was given in Tokyo to the 2nd Asia-Pacific IPA Conference in 2018.

Chapter 5 was commissioned for the Controversies Section of the *International Journal of Psychoanalysis*. My thanks for the *IJP* invitation and for permission to re-publish it here.

Chapter 6 was invited by the EPF programme committee for the 26th Annual EPF conference on the theme of Formlessness in Basel. It was presented in English and published in the *EPF Bulletin* in 2013 (67). I am grateful to the EPF programme committee for the invitation.

Chapter 7 was originally prepared for an atelier led by Haydée Faimberg who had invited me to offer a paper in her atelier for the French Speaking Congress CPLF (2013) held in Paris on the theme of Le Paternel. A short version of the main argument was presented in French at that conference. A longer version was developed in 2014. This version was published in French for *the Journal de la psychanalyse de l'enfant*, commissioned by Didier Houzel, in 2015. It was later translated into German for the 'Zeitschrift für psychoanalytsch Theorie und Praxis' and published in 2016. It was subsequently presented at a Scientific meeting of the British Psychoanalytical Society in July 2015 and published in the Society's in-house *Bulletin*. It was also presented to the Japanese Psychoanalytical Society, in Tokyo and Fukuoka, and at a conference for the Japanese Psychoanalytic Association in Osaka in September 2016 during my sabbatical at the University of Kyoto.

Chapter 8 was commissioned by Johannes Picht for the German journal *Psyche* and it was translated into German and published

Acknowledgements

in 2018. I am grateful to Johannes Picht for the invitation. While Chapter 8 in this book is the first part of the original paper, which has only been published in German, I have slightly amended the Appendix of that publication to become the Appendix for this book, illustrating the value I hold for archival work.

The Afterword – 'Psychic *survival-of-the-object* in the Context of Covid-19' – is a short contribution prepared during 2020 originally prepared for a presentation to the Swiss Psychoanalytical Society, Zurich branch, in June 2020 by Zoom. Thank you to Susanne Richter who invited me. I also wish to acknowledge and thank Eva Schmid-Gloor of Zurich, recent Vice President of the EPF, for her longstanding support of my work and her encouragement for me to publish this book.

My warm thanks to Ofra Eshel for inviting me to present my work to the University of Tel Aviv, which was held online in 2020 because of the pandemic. I am grateful to Ofra Eshel, not only for her support of my work but also for her shared passion for Winnicott's work and thought and her own significant contribution to the advances in Winnicott's work.

Later, in November 2020, I was invited by Liz Allison and David Taylor to present the paper in a panel, alongside Claudia Frank, for the UCL virtual Conference – 'Contagion, Containment and Staying Connected'. Thank you to both Liz Allison and David Taylor for their invitation not just to present at the online conference but also to develop the paper for the book they are compiling of the conference. This short version seems to be well placed as an Afterword in this book and I look forward to elaborating on it for a longer version for the UCL book in 2021/22.

I would like to thank very many people who have supported my work over the years in a variety of ways and my apologies for not being able to name every single person. Students and supervisees, colleagues and friends, offer me much stimulation in my work on Winnicott and psychoanalysis. Special thanks regarding the preparation of this book go to Louise Lyon whose comments on the first draft of this book encouraged me to carry on with the project; Jing Wang, whose comments and questions at the early stages, helped me to clarify many points in my arguments; and Kathleen Kelley-Lainé, whose reading of the early chapters assisted me with me making more clarifications.

Acknowledgements

I am also very grateful to the three unnamed reviewers for the New Library of Psychoanalysis whose reviews were generous and rigorous and offered many ideas for some necessary revisions that improved the chapters. Alessandra Lemma's thorough critique and advice stimulated me to make some significant revisions during the summer of 2020. I am very grateful to her for seeing this book through as one of the final books she worked on in her role as Editor for the New Library of Psychoanalysis Main Series.

My very warm thanks also go to my psychoanalytic colleagues who agreed to write an endorsement: Dr Thomas Ogden from San Francisco; Dr Sølvi Kristiansen from Oslo, Norway; Professor Osamu Kitayama, from Tokyo, Japan and Dr Michael Parsons from London. I was very moved and most appreciative of their work on reading the manuscript and writing their endorsements.

Clinical work as an analyst would not be possible without the analysts who showed me the real meaning of psychic *survival-of-the-object* over many, many years. I will be forever in their debt. As well as my previous analysts I wish to thank my analysands, past and present, for their courage and trust in the psychoanalytic process with me. Thank you also to all supervisees, students and audiences for their searching and stimulating questions and comments.

As always, my infinite indebtedness goes to my husband John, as well as my mother and sister, and indeed every member of our thriving family, all of whom demonstrate how they intuit the true meaning of *survival-of-the-object*.

Preface

At the heart of this book is my proposal for the dual concept of an intrapsychic surviving and non surviving object. This proposal emanates from my interpretation of Winnicott's late formulations on the 'fate of aggression' in the psyche. 'Psychic *survival-of-the-object*' places the primary maternal relationship at the core of healthy emotional development before innate factors are relevant.

The themes and concepts presented in *The Language of Winnicott* (1996; 2007) and *Donald Winnicott Today* (2013 New Library of Psychoanalysis) constitute the framework for this book. My main aim in *The Language of Winnicott* was to clarify Winnicott's particular use of the English vernacular. In *Donald Winnicott Today* I set out to demonstrate the specificity of Winnicott's r/evolution in psychoanalysis. Both volumes illustrate how Winnicott's discourse with both the classical Freudian paradigm and the developing Kleinian paradigm of his epoch led to significant advances in psychoanalysis.

Further elaborations permeate the chapters of this book towards an amplification and extension of Winnicott's paradigm: the incommunicado self; violation of the self and the paradox of communication; terror at the roots of non survival; an implicit theory of desire; the fear of WOMAN underlying misogyny; the meaning of infantile sexuality; the father in the nursing mother's mind as an integrate in the nascent psyche; formlessness preceding integration; a theory of madness; and psychic *survival-of-the-object*.

The Appendix offers an account of recent archival research to expound my perspective on Winnicott's final conceptual preoccupations. The Afterword is a short clinical piece written during the pandemic of 2020.

A word on the pictorial representations of the surviving object and the non surviving object

In the 1990s I came across the painting by René Magritte of *L'esprit de géometrie* in a newspaper article that was reviewing an exhibition of his work in London. Underneath the photo of the painting the reviewer had written KEEPING MUM. I found the painting, especially with that caption, breathtaking. It seemed so evocatively to epitomise everything that Winnicott writes about in relation to early psychic trauma at the start of life. I've had a reproduction of the painting for many years and use it for seminars and teaching. As the concept of the non surviving object evolved, I found myself enlisting this picture to represent the intrapsychic non surviving object.

As I have mentioned in the Acknowledgements, I first came across the Ukiyo-e by Yōshū Chikanobu when I participated in a workshop during my sabbatical in Kyoto, with Professor Osamu Kitayama. I was very taken by the dynamic beauty of the picture to depict Winnicott's concept of holding and object presenting. A little later, while teaching students at UCL, I found myself enlisting the print to depict the intrapsychic surviving object. Later, in preparation for this book, it seemed to me the act of object presenting by the mother illustrated the themes related to the paternal integrate as I set out in Chapters 6 and 7 of this book. Without the mother's introduction of the third the developing infant will struggle to reach the capacity to discern the other as separate with a mind of her own. There are some further associations with the picture, as Osamu Kitayama has pointed out in his work on transience. Ukiyo conveys a sense of transience and 'e' means picture in Japanese. Kitayama has used this picture in his book *Prohibition of Don't Look: Living Through Psychoanalysis and Culture in Japan* (2010 Iwasaki Gukujutsu Shuppansha Co. Ltd.) on page 106.

The multitude of meanings that could be developed about my selection of these two pictures to represent the dual concept of the surviving and non surviving objects will have to wait for another day.

Jan Abram Vale of Glamorgan, January 2021

WHY WINNICOTT?

Everyday psychoanalytic practice alongside my work on Winnicott continues to be an inspiring and complementary adventure. The meaning of psychic *survival-of-the-object* has long been, for me, the vital Ariadne thread for my becoming and being a psychoanalyst. The themes related to Winnicott's final major conceptual achievement, central to my clinical and theoretical trajectory, is woven into each chapter in this book.

Winnicott suggested that the core problem for the human being was not primarily psychosexuality (as it was for Freud); nor was it the death instinct, (as it was for Klein); rather, it was the 'fact of dependency'. This observation placed the earliest relationship and the essential elements of the early psychic environment at the heart of the healthy development of the individual.

In 'The Use of an Object' Winnicott investigated how the human infant moves from object relating to object usage (Winnicott 1969), and identified the specific elements that facilitate such a development towards the capacity to discern the Other as separate. Formulating concepts on the specific dimensions of emotional development was his lifelong quest and took into account a 'recognition of the destructive element in the crude primitive excited idea' without resorting to Freud's notion of the 'death instinct'. I have suggested that while not being explicit Winnicott was referring to his major concept 'survival of the object' (Abram 2012 in Abram 2013: 308). Here, for the first time, I propose to write this concept as psychic *survival-of-the-object*, in order to designate its fundamental role as the core concept in Winnicott's theoretical matrix (Abram [2012] 2013: 308).

Survival-of-the-object refers to the crucial processes involved between object and subject that initiate healthy psychic development. Because it is only due to the object's psychic survival of the subject's primitive benign aggression, that the subject will be able to place the object outside in the world. This emotional achievement means the subject starts to be able to perceive the object as separate and differentiated. This achievement evolves from infantile apperception.

From this perspective, the subject's experience of the object's consistent psychic survival leads to an internalisation of the dynamics of this process. My interpretation of this process is at the root of my proposal of an intrapsychic subjective surviving object. The Japanese Ukiyo-e of a mother and infant, presented in Figure 1, is a pictorial representation that I have enlisted to depict the intrapsychic surviving object as an ongoing intrapsychic dynamic formed through the original interpsychic relationship. Conversely, the object's psychic non survival causes the dynamics of an intrapsychic non surviving subjective object that will also be internalised, as I expound in **Chapter 3**. The René Magritte painting as shown in Figure 2 thus represents an intrapsychic non surviving object rooted in the newborn's trauma and petrification in which the psychic environment had not survived.

As I propose in **Chapter 2** without the ongoing development of the intrapsychic surviving object, reinforced through the interpsychic relationship of a good enough parental environment from the start, the infant will not be facilitated to reach the stage of development that constitutes Freud's Oedipus Complex and what André Green has referred to as 'thirdness' (Green 1991). Without this facilitation the subject is consigned to remain in the phase of object relating in which there is a deficient capacity to distinguish Me from Not-me (Abram 2007: 34–38).

In the process of selecting and revising these clinical essays, I am ever more convinced that Winnicott's clinical-theoretical paradigm truly advances the fundamental themes in Freud's work. That is not to say his new paradigm negates Freud's monumental achievements; in fact, I do not think it possible to fully appreciate Winnicott's work without an in-depth understanding of the Freudian paradigm. However, I believe that Winnicott's final theoretical matrix offers new horizons for psychoanalysis in practice and theory. These new perspectives, therefore, constitute an expansion and advance on Freud's work.

The aim for this collection – *The Surviving Object* – is two-fold: firstly, to offer an account of how I understand some of Winnicott's specific advances in psychoanalysis and secondly to highlight the ways in which I interpret and utilise his language in my clinical psychoanalytic practice that have led to some further elaborations.

Chapter 1 illustrates how the notion of a surviving object was initiated predicated on Winnicott's core concept – psychic '*survival-of-the-object*' – in his late paper, 'The Use of an Object' (1969). The chapter starts with a reflection on Winnicott's concept of the Self and how it comes into being through the parent–infant relationship. This is followed by a consideration of the paradox at the heart of Winnicott's theory of communication in which he introduces the human need for an incommunicado self. These themes relate to his focus on the environment's powerful role for the formation of the nascent psyche, the sense of Self and the potential problems related to 'violation of the self'.

The clinical example depicts a specific situation in the therapeutic relationship that alerted me to the patient's experience of psychic violation. In identifying my affect as a countertransference response, I was gradually able to make a reflective interpretation to the patient that instigated a memory of a traumatic event in her childhood. This memory illuminated an intense maternal transference, and in my Discussion, I refer to how the subsequent incremental working through of early environmental and Oedipal elements led to changes in the patient's life.

To complete **Chapter 1** I reflect on Marion Milner's challenge to Winnicott about his concept of an incommunicado self, and I highlight some of their different perspectives. In my conclusions I argue that Milner follows Freud and disagrees with Winnicott on the notion of an incommunicado self. I suggest that Winnicott offers a perspective which has implications for technique in clinical work in relation to the patient's need not to communicate.

Chapter 2 is my early attempt to develop the notion of an intra-psychic surviving object. This formulation was instigated by working with a patient who struggled to survive psychically, indicating that her non surviving object was more powerful and eclipsed her surviving object. Over the course of several years' analysis at 4 x weekly I highlight the way in which the patient's screen memories depicted an oscillation between psychic survival and non survival of the object in her childhood and how this was manifested in the transference. In the Discussion to **Chapter 2** André Green's work is referred to especially his concept of the 'dead mother complex' that resonated strongly with the patient's psychic history (Green 1986). In my conclusions I link Green's 'dead mother complex' with the notion of non survival of the object.

My personal experience of almost total non survival occurred when working with a patient who became violent in the 2nd year of analysis. This led to a focus on the meaning of non survival and the intrapsychic non surviving object as a concept is elaborated in **Chapter 3**. In that analysis I was taken to an extreme countertransference reaction that made me question the value of psychoanalysis as a treatment. The sense of dread and terror experienced by both patient and analyst led me to consider terminating the treatment. But a turning point arose which changed the course of the treatment. In **Chapter 3** I propose that the roots of terror are founded on the early parent–infant relationship in which the m/Other has not psychically survived the infant's raw needy communications. Thus, an intrapsychic non surviving object is necessarily ignited in the transference of the analysing situation.

In the Discussion of **Chapter 3** I refer to the theories of early female analysts on the dread of women, the perforation complex and the maternal erotic transference. While some of these theories assisted in understanding what had occurred in the transference, the main theme again centres on Winnicott's notion of psychic *survival-of-the-object* and how non survival has to occur in any given analysis before there is a chance of working through the early environmental failures. Some questions on Winnicott's perspectives concerning Freud's concept of the Oedipus complex as a developmental achievement are also included in this chapter to show that for Winnicott the Oedipus complex is not a given in human development. The issue of the 'turning point' in this chapter was explored a few years later as illustrated in **Chapter 7**.

In **Chapter 4** I examine the ways in which Winnicott's emphasis of psychic survival extends Freud's core theory of psychosexuality. The inspiration for this exploration was initiated in discussion with André Green in 2003 who thought that Winnicott's theory ignored psychosexuality (Green 2003). But I argue that because of Winnicott's focus on early psychic development, psychosexuality is not primary but secondary. In my work with a female patient whose fear of analysis was inextricably linked with her fear of dependency I show how sexual development was terrifying due to the deficiencies in the early parent–infant relationship.

Very similar to the patients discussed in **Chapters 1 and 2** the central anxieties emerging in the transference were wholly caught up with the developmental step of becoming a woman. The patient's fear of her hidden feelings of (Oedipal) desires led to my reflections on the concept of desire in Winnicott's work.

In this chapter I propose there is an implied theory of desire in Winnicott's work in which he distinguishes between needs and wishes. Winnicott had latterly proposed that the fear of WOMAN was rooted in the fear of dependency (see Abram 2007: 135). In reference to the patient's wish to hide her desire from her analyst, for fear of envy and rivalry, I try to illustrate the way in which psychic *survival-of-the-object* operates in analysis. While Oedipal development in the context of the transference is ever-present, my attempt is to show how prior to Oedipal issues being addressed the patient needs to evolve a capacity to develop an intrapsychic surviving object. In the Discussion I elaborate on Winnicott's late ideas about the fear of WOMAN and develop my original proposal (in the first edition of *The Language of Winnicott* in 1996), that the roots of misogyny in both men and women are located in the fear of WOMAN (Abram 2007: 135). This is finally linked with a different concept of desire to illustrate how Winnicott's ideas build upon Freud's classical paradigm but with a different emphasis.

Chapter 5 traces Winnicott's clinical approach in his 1962 paper 'The Aims of Psychoanalytical Treatment' and draws attention to some of his major clinical innovations that extend and elaborate Freud's metapsychology (Winnicott [1962] 1965). To this end I draw on the work of the French analyst René Roussillon, who shows how Winnicott made Freud's concept of narcissism a clinical concept by introducing how the mother's role in the formation of the Self is intrinsic to primary narcissism (Roussillon 2010 in Abram 2013). This is in contrast to Freud's concept of narcissism as solipsistic. I also enlist the work of Haydée Faimberg, who argues that Winnicott's concept 'fear of breakdown' intuited Freud's concept of nachträglichkeit and the technique of constructions in analysis (Faimberg 2009 in Abram 2013). A specific clinical example from Winnicott's late work is examined to illustrate the way in which he conceptualised and applied his countertransference with the meaning of nachträglichkeit.

Following on from the themes of temporality in Winnicott's work, **Chapter 6** examines the necessity for the early experience of 'formlessness'. The Discussion raises my questions about Winnicott's technique related to the analytic frame in relation to paternal and maternal functions. The notion of an 'integrate' from Winnicott's very late paper, 'The use of an object in the context of *Moses and*

Monotheism' (Winnicott [1969] 1989), and my proposal for a 'paternal integrate' starts to take shape.

In **Chapter 7** I develop the notion of a 'paternal integrate' that interprets and extends Winnicott's very late proposal of the father as a whole object from the start of psychic life. Following Winnicott saying 'there's no such thing as a baby' (Winnicott [1952] 1958: 99), André Green suggested there's no such thing as a mother and baby and proposed the notion of the 'other of the object' in the mother's mind (Green 1991 in Abram 2016). In **Chapter 7** I argue that the 'other' is de facto 'paternal'. With reference to **Chapters 2 and 3** in which I first proposed the dual conception of an intrapsychic surviving and non surviving object, I suggest in **Chapter 7** that the concept of a paternal integrate reinforces the notion of the surviving object. Conversely, the non surviving object indicates paternal integrate deficiency.

At the centre of **Chapter 7** I re-visit the clinical work with the patient K. as narrated in **Chapter 3** and focus on the turning point when a significant affective change occurred in me. It is that turning point in the treatment that I suggest was related to the necessity for the analyst's psychic work. I argue that it was the paternal factor, related to discussing the case with a colleague (who was enlisted as the third), that I believe instigated psychic change in the analyst that led on to psychic change in the analysand.

In my conclusions I explore the notion of the third in the analyst's mind that stems in origin from the analyst's paternal integrate. Drawing on Strachey's well-known concept of the 'mutative interpretation' I furthermore suggest that the analyst's third constitutes an essential ingredient of psychic *survival-of-the-object* and the mutative process (Strachey 1934). Thus, I aim to illustrate the role of the paternal integrate in the analysing situation.

Chapter 8 explores Winnicott's psychoanalytic theory of madness and breakdown that is firmly located in the earliest psychic environment in which the infant suffered unthinkable anxiety due to deficient ego protection from the m/Other. The psychic history of non survival will inevitably emerge in the transference and needs to be lived through in the analysing situation. Winnicott's term 'breakdown' essentially refers to the deconstruction of a fragile defence that has not yet evolved in the traumatised infant and therefore only thinly covers the underlying 'madness'. Madness is a state of mind in which nothing can be comprehended because the subject has no ego functioning due to a serious lack of ego protection from the psychic environment. Winnicott makes a specific distinction between psychosis and psychotic defences.

Emanating from work with a patient whose fear of death, murder and madness was a predominant feature, the psychoanalytic notions of nachträglichkeit and the negative therapeutic reaction were invoked. Drawing on Freud's concept of the negative therapeutic reaction and Riviere's extension of that concept I explore the work of Haydée Faimberg, where she makes a plea for a broader conceptualisation of nachträglichkeit (Faimberg [1998] 2012 in Abram 2013). **Chapter 8** offers some reflections on Winnicott's late theory of madness. While Winnicott's thesis has its roots in Freudian thought I propose that his specific psychoanalytic advances concerning the 'psychology of madness' argues against the notion of a death instinct.

Thus, I wish to propose that Winnicott's contribution to the concept of breakdown and madness in psychoanalysis offers a significant dimension that constitutes the essential hallmark of his work, i.e. the vicissitudes of the parent–infant relationship. And it is this hallmark that illuminates how his innovative contributions to psychoanalysis are radical – in practice and in theory – and are still in the process of being expanded.

In the **Appendix** I offer an account of my archival work on the dating of Winnicott's late paper 'Fear of Breakdown' and its twin paper 'The Psychology of Madness'. This work brought me to a different conclusion than that of both Clare Winnicott and Thomas Ogden on the year that Winnicott wrote 'Fear of Breakdown'. My findings correlate with André Green's Discussion to my original presentation of 'The Surviving Object' in 2003 (Green 2003) (see Acknowledgements). In his Discussion he stated that he certainly considered that the themes in 'The use of an object' preoccupied Winnicott's final years. In Part 1 of Chapter 14 in *Donald Winnicott Today* I have argued how my archival findings offer some important evidence on Winnicott's final preoccupations (Abram 2012 in Abram 2013).

The submission of the manuscript for this book, in early March 2020, coincided with the new global situation that arose from the corona virus pandemic. My reflections on having to exclude my patients from the consulting room, with no clear date of a return to normal practice, has forced me to think further on the meaning of psychic *survival-of-the-object* while undertaking what has become referred to as 'remote' analysis but which I prefer to refer to as 'online' analysis. In the **Afterword** I examine one of Winnicott's footnotes that he added to his paper 'The Use of an Object' when it was slightly revised for the 1971 publication of *Playing and Reality* (Winnicott 1971). The footnote states that it is impossible to avail the patient the opportunity for maximum destructiveness in the analytic work if the patient arrives to the session carrying a revolver. During the pandemic the analysing situation was initially a place in which it was as if both patient and analyst were carrying a revolver. This was more so for the older analyst. This raised, I suggest, one of the vital questions about analytic work during the pandemic of 2020. How is it possible, to offer the patient an opportunity for an authentic experience of psychic *survival-of-the-object* when the analyst is either online or at two metres' distance and wearing a mask?

References

Abram, J. (2007) *The Language of Winnicott: a dictionary of Winnicott's use of words*, 2nd edition. Routledge.

Abram, J. ([2012] 2013) D.W.W. Notes for the Vienna Congress 1971: a consideration of Winnicott's theory of aggression and an interpretation of the clinical implications. Chapter 14 in Abram 2013.

Abram, J. (editor) (2013) *Donald Winnicott Today*. New Library of Psychoanalysis. London: Routledge and the Institute of Psychoanalysis.

Faimberg, H. ([1998] 2013) Nachträglichkeit and Winnicott's Fear of Breakdown Chapter 8 in Abram, J. (2013).

Green, A. (1986) The Dead Mother in Green, A. *On Private Madness*, London: Hogarth Press 1986, pp. 142–173. Translated by Katherine Aubertin from 'La mère morte' *Narcissisme de vie, narcissisme de mort*, Éditions de Minuit, 1983.

Green, A. (1991) On Thirdness 39–68 in (2016 2nd edition) (ed. Abram, J) André *Green at the Squiggle Foundation* Karnac Books.

Green, A. (2003) Discussion of the Surviving Object Le Compte Rendu G.E.R.P.E.N. (2003 Volume 55).

Roussillon, R. ([2010] 2013) Winnicott's deconstruction of primary narcissism in Abram 2013.

Strachey, J. (1934). The Nature of the Therapeutic Action of Psychoanalysis. *Int J Psychoanal* 15: 127–159.

Winnicott DW ([1952] 1958) Anxiety Associated with Insecurity 97–100 in Winnicott DW (1958) *Collected papers: Through paediatrics to psychoanalysis*, 1st edition. London: Tavistock.

Winnicott DW ([1962] 1965) The Aims of Psychoanalytical Treatment 166–170 in Winnicott DW (1965) *The Maturational Processes and the Facilitating Environment Studies in the Theory of Emotional Development*, The Hogarth Press and the Institute of Psychoanalysis.

Winnicott DW ([1969] 1989) The Use of an Object in the Context of *Moses and Monotheism* in Winnicott DW *Psychoanalytic Explorations* Winnicott C, Shepherd R, Davis M, editors. Cambridge, MA: Harvard UP.

Winnicott DW (1971) The Use of an Object and Relating Through Identifications. Chapter 6 in Winnicott DW *Playing and Reality*. London: Tavistock.

1

SQUIGGLES, CLOWNS AND CATHERINE WHEELS

Violation of the self and its vicissitudes (1996)

Prelude

While all Freudian analysts expect their patients to lie on the couch and to say whatever comes to mind, why did Winnicott suggest that it was the patient's prerogative not to say whatever comes to mind? Despite his agreement on free association as an invaluable method for psychoanalysis his late proposal emphasised a paradox. While communication is essential and enriches relationships at the same time each one of us also has the right not to communicate even, and perhaps especially, at the very beginning of life and on the analyst's couch. Winnicott addresses the topic of communicating and not communicating and raises another important question on intrapsychic and interpsychic communicating: '…how to be isolated without having to be insulated?' (Winnicott [1963a] 1965a: 187).

What are the key elements to the capacity to feel real and to feel seen and recognised? Towards the end of his life Winnicott wrote a short and succinct poem to highlight his ideas on how a subjective sense of self comes into being. The process is contingent on being seen.

> When I look I am seen, so I exist.
> I can now afford to look and see.
> I now look creatively and what I apperceive I also perceive.
> (Winnicott [1967a] 1971: 114)

These lines speak for the infant who cannot use words and yet has reached the major psychic developmental point of being able to distinguish between Me and Not-me. The baby in the Ukiyo-e wood print (Figure 1) represents a good example of that developmental moment in which they had reached the stage of Relative Dependence (Winnicott [1963] 1965: 84). The baby still requires holding by the mother, but the mother intuitively knows that her baby is ready to be introduced to a third – represented by the carp fish streamer.[1] It indicates that this particular baby has internalised the experience of their mother's 'ordinary devotion' to every infantile need to such an extent that the ability to perceive Me from Not-me has been reached. Subsequent to that psychic achievement they are able to start the process of seeing another Not-me. The details of how the newborn achieves this psychic capacity was Winnicott's lifelong quest to understand and to formulate. The key to the analyst being able to discern the 'clinical infant' (Green & Stern 2005) in the adult lying on the couch is based on the profound appreciation of early psychic processes that emanate from the analyst's own 'clinical infant' (Winnicott [1967b] 1989).[2]

★ ★ ★

Even his name – Winni – cott – conjures up Christopher Robin's favourite transitional object and every baby's holding environment outside of mother's arms.[3]

In 1972, a year after his death, Marion Milner shared memories of her friend and colleague Donald, at a Memorial Meeting held by the British Psychoanalytical Society. 1957 – somewhere in France – the little clown she saw in a small town square, who appeared not to be able to do what the other acrobats were doing as he jumped up to the trapeze bar, but then suddenly when he finally did reach the bar, he whirled himself round faster than anyone else – delighting and thrilling the crowd – like a Catherine wheel. This was another of Marion Milner's images reminding her of Winnicott. The dark centre of the spinning firework reminded her of Winnicott's writings on the unknowable core self (Winnicott [1962] 1965c: 187).

One of the images I particularly enjoy of Milner's is a cartoon from the *New Yorker* of two hippopotami surfacing from the water with one mouth wide open. The caption underneath reads: 'I keep thinking it's Tuesday'. She showed this to Winnicott during WW2, and it was a joke they shared for years after.

The cartoon resonates with psychoanalytic preoccupations concerning the threshold of consciousness between the surface of the water as the place of submergence or emergence. There are several other Winnicottian themes depicted by this simple cartoon: transitional space, aggression, communication and friendship; the sharing of an experience of absent-mindedness, which is something that Milner herself was preoccupied with when she suggested that 'ordinarily' human beings 'think on two different levels in an oscillating rhythm' and emerging from absent-mindedness into a more conscious state of mind makes it difficult to know where we had been (Milner 1972: 195).

Good clowns, like good jokes, strike home, taking us to the essence of something inside us that is felt but may not yet be thought in the conscious mind. This is true of great poets, writers and artists and, to my mind, why André Green once said of Winnicott 'that he was the next greatest mind in psychoanalysis after Freud'.[4]

This essay is a reflection on Winnicott's concept of the Self and pays particular attention to the 'incommunicado self', as Winnicott describes it in 1963, and how this relates to Marion Milner's comments from her 1972 paper, 'Winnicott and the Two Way Journey' (see Milner 1972 in Abram 2013). The clinical example aims to illustrate these themes in the context of the analytic setting.

The Self

Winnicott writes that during a Scientific Meeting (of the British Psychoanalytical Society), he suddenly realised 'there's no such thing as a baby' (Winnicott [1952] 1958b). This realisation led to him to formulate his thinking on the nascent psyche at the very beginning of life in which he proposed a stage of development that preceded object relationships. This has become one of the hallmarks of his work and it was a radical proposal. At that time (circa 1942) object relations according to Kleinian theory were seen to exist from the start of life. By focusing on the merger between infant and mother at the beginning, Winnicott advanced the concept of primary narcissism (Roussillon 2010 in Abram 2013; cf. Abram & Hinshelwood 2018: 29–35). In 1952, Winnicott clarified what he meant by 'there's no such thing as a baby'. He considered that the 'centre of gravity' of each individual started off in the 'environment–individual set-up' or what he also described as the 'total set-up'. He referred to the shell as the parents who were gradually taken over by the kernel, 'which has looked like a human baby' ([1952]1958b: 99).

In the same year as presenting 'Anxiety Associated with Insecurity' he wrote another paper 'Psychoses and Child Care' and set out clearly what he suggested as the earliest patterns of relating. There is a healthy pattern of relationship and, conversely, a pathological pattern of relationship (Winnicott [1952] 1958c).

The essential point Winnicott stresses is that the pattern of relationship is set up from the very beginning and is absolutely contingent on the environment. In his late work he categorised two types of babies based on these proposals in both papers. Either the baby had been held or not. Up until the end of his life he maintained this position, i.e. that the mental health of the individual is founded on the earliest environment. Based on this theory, I have recently suggested that there are two Winnicottian babies: a baby who knows at a corporeal level what it means to be held and a baby who does not (Abram & Hinshelwood 2018: 46). This contrasts with Klein, who proposed that the paranoid-schizoid position is universal. For Winnicott, the state of mind depicted by the paranoid-schizoid position demonstrated a failure of the earliest stage of psychic development in which the infant had suffered gross impingement.

For Winnicott, there are two qualities of environmental impingement. A benign impingement is accepted by the infant because in the context of being held the baby is ready for an experience and therefore will be enriched by the impingement. Whereas, in the pathological pattern of relating, the infant is not emotionally ready and is obliged to react to the impingement. The impingement thus becomes a 'gross impingement', as Winnicott described because the infant's reaction (without thought) constitutes trauma. The emphasis here is that the subjective reaction to impingement is the cause of internal breaks in the continuity-of-being which distorts ordinary development.

From this same paper Winnicott introduces the notion of the 'isolate core self'. Here we see what could be described as a divided self.[5] Winnicott refers to the 'basic split in the personality' that is pathological and as a result of a failing environment. He suggests that a failing environment causes the individual to create a 'secret inner life' and this inner life is truly incommunicado because it has 'very little in it from external reality' (Winnicott [1952] 1958c): 224–225).

In the following diagram, based on Winnicott's original 1952 diagram, I add Winnicott's later concepts on the self: the true self in

BASIC SPLIT IN PERSONALITY

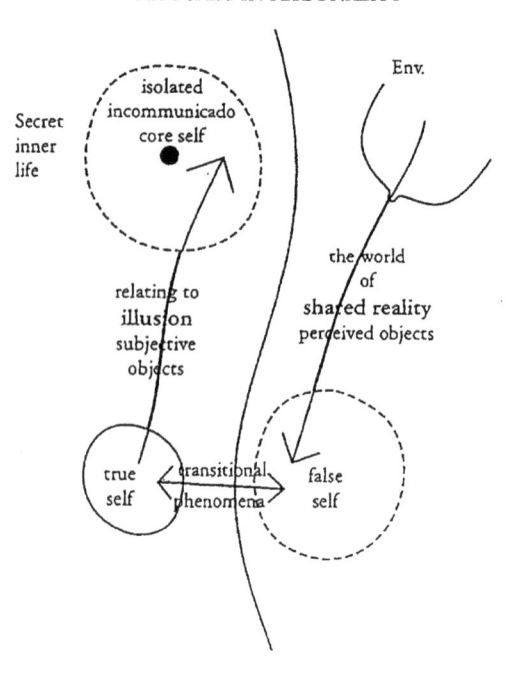

Figure 3 Basic Split in Personality Abram elaboration (1996) of Winnicott's Basic Split in Personality (1952) (Chapter 1).

relation to the false self and the incommunicado, core self as outlined in his paper on Communication in 1963 (Winnicott [1960b] 1965c, [1963b] 1965d).

Let me elaborate. In 1960, Winnicott writes 'Ego Distortion in Terms of True and False Self'. In this paper he outlines five different classifications of the false self that span from pathological to healthy. The false self is set up in the individual to protect the true self. At the pathological end there is a total dissociation in which the false self is not connected to the true self. But the 'healthy' false self signifies the individual's capacity to set up a necessary boundary between the outside world and the inside world. Therefore, there is a false self that constitutes a 'healthy split', because it protects rather than dissociates. Winnicott develops this notion later in his paper 'Communicating and Not Communicating Leading to a Study of Certain Opposites' (Winnicott 1965d) and introduces the notion of a healthy corollary to the pathological basic split of 1952. He proposes that there is a core self that 'never communicates with the world of perceived objects'. Furthermore, he suggests that this core self should never be touched by external reality because 'each individual is an isolate, permanently non-communicating, permanently unknown, in fact unfound' ([1963b] 1965d: 187). And this, he emphasises, is his main point i.e., communication for each human being is paradoxical: we need to communicate with each other and to be recognised but at the same time we are isolates and need to protect our inner core self.

For Winnicott, it is the failure of the environment in the earliest stages of life and the subsequent accumulation of painful, traumatic experiences that will lead to the individual organising primitive defences in order to protect the 'isolated core'. And to emphasise that violation of the self is more psychological than physical, he writes 'rape, and being eaten by cannibals, are mere bagatelles as compared with the violation of the self's core…' (idem. 187). Thus, the additions in my diagram (Figure 3) illustrate the healthy corollary of the pathological basic split in which the individual is engaged in the struggle of inter-relating 'without having to be insulated' (Winnicott [1963a] 1965a: 187).

Let us now turn to Winnicott's notion of the 'isolated incommunicado self'. Why must it never be communicated with and why must it always be 'permanently isolated'? Marion Milner was not convinced by this notion and questioned Winnicott's formulation.

In health, the withdrawal from relating is what Winnicott described as a 'resting place', and a place to 'be' and 'feel real'. This is something that preoccupied Winnicott's thought in his last decade, as seen in the collection of articles in *Playing and Reality* (1971). 'To be' and 'to feel real' are based on the experience of unintegration during the holding phase when, in health, the mother is in a state of primary maternal preoccupation. This experience of unintegration is a precursor to the capacity to enjoy, as we shall see.

Pathological withdrawal, however, is based on the experience of gross impingements from the environment in which the baby, who is not being held, has no other option but to react. This reaction, as indicated above, interrupts the continuity-of-being so that the place that should be for rest becomes a place of retreat from persecutions. Thus, violation of the self, according to Winnicott, constitutes 'communication seeping through to the inner core' of the self and later, in 1960, in his paper 'Theory of the Parent–Infant Relationship' he states that the impingements that the infant is not ready to respond to (rather than react to) will penetrate the 'central core of the ego' and this he adds 'is the very nature of psychotic anxiety' (Winnicott 1960a: 585). This infers that the core of psychotic anxiety is thus made up of accumulated cataloguings[6] of violation [of the self] from the beginning of life. This conceptualising is reminiscent of Marion Milner's image of the Catherine wheel, which has its origins in torture, punishment and death.[7] Milner questions Winnicott's notion of the incommunicado core self and while she understands what he means by integration emerging out of unintegration she writes that 'she feels fairly certain that, in the right setting' the core of the being can be connected with and can even find a place of re-birth. She follows this with her question on the body. What is the relation of the sense of being to the awareness of one's own body? (Milner 1972; 1987: 250)

If we turn to Winnicott's paper 'Psychoses and Child Care', as cited above, perhaps the beginning of an answer to Milner's question can be found in a footnote when Winnicott says that the awareness of one's own body is inextricably related to the environment–individual set-up ([1952b] 1958c: 222). By that time, he had already developed his notion of the psyche-in-dwelling-in-the-soma in his paper of 1949, 'Mind and its relation to the psyche-soma' (Winnicott [1949] 1954). For Winnicott, the awareness and relationship of the Self to one's own body is always associated with the environment-mother, i.e. the mother's body.

Survival of the object

Let us now turn to look in more detail at Winnicott's paper, 'The use of an object' (Winnicott [1968] 1969: 711–716), where he develops the above themes. In this paper, and across the whole of his work, Winnicott states that there can be no true self living, no creative living, no sense of feeling real, without the subject's experience of the destruction of the object and, absolutely crucial, the object's survival of the infant's destruction. The failing environment is one in which the object has not survived the subject's destruction. Whereas a facilitating and holding environment is one in which the object survives the subject's destruction, in the former it is the subject's experience of non *survival-of-the-object* that violates the core self.

The fortunate subject, born into a facilitating environment, is enabled, through *survival-of-the-object*, to feel real, to discover the sense of self in relation to the body and outside world and, above all, is able to enjoy life. For it is only through the enjoyment of life, through relating to others and Self, that the individual can be enriched and continue to develop and grow. It's important to remember that Winnicott stresses 'there is no anger in the destruction of the object': rather, there is a sense of 'joy at the object's survival' (Winnicott [1968] 1969: 93). This experience of joy is invaluable because it contributes to the subject's sense of reality and 'strengthens the feeling tone' ([1968] 1969: 716). As a consequence of this process, the object can then be used.

As stated above, Winnicott is very categorical about the distinction between a good enough and not good enough beginning. And later in his work he was very clear that there were two categories of people – those who had experienced a good enough holding environment from the start and those who had not. In terms of *survival-of-the-object* this infers there is only an experience of survival or non survival.

Here I want to suggest that in an infinite variety of ways the experience of survival and non survival is universal to a greater or lesser degree. Thus, the experience of 'violation of the self' and its vicissitudes could be seen to be an aspect of the human condition. But if we reflect on Winnicott's notion of the isolate/core self that must never be communicated with we will see a significant difference between the inner world of an individual who has experienced early trauma and an individual who has not. For example, if the intrapsychic surviving object (as depicted in the Ukiyo-e; Figure 1) is alive in the adult who is then traumatised for whatever reason in adult life, the surviving object will equip the individual to cope emotionally. In contrast, the adult whose intrapsychic non surviving object (as we see in Figure 2) eclipses their surviving object and who is then traumatised in adult life will cope less well. The present-day trauma will tune into earlier psychic deficiencies, amplifying the trauma. It therefore follows, I suggest, that because violation of the self is a result of the object not having survived the subject's raw aggressive needs, the patient seeking analysis will be motivated by an unconscious search for an object who will survive.[8] Winnicott's theory lends credibility to this notion despite the profound difficulties of working with borderline and psychotic patients with whom the analyst experiences a powerful unconscious motivation from the patient to prove that the analyst is completely ineffective. This is certainly the case in work with the extreme narcissist and the malignant hysteric in which the (so-called) 'negative therapeutic reaction'[9] dominates the analytic work. Winnicott's theories go beyond this manifest problem to show that these classifications are in fact defenses and thus the individual's negative therapeutic reaction may indeed be the only way in which they have to protect themselves from ever having to re-experience violation of the self. In **Chapter 8** I explore in more detail Winnicott's perspective on Freud's concept of the negative therapeutic reaction.

If we apply the notion of an unconscious search for an object who will survive, can we postulate that at the root of all creative endeavour the artist is searching for the object who will survive which, in turn, will bring about joy and enable the subject to 'feel real' and to 'live creatively'? The alternative to the artistic endeavour, or alongside it, is the analytic setting that constitutes a particular environment in which, through the transference, there is the potential for a patient to find an object who will survive. And this possibility could be available for them for the first time in their life. But psychic work is necessarily painstaking and cannot guarantee such a transformation.

In Figure 4, I attempt to illustrate the ideal integrated self who is able to distinguish between Me and Not-me, can meet the impingements of everyday relationships and can continue to develop, evolve and blossom.

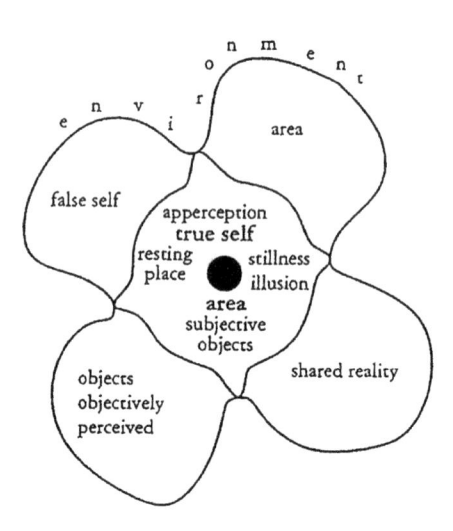

INTER-RELATED SELF

environment area

false self
apperception
true self
resting place • stillness illusion
area
subjective objects

objects objectively perceived

shared reality

enrichment through relationship

Figure 4 Inter-Related Self – enrichment through relationship Diagram (1996) by Jan Abram (Chapter 1).

The outer line of the diagram is the boundary between the environment and the healthy false self area which includes shared reality and the mature ego's ability to discern objects objectively perceived. The line that defines the inner self depicts the true self area in which the states of apperception reside with the layer of illusion and subjective objects. This innermost area constitutes the unconscious memories of 'being' that relate to the infantile in each human being. This is the area in which the 'clinical infant' resides. The analysing situation invokes the clinical infant to speak through the 'false self area'. If we take the diagram as a whole, we see an inter-related self who inter-relates between an infantile self who is historic, and an evolving self who continues to grow through an oscillating journey between inner and outer; between being and doing; and between past and present. At the centre of the Self, Winnicott proposes, there is an incommunicado self who must never be communicated with.

Winnicott makes a distinction between the 'incommunicado self' and the psychotic core self. Gross impingements on the newborn's incommunicado self causes the infant to defend himself, as we have seen, in the early pattern of relating. Thus, the psychotic core comes about as a result of cumulative trauma. This, following Winnicott, I suggest constitutes non *survival-of-the-object*, i.e. an environment that traumatises through gross impingements.

But, as we have seen, Marion Milner's perspective is that the incommunicado self, like the unconscious, surely 'in the right setting,... may be related to by the conscious ego discovering that it can turn in upon itself, make contact with the core of its own being, and find there a renewal, a rebirth?' Before addressing Milner's question, let us first of all reflect on the case of Faith.

Clinical example

Faith is the second child and the only daughter of parents who belonged to a fundamentalist sect whose philosophy was totalitarian. Their beliefs and membership of this sect rationalised their need to lead an extremely controlled family life that was completely predictable, down to which meal they would eat on a given day of the week. The children, Faith and her siblings, were assigned quite specific roles, which included the way in which they were named.

Faith says she always seemed to know that she was expected to be the perfect compliant daughter. According to her mother she was 'so good' even as a small baby, and as a little girl she remembers always trying to be as good as she possibly could be with the hope that she would be noticed. And people did notice her for a while, but Faith never felt it was enough, because, in reality, her good behaviour meant that she was mostly ignored. Therefore, if any of her thoughts were bad then being ignored exacerbated her feeling that she was indeed bad. These feelings had to be hidden by 'being good'.

According to Faith, her mother dominated the family. Her father, she said, was quiet and withdrawn and also compliant. Disagreement and anger were emotions that were never openly expressed. Faith had one memory of disagreeing with her mother. She was at the beginning of her adolescence and protested that she was surely old enough to go to the shops alone. Her mother sulked, as if mortally wounded, and ignored her for a while. In contrast to this memory, Faith said she had one memory of warmth from her mother. She remembers that her mother kissing her on the cheek one time. She giggled and ran away, feeling embarrassed. But she remembered that this kiss made her feel good inside. Momentarily, she felt that her mother had noticed her. This made her feel special and loved.

Throughout the years of twice-weekly psychoanalytic psychotherapy I came to learn of Faith's version of her well-meaning parents. The mother came across as cold, narcissistic and controlling while the father seemed remote and depressed. I had the impression they were both afraid of their own emotions and Faith said her father had a hidden secret past that nobody must ask about.

Faith's presentation of her original family life seemed plausible because her compliance and the anti-life atmosphere of the family were quite palpable in the transference. I was very struck how still she lay on the couch and, at first, I couldn't work out whether she didn't dare move or simply could not move. The atmosphere of each session was as if we were in a very sacred place where we had to be very still and very quiet. I found myself, at first, fearing to move too much, talk too much or even feel too much.

Faith sought therapy, she said in the first session, because she felt she needed some help with the thinking that she'd had to do on her own all her life. She said she knew at a deep level that she was not really living her life. The thinking she talked about in the first session, I believe, was linked with, among other things, a sense of a profound depression at having to stay so hidden ('disaster not to be found') (Winnicott 1963b) and a profound sense of guilt because she did not believe in her parents' staunch beliefs and could not accept from a very young age the fundamentalist teachings of this particular sect. This was the manifest reason why her sense of guilt also related to her 'bad' feelings, such as her rage, envy, hate and sadism. These feelings, though, took some time to come to the fore in our work. Initially, the help Faith knew she needed was to live her life so as to set herself free from the stifling atmosphere of her childhood that caused her, in some ways, to hide from herself the lurking aggressive emotions.

At some deep level, however, I felt that she had indeed found herself because she knew she was different from her parents. But she had not yet found a way of being herself with others and to declare herself to the world. For instance, on the rare occasions her parents visited her in her flat she would hide everything that she felt they would disapprove of. This would require quite an upheaval and several hours of going through her things with a fine toothcomb. She had long thought and accepted that this was normal.

There was a parallel process that also occurred in the therapeutic relationship. Her habit was always to arrive five minutes before time. On one occasion she arrived late, because of heavy traffic, and she felt flustered and afraid because she had not had the five minutes in the waiting area to prepare herself. We worked on the meaning of this and came to understand that it related to her fear of being exposed. While it was clear to me that this indicated Faith's fear of her aggressive feelings, all Faith could say in the early stages of therapy was that she was afraid of things inside herself that felt bad. So, the five-minute preparation time before the session started was a way in which she could tidy things away that she thought I would not approve of.

In the transference I alternated between her mother and the political leader of their sect: controlling, judgemental, and authoritarian. The atmosphere of each session was not dead exactly, but also not alive, and although there were some important changes occurring in her life, I wondered whether Faith would ever be able to break free of her past and feel she had the right to experience joy and happiness. Or was she going to live a life of deathly compliance, never daring to acknowledge her desires and how to achieve them (see Chapter 4)?

Faith was quite psychologically minded, and, despite her family background, I was impressed by how deeply she had been thinking on her own. She was highly intelligent and intuitive. Despite her extreme inhibition in the therapeutic relationship, as far as I could tell she had had a good education and had achieved a certain success in her vocational work. She talked about female friends she had, but I had the impression that she was lonely – even isolated – and longed for something else. Of course, as a woman in her mid-twenties she must have had concerns about her sexuality, but she talked about this rarely and had conveyed from the start of treatment that she could not imagine any man ever desiring her.

About four years into the therapy, I started to find the sessions more and more difficult to tolerate in relation to my concentration and had the experience of not being able to listen to what Faith was saying. For a period of several months, this experience increasingly dominated each session. She would enter the room, go to the couch and I would start to listen and then realise that time had gone by and I had not heard anything, and I would not know what she was talking about. On realising that I had not heard I would then make a concerted effort and for a while could hear the content of the first few sentences, but then the same pattern would recur.

The peculiar aspect of my reaction was that I did not really go into my own reverie whilst not being able to hear. It really felt as if I was disabled, almost as if I had lost my ability to hear. I had an image of an insulated glass wall in the middle of the consulting room dividing Faith on the couch and me on the chair behind her that prevented any possibility of sound getting through. As if we were both incommunicado. My desire to listen had not disappeared; in fact, I struggled painfully to listen and hear at each session. Gradually, it became clear that my inability, this loss of hearing, was a symptom occurring in the countertransference.

Faith had told me at a conscious level about her experience of her mother, but now it seemed that something was happening at an experiential level that, at this particular stage of treatment, could not be articulated. I wondered whether it indicated that I had become the mother who did not or could not listen to her daughter. Did this countertransference reaction make me feel Faith's confusion about who was who and whose pain was she feeling – her own or her mother's? Were we now reaching the layer of experience at the very core of the Catherine wheel, where, in a quasi-autistic state, I could not respond because I was so insulated? Insulation is caused by the need to withdraw from a grossly impinging environment, as Winnicott indicated.

At this point in the therapy, however, I did not know precisely how to deal with the situation because I had a feeling of paralysis.

While I was trying to understand I observed that Faith did not seem to notice that I had a problem with listening to her. On the contrary, she seemed to carry on as if I was listening. It subsequently became clear that Faith did not expect me to listen to her and indeed nor did she expect me to notice her. In fact, it gradually dawned on me that although she was arriving and departing for her sessions she was hoping (at some level) that I would not notice her.

But there was something paradoxical occurring: I was receiving double messages. On the one hand, I could not hear her and hardly noticed her and at the same time I came to notice, through my countertransference reaction, that she did not want to be noticed, and yet at the same time needed me to notice that she could not bear to be seen.

'It is a joy to be hidden but disaster not to be found' ([1963b] 1965b: 186). Winnicott reminds us of how we can be affected by the game of hide and seek. Somehow there is a length of time, which is just right between hiding and being found, and the game can be played satisfactorily. To be found too soon is tedious and humiliating, but never to be found can be agony. If the seeker gives up, gets bored, goes away and the hider has still not been found this can feel disastrous.

So, the session arrived one day when I found myself saying, just as the symptom of not being able to listen began to occur in the session:

JA: Although you are talking to me now, I think you do not expect me to listen to what you are saying.

There was a rather long pause. This did not disconcert me because it was characteristic of Faith's way of responding after I had spoken. On this occasion, rather than waiting for her response I decided to continue:

JA: In fact, I wonder sometimes if you do not expect me to even notice that you are here in this room with me.

There was another long pause and this time, although Faith was not speaking yet, through silent communication I felt the atmosphere changing in which she gained my full attention. She then said quietly:

FAITH: When I was little, I was in a car crash. My father was driving and my sister and myself were in the back of the car. It wasn't a serious crash, but I had a cut on my face which was bleeding slightly. I had to go to hospital to have it stitched. My mother was called, and she came to the hospital and when she saw me, she fainted. After I had the stitches put in, we all went home but I knew that my mother would not be able to bear seeing my face, so every time she came into the room I would go to the window and look out so that she didn't have to see my face.

In my consulting room at that time, both the couch and my chair behind it, faced the window. As Faith reported this scene, we were both facing the window and it became clear to me that my setting – the analytic space – was uncannily replicating Faith's experience of her mother after the car crash.

However, the incident (although it was an actual traumatic event) had become a condensation of Faith's psychic pain, i.e. that her mother could not bear to look into her daughter's face.

This moment in the therapy marked a significant turning point for Faith and heralded a more authentic transformation than had occurred hitherto. Following on from this session the work focused on Faith's exploration of her feelings that I, like her mother, could not bear to see the scar on her face. There were many sessions when she was able to explore more fully her associations to her scar related to femininity, sexuality, damage and menstruation. Faith began to talk about her wish to find a man and have a baby. In talking about her innermost desires, she could also report how afraid she was of discussing her feelings and felt afraid that I would not be able to bear hearing whatever she had to say. Alongside these fears were her real fears about something very bad emerging; for example, she had rather child-like images of monsters locked in cupboards. If the cupboards were opened, chaos would reign.

It became apparent to me that there was an aspect of the transference in which Faith had complied by lying on the couch from the start of treatment. In the early years of my practice, I had told new patients that I expected them to lie on the couch. Later in my practice I did not make this demand explicit and instead chose to wait and see how each new patient would respond to the couch in the room. This felt more facilitating.

Although Faith was lying down at the point of a breakthrough in the treatment, when my sense of not being able to listen to her faded, I nevertheless began to feel she was hiding on the couch due to being gripped by the maternal transference that made her convinced that I could not bear to see her face. After some interpretations that addressed my sense of the transference, for several months Faith explored her fantasies of what might happen if she were to sit in the chair. And there came a moment when she seemed to wish to make a move to the chair. I felt this had evolved in the work in which she could take the risk of seeing what would happen face to face. So, at the end of a session we agreed that she would sit in the chair for the subsequent session.

Faith was initially shy and embarrassed and found herself giggling like a small child. But it seemed to me for the first time, I saw her smile and laugh and demonstrate something akin to happiness. It reminded me of what she had said about her mother's kiss. Was it healing the wound through acknowledging the damage? Was the transference beginning to transform and could I now be the mother who would not faint facing the bleeding wound, but rather see her as a female in her own right and in being seen she could feel she existed?

After the initial novelty of using the chair, where I certainly began to witness a more alive patient, she occasionally went back to the couch, and each time I would experience something of the same inability to listen (although never quite as before), and she would feel she was hiding again and then return to the chair. Here was some sort of playing out of Winnicott's paradox of being a joy to be hidden but disaster not to be found.

Within a few weeks of Faith's use of the chair, our work focused on appetite, greed and an exploration of her aggression in all its forms. Faith was gradually able to show me many more faces and to talk about her desires and dreams. Her life began to change in a dramatic and remarkable way. For the first time in her life, she was beginning to show all the signs of living a life from her true self as she was in contact with her own desires. And her feelings of true happiness were also becoming apparent in all sorts of ways. This ability to experience 'jouissance' began to become a regular part of her life, and she came to understand her feelings of happiness as very much feeling good about being female. At last, she felt she could allow her true self to evolve. And while she was still isolated, as we all are, she no longer had to be insulated.

Discussion

At the beginning of the treatment Faith was suffering from an unidentified depression. She was not clinically depressed, I believe, because she was able to function quite well at work and she was able to develop good friendships. But her inhibitions and low self-esteem indicated that during her early psychic development she had internalised a non surviving object, i.e. an internalised experience of consistent non psychic *survival-of-the-object*. In the context of this essay and in Winnicott's language this would indicate that Faith's basic split in her personality came about through a deficient early psychic environment and therefore her pattern of relating was defensive. She had formed an intellectual false self that protected her true self, but it meant that she was not 'living creatively' and living in the world of real objects. However, her hidden true self was connected to the life force within her that stimulated her to search for an object who would survive. This search brought her to therapy, in the first place, and her intellect and intuition stood her in good stead to make use of the therapeutic relationship.

My countertransference experience of the sense of not being able to listen is an example of an actualisation, as described by André Green, which is related to the historical process that the analysing situation stimulates (Green 1987 in Abram [2000: 2016] 2016: 2) (cf. Chapter 2).

Faith's psychic pain represented by the traumatic memory of the car crash and her mother fainting at seeing her daughter's face in the hospital was actualised in the transference-countertransference. This affective experience indicated that Faith, probably from a very early age, had found herself protecting her mother emotionally (see Figure 2). In Winnicott's theory, this strongly suggests that Faith had suffered violation of the self because the mother's demand on her infant constituted a gross impingement. Faith had internalised non survival from her primary object throughout her development. This became manifest in the transference during the analytic treatment. This occurred not only at the moment when it was clear that she was hiding her face from me, but also after the experience of sitting up and returning to the couch whenever she wanted to. She felt free to experiment in her therapeutic treatment either on the chair or couch. This facilitated her own realisation that she felt safer on the couch because I could not see her scar. Returning to the chair continued for a while up to the point that she genuinely felt I could tolerate seeing her face. Once this alternating between chair and couch had functioned in quite a literal way Faith spent the rest of her treatment on the couch.

The unconscious communication of the primitive internal object relationship brought the traumata of the past into the centre of the analytic setting when I experienced the countertransference symptom, and this was how the 'the traumatic factors entered the psychoanalytic material in the patient's own way…' (Winnicott 1960a: 585 & 37).

When I was able to realise that the symptom, I experienced was actually the countertransference in relation to something Faith was unconsciously projecting (of the past traumata), I was then able to find a way of interpreting by simply verbalising my experience. When I acted on my countertransference experience by saying to Faith:

> 'Although you are talking to me now, I think that you do not expect me to listen to what you are saying' and after a pause when I felt she was listening, adding 'In fact, I wonder sometimes if you do not expect me to even notice that you are here in this room with me', a traumatic memory was invoked.

I suggest this was because Faith felt that I wanted to hear what she had to say which meant she could take a risk to tell me about her experience with her mother after the car crash. It is striking that she said the car crash was not serious and although this 'fact' may be true I think it illustrates that for Faith the most traumatic memory was that she had to hide her face from her mother for fear she would make her mother faint again (as she had the first time in the hospital). This past 'event', as I have tried to make clear, is a manifestation of something Faith had already experienced with her mother in early psychic development.

I would like to think that my interpretation at that particular moment of what felt like authenticity, was, in Winnicott's words, '… alterative' because it was 'made in terms of projection' (Winnicott 1960: 585 & 37). All analytic clinicians are obliged to go through a process of personal psychic work before they are able to make an intervention that has the potential to stimulate change in the patient. I elaborate on this further with all the clinical examples in this book.

The decision to facilitate Faith's wish to move to the chair from the couch was, I have argued above, based on my countertransference experience of her hiding on the couch. Interpreting how she had complied with my demand for her to use the couch at the beginning of treatment led her to explore the possibility of using the chair. I believe this freed her to experiment between the chair and the couch. It seemed to me that as long as she stayed on the couch her conviction of damaging me with her aggressive feelings would not shift. At that time in the treatment, I felt she needed to see the reality of my eyes looking at her face in order to feel safe enough to explore and work through her primary aggressive, hungry feelings. If she had not sat in the chair face to face, I felt there was a risk that either the therapy would have continued at a false self and dissociated level or that she may have retreated further into the psychotic, unthinkable anxiety of her isolated core self with the risk of becoming ever more withdrawn and possibly psychotic.

The experience of relating to another maternal figure who proved to be different from her experience of her mother seemed to enable Faith to experience, probably for the first time, a real experience of *survival-of-the-object* which vindicated the change. Face to face, she could destroy me (a de-construction of me as her mother in the past) that helped her start to discern the reality of her object world, i.e. an object objectively perceived rather than apperceived (Winnicott [1968] 1969). Once this psychic work had been set in process, face to face, Faith did return to the couch where, still destroying me (in unconscious fantasy), she could enjoy the value of a free association.

Milner's question about Winnicott's incommunicado self

Let me finish this essay with a word on Marion Milner's disagreement with Winnicott's formulation of an 'incommunicado self'. Her question suggests to me that she interprets Winnicott's concept as the Freudian unconscious and I think she is referring to the nature of the analytic work in analysis.

In reference to the work with Faith perhaps we could think about it in this way – that she had made contact with the core of her being and found there a re-birth. There is this potential for every analytic treatment when the traumata are re-visited in a different way because of being with a different object. This relates to Freud's notion of nachträglichkeit and the negative therapeutic reaction (see **Chapter 8**).

However, Milner's way of interpreting Winnicott's concept, it seems to me, does not take account of something fundamentally radical about his ideas that emanated from his clinical work. Let's examine this statement from 'Communicating and Not Communicating':

> At the centre of each person is an incommunicado element, and this is sacred and most worthy of preservation.
>
> ([1963b] 1965d: 87)

My reading here is that Winnicott is referring to the uniqueness of each human being that must be respected and left alone. This notion is related to the human right for privacy and, indeed, it follows that this has implications for psychoanalytic technique. Free association is what we want our patients to do and preferably on the couch. But recognising how some patients have been violated at the core of their being led Winnicott to advocate that all patients deserve the analyst's respect not to have to say everything that comes to mind. This also applies to the baby's need to be recognised for who she will become. One of the first reasons a mother hates her baby from the start, Winnicott proposed in 1947, is because the infant is not her own (mental) conception (Winnicott [1947] 1949: 73). The narcissistically disturbed mother is not able to recognise the uniqueness of her baby and has a need to mould him into something she feels she has created.

The defences that are built up by the individual who has suffered violation of the self emanate from a need to protect the isolated core self. This is why Winnicott refers to psychosis as a defence. It is a defence against the very real experience of violation and thus the psychotic defences are set up to protect the individual from infinite exploitation by an invasive and traumatising object.

Notes

1 While preparing this book I was in contact with Professor Osamu Kitayama, who kindly offered to write an endorsement (see inside cover). He told me that his wife and daughters did not think the infant in the Ukiyo-e was three months old but rather a little older, more like seven or ten months old. Mr Yoshizawa, who is the curator at the Museum in Tokyo where this particular Ukiyo-e by Yoshu Chikanobu is conserved, thinks the infant is at least one year old. We all agree that we don't really know. Still, I feel sure that the infant is at the earliest three months old and the latest ten months old. Whatever the age the print maker Chikanobu had in mind when he cut the wood, for me, the infant's stage of development depicts Relative Dependence (see the Entry on Dependence in *The Language of Winnicott*) (Abram 2007: 130–147). Another interesting piece of information from Professor Kitayama written to me in November 2020 was a confirmation that my interpretation that the mother was introducing the third to the infant with the carp-streamer, he said, 'is very appropriate', because the toy of the black Carp-Streamer that the mother waves in front of the baby is used to display good health and happiness for boys and is at the

2. Winnicott said that the 'chief result of the first five years of analysis' meant he was able to see that the baby is a human being (Winnicott [1967b] 1989: 576).
3. Christopher Robin is the child who was created by A.A. Milne in his book for children *Winnie-the-Pooh* (1926). Winnie-the-Pooh is a teddy bear and depicted in the illustrations as Christopher Robin's favourite toy bear. In the light of Winnicott's theories, Winnie-the-Pooh represents a transitional object. All British children would know this story and character. Winnie-the-Pooh has become more famous since the books have been translated into many languages and his fame as a star of Disney films has established him as a character most children are familiar with in the 21st century. 'Cot' is the name of the bed with safety rails for small babies.
4. Personal Communication 1996.
5. R.D. Laing published his book *The Divided Self* in 1960 about the same time he was in supervision with DW Winnicott, as he completed the analytic training at the Institute of Psychoanalysis.
6. 'By cataloguing, Winnicott is referring to an unconscious memory of a reaction to gross impingement, based on his belief that we remember everything that has happened to us, bodily and emotionally' (Abram 2007: 269).
7. This firework is named after St Catherine who was a Christian who converted many people to Christianity. She was condemned to death by the 'breaking wheel', which was an excruciatingly painful capital punishment in which the victim was tied to the wheel and then bludgeoned to death. In fact, Catherine did not die this way because when she touched the wheel it was shattered into pieces (wikepedia.com).
8. I developed this theme several years later in 2014 in a paper entitled 'From communication to non-communication: a search for an object who will survive' (see Abram 2014).
9. In Chapter 8, I argue that Winnicott's concept 'fear of breakdown' indicates that the so-called negative therapeutic reaction is related to the phenomenon of nachträglichkeit as opposed to the death instinct (Abram 2018).

References

Abram, J. (1996) *The Language of Winnicott: A Dictionary of Winnicott's Use of Words*, 1st edition. Routledge & P.E.P. Classic Books.

Abram, J. (2007) *The Language of Winnicott: a dictionary of Winnicott's use of words*, 2nd edition. Routledge & P.E.P. Classic Books.

Abram, J. (ed) (2013) *Donald Winnicott Today*. New Library of Psychoanalysis, Routledge, US & UK.

Abram, J. ([2012] 2013) D.W.W.'s Notes for the Vienna Congress 1971: a consideration of Winnicott's theory of aggression and an interpretation of the clinical implications In: *Donald Winnicott Today*. New Library of Psychoanalysis, Routledge, US & UK.

Abram, J. (2014) De la communication et de la non-communication, recherche d'un objet qui survivra, *Revue Belge de Psychanalyse*, no. 64.

Abram, J. (2018) Angst vor der Verrücktheit PSYCHE Zeitschrift für Psychoanalyse und Ihre Andwendungen 4/2018.

Abram, J. & Hinshelwood, R.D. (2018) *The Clinical Paradigms of Melanie Klein and Donald Winnicott: Comparisons and Dialogues*. Routledge.

Green, A. and Stern, D. (2005) *Science and science fiction in infant research in Clinical and Observational Psychoanalytic Research Roots of a Controversy* ed. Joseph Sandler, Anne-Marie Sandler & Rosemary Davies Karnac Books.

Green, A. ([1987] 2000; 2016 2nd edition) Experience and Thinking in analytic practice In: Abram, J. (ed) *André Green at the Squiggle Foundation*. Routledge.

Laing, R.D. (1960) *The Divided Self*. London: Tavistock.

Milne, A.A. (1926) *Winnie-the-Pooh*. Methuen & Co. Ltd.

Milner, M. (1972) Winnicott and the Two Way Journey. In: Milner 1987.

Milner, M. (1987) *The Suppressed Madness of Sane Men*. New Library of Psychoanalysis, London: Routledge.

Roussillon, R. ([2010] 2013) Winnicott's deconstruction of primary narcissism in Abram 2013.

Winnicott DW ([1944] 1945) Why do babies cry? *New Era in Home and School*, 1945, 26. In: 1964.

Winnicott DW ([1947] 1949). Hate in the countertransference. *Int J Psychoanal* 30: 69–74.

Winnicott DW ([1949] 1954). Mind and its relation to the psyche-soma. *Br J Med Psychol* 27: 201–209 & In: 1958a: 243–254.

Winnicott DW (1958). *Collected papers: Through Paediatrics to Psychoanalysis*, 1st edition. London: Tavistock.

Winnicott DW ([1952a] 1958b). Anxiety associated with insecurity. In: 1958a, 97–100.

Winnicott DW ([1952b] 1958c). Psychoses and Child Care. In: Winnicott 1958a.

Winnicott DW (1960a). The theory of the parent–infant relationship. *Int J Psychoanal* 41: 585–589 & In: 1958a.

Winnicott DW (1964). *The Child, the Family and the Outside World*. Harmondsworth: Penguin.

Winnicott DW (1965). *The Maturational Processes and the Facilitating Environment: Studies in the Theory of Emotional Development.* London: Hogarth. (International Psycho-analytical Library, No. 64.)

Winnicott DW ([1963a] 1965a). From dependence towards independence in the development of the individual In: 1965a, 83–92.

Winnicott DW ([1960b] 1965c). Ego distortion in terms of true and false self [1960]. In: 1965a, 140–52.

Winnicott DW ([1963b] 1965b) Communicating and not communicating leading to a study of certain opposites. In: 1965: 179–92.

Winnicott DW (1967a). Mirror-role of mother and family in child development. In: Lomas P, editor. *The Predicament of the Family: A Psychoanalytical Symposium*, 26–33. London: Hogarth and In: 1971 Chapter 9.

Winnicott DW ([1967b] 1989) Postscript: DWW on DWW In: 1989: 569–582.

Winnicott DW ([1968] 1969) The use of an object. *Int J Psychoanal* 50: 711–716.

Winnicott DW (1971). *Playing and Reality.* London: Tavistock.

Winnicott DW (1989) *Psychoanalytic Explorations.* Winnicott C, Shepherd R, Davis M, editors. Cambridge, MA: Harvard UP.

2
THE SURVIVING OBJECT (2003)

Prelude

This chapter sets out a more detailed proposal for the dual concept of an intrapsychic surviving and non surviving object. At the centre of my proposal is the case of Jill whose account of her childhood history was vividly lived out in the transference-countertransference and elaborates many of the themes introduced in Chapter 1. The focus in this narrative is how the patient's screen memories depict an oscillation between psychic survival and non survival that was intensely played out in the context of the clinical situation. In my Discussion, I refer to André Green's concept 'projective actualisation' and the 'dead mother complex'. I link both with the notion of psychic non *survival-of-the-object*.

★ ★ ★

In his late work Winnicott wrote that '…it is not possible to be original except on a basis of tradition' (Winnicott 1967: 370). This was aimed at his appreciation of Freud's work and I suggest indicates the gratitude he had for his first analysis with James Strachey. This is why the originality of Winnicott's work can only be fully appreciated through recognition that the theoretical foundations reside in Freud's metapsychology and symbolic matrix of psychosexuality. Nevertheless, Winnicott's theoretical innovations led to his view that psychosexuality and instincts in emotional development are secondary, as I referred to in the introduction to this book, in comparison to the effect of primary dependency on the evolving psyche. This focus draws on Freud's recognition that the infant's sense of helplessness (hilflosigkeit) has a significant influence on the structuring of

The surviving object

the psyche (Laplanche & Pontalis 1973). Klein's presence in his work is different. His discourse with the Kleinian development during the 1940s and 50s shaped many of his seminal concepts.[1] Therefore, in my view, Winnicott's theories offer such new perspectives that in the final analysis his work offers a new paradigm for psychoanalysis as I have proposed in *Donald Winnicott Today* (2013).[2]

The distinctiveness of Winnicott's epistemology is that at root psychoanalysis is a study of human nature. *Human Nature*, posthumously published in 1988, is a succinct account of Winnicott's contribution to the development of psychoanalysis. André Green has described human nature as a 'classical concept of philosophy' (Green 1997 in Abram 2016), and it is important to note that although Winnicott valued the complement of paediatrics and psychoanalysis, what he affirms (in the Introduction to *Human Nature*) is that there is more to learn about early infancy from the deeply regressed adult who is in analysis than there is from direct infant observation or even working with a very young child. In a late paper he clarifies this point when he says that 'early is not deep' ([1967a] 1989: 581). This is because of the factor of time in infant development. Depth starts between the ages of 1–3. Schizoid mechanisms belong to early and depression belongs to deep. The underlying message from Winnicott contains an oblique criticism of Klein's conceptualisations of early psychic development which he considered imbued the newborn infant with too much development.

Winnicott's theoretical matrix includes early and deep, but the essential core amounts to a clinical-theoretical model of Self-experience. The emphasis on subjectivity is one of the features of Winnicott's work that perhaps means more to the French intellectual tradition than the English empirical tradition and this is one of the reasons that his work has long been more appreciated in France than in London. In fact, Pontalis said that Winnicott's work rescued French psychoanalysis from the domination of Lacan (Birksted-Breen et al. 2009).

As I surmised in *The Language of Winnicott* there are three principal conceptions that structure Winnicott's work: the parent–infant relationship, primary creativity and transitional phenomena. These principal conceptions carry a range of nodal points across the whole of his work that constitute the fabric of the entire theoretical matrix (cf. Ogden 1986). Some of the nodal points are concepts in embryo, waiting, as it were, to be developed. Several have already been developed. For example, André Green has written about how his development of the concept 'the work of the negative' was inspired by Winnicott's 'intuition' of the negative when discussing the themes of absence and loss in *Playing and Reality* (Green 1997). As I hope to show here in my Discussion of Green's concept of the 'dead mother' the latter concept was also strongly influenced by Winnicott's late work.

The parent–infant relationship

Intrinsic to the sense of self is always the Other as first suggested by Freud through 'the shadow of the object' (Freud [1915] 1917). In 1942 Winnicott realised that *'there's no such thing as a baby'* ([1952] 1958b). Winnicott knew that Mrs. Klein and her followers dismissed his work and refused to acknowledge his thinking about the environment (Abram 2007: 164–181). Towards the end of his life he references their main criticisms when he asked, '…how to get back to the environment without losing all that was gained by studying the inner factors' (Winnicott [1967a] 1989: 577). But it may be easy to misunderstand Winnicott's use of the term 'environment', which actually refers to the m/Other's emotional attitude and feelings about her infant.

Primary creativity and the theoretical first feed

'Primary creativity' is Winnicott's term to describe the infant's biological instinctual force, i.e. the energy the baby brings to the mother from the beginning in the context of absolute dependency. The mother's reception of her infant's life force conveys the message, 'Come at the world creatively… it is only what you create that has meaning for you' (Winnicott 1967b: 101). Winnicott postulates three stages of dependency: absolute dependence (up to about three months); relative dependence (up to about nine months); and towards independence (for the rest of life).[3] For Winnicott, there is no such thing as independence but only ever inter-dependence. This emphasis on dependency in Winnicott's work is central to his theory (see Abram 2007: 130–147) and I suggest, as previously stated, that he was inspired by Freud's work on helplessness. The term 'theoretical first feed' refers to the process of internalisation: a gathering of feeding experiences which means the 'baby begins to have material with which to create' (Winnicott ([1953] 1988: 106). This is another important distinction between Klein and Winnicott. In Kleinian theory the infant is born with internal objects already in place. For Winnicott the infant is born with 'inherited tendencies' and a 'life instinct' because internal objects are not innate; rather they evolve out of the primary relationship with m/Other.

This quality of contact between mother and infant contributes to the baby's 'illusion of omnipotence'. This 'illusion' depicts the baby's belief, through experience of his needs being met, that his need (hunger) creates the breast (food). The mother's empathic attention to her baby's dependence and needs (rather than wishes) facilitates the 'illusion of omnipotence'. This is the crucial moment that propitiates all further development and is the outcome of the theoretical first feed. It is all dependent on the mother's ability to adapt well enough so that the baby 'assumes that the nipple and the milk are the results of a gesture that arose out of need, the result of an idea that rode in on the crest of the wave of instinctual tension' (Winnicott [1953] 1988: 110).

The wave of instinctual tension, e.g., hunger, is precisely what the mother has to adapt to. As long as she is able to meet these early and primitive needs then she is able to provide the 'theoretical first feed' but without consciously knowing she is providing this. At this stage the newborn baby is in a state of pre-ruth which is another way of defining primary aggression: it is benign. In Winnicott's late work, as we shall see, he describes the necessary destruction of the object and explores how the good enough object survives the baby's primitive need. Needs being met, as distinct from wishes being fulfilled, are essential to survival – physically and psychically. The stress in use of an object is that the actual destruction of the object and the object's survival of that destruction amounts to a complex psychic process.

Transitional phenomena

The concept of transitional phenomena refers to a dimension of living that belongs neither to internal nor to external reality; rather, it is the place that both connects and separates inner and outer. Winnicott uses many terms to refer to this dimension – the third area, the intermediate area, the potential space, a resting place, and the location of cultural experience.

Developmentally, transitional phenomena occur from the beginning, even before birth, in relation to the mother–infant dyad. This will occur in a good enough situation in which the mother's primary maternal preoccupation constitutes an unconscious transmission that facilitates transitional phenomena. And here is the location of culture, being and creativity.

As the infant begins to separate Me from Not-me, moving from absolute dependence into the stage of relative dependence, s/he makes use of the transitional object/s. This necessary developmental journey leads to the use of illusion, the use of symbols, and the use of an object. Transitional phenomena are inextricably linked with playing and creativity (Abram 2007: 337).

The intrapsychic subjective surviving object

Elsewhere I have written a detailed account of my interpretation of Winnicott's late paper 'The Use of an Object' (Abram 2012 in Abram 2013) in which I have proposed that it constitutes Winnicott's final theory of aggression. In this volume I have re-visited my interpretation of Winnicott's words on object usage in Chapter 1. In this chapter, while re-visiting the same themes I will elaborate on the specifics of the sequence Winnicott sets out in 1968 in order to highlight my proposal of an intrapsychic surviving object. In my view this concept is implicit in Winnicott's finely attuned observation of early psychic development.

At the core of 'The Use of an Object' Winnicott emphasises the relationship between the subject's destruction of the object and the object's survival '…after 'subject relates to object comes subject destroys object (as it becomes external); and then may come "object survives destruction by the subject"…'. The m/Other who survives her infant's (unintentional) destruction defines, for Winnicott, the 'new feature in the theory of object relating' (Winnicott [1968a] 1969: 713). This new feature in terms of psychoanalytic theory is, I have suggested, at the heart of Winnicott's theoretical matrix in which subjectivity is inscribed with the m/Other (Abram 2013: 1). This was a radical proposal because it shifted the psychoanalytic paradigm. In this new paradigm it is the external Other who significantly shapes the infant's nascent psyche rather than instincts or endowment. Let me add here that subjectivity is inscribed with the m/Other who both survives and does not survive. I address the notion of the non surviving object in Chapter 3.

Then Winnicott speaks for the infant when he writes, 'The subject says to the object: "I destroyed you", and the object is there to receive the communication' (Winnicott [1968a] 1969: 90). This is the point, I suggest, where Winnicott implicitly ushers in the notion of an intrapsychic surviving object. The key part of the sequence is that the object is there to receive the communication, i.e. the object who is able to receive the subject's loving destruction constitutes the object's psychic survival. Because of the object's ability, i.e. her primary maternal preoccupation, the subject is thus facilitated to experience that the object has survived her destructiveness. This constitutes a developmental achievement and from this point onwards the subject can relate in a new way.

The essential infantile experience as outlined above, I propose leads on to the establishment of an intrapsychic surviving object. Without the experience of the object's survival the subject is not able to internalise the specific experience that facilitates the evolution of an intrapsychic surviving object. Once internalised, the infant can slowly develop the capacity to distinguish between her projections and the integrity of the other. In other words, to discern the world rather than to project.

At first the intrapsychic surviving object is a 'subjective object'. The term 'subjective object' is the term coined by Winnicott to distinguish it from Klein's 'internal object'. The subjective object comes about in the stage of development that precedes object relations when the infant feels that everything she sees is Me (Abram 2007: 70). Therefore, the intrapsychic surviving object denotes that it is initiated through the experience of her needs being met during the earliest stages of merger. In that sense the newborn's surviving object has not yet become an internal object. It will become an internal object in the later stages of development when awareness of Me and Not-me is achieved. The ability to discern Me from Not-me is a sign that the infant has reached a stage of development beyond subjective objects. This means that the memories of having been survived by the object are established to form the intrapsychic surviving object. Therefore, the early 'intrapsychic subjective surviving object' is the foundation of the later established internal surviving object; provided the process of *survival-of-the-object* is consistently ongoing throughout infancy and subsequent childhood. In other words, the parents have to continue to survive the growing child's changing developmental needs based on the early interpsychic–intrapsychic dynamic of relating. A different quality of adaptation is required for each stage that depends on the growing child's needs at each stage.

Based on the proposition that the intrapsychic surviving object continues to grow due to a consistent psychic survival of the facilitating environment, I suggest that the surviving object continues to establish itself internally and that the complex emotional tasks during adolescence contribute to it becoming whole. I suggest that an internal whole surviving object only becomes fully established once the emotional tasks of adolescence have been completed (Abram 2014).

So, an established internal surviving object comes into being as a result of a developmental process that is ongoing from the beginning of life throughout childhood and reaches a particular peak of growth at the onset of adulthood. This constitutes, in parallel with the body and ego functioning, an essential feature of the internal world of object relationships, that, from the final stages of adolescence onwards, facilitate further consolidation, enrichment and growth (see Figures 1 and 4). The quality of the surviving object will come about through ongoing interpersonal relationships that feed internal objects which make up the individual's inner world of vital inner resources. This contributes to a meaningful life related to the capacity to live creatively (Winnicott 1970).

'Destruction' is intrinsic to the subject's capacity to move from object relating to object usage. The object has to be destroyed by the subject before it survives the subject's destructivity. Primary aggression and ruthlessness are intrinsic to primary destructiveness in Winnicott's language and inherently the life force in action. The infant needs an object to survive his destruction. Let me now explicate my interpretation of the five stages in the sequence Winnicott sets out in 'The Use of an Object'.

Subject relates to object

This is the newborn infant who is unaware of the care s/he receives and is merged with the mother during the phase of absolute dependence. The newborn is ruthless during this stage which is a state of pre-ruth, and cannot know the demands s/he puts on the environment; indeed, it is paramount that the baby is not made aware of what they are doing. The mother must protect them from being aware of how demanding they are. This ego protection allows the infant to get on with the tasks of being out of the womb and adjusting to the new predicament.

Object is in the process of being found instead of placed by the subject in the world

In a good enough environment, the baby's needs are met and this leads to the object being taken in and experienced, although this is not yet conscious. The baby cannot yet be aware that the mother/object is a separate Other. The process of finding out and moving towards more conscious awareness has to be given space and time. Further crucial processes need to take place before the infant will be ready to 'place the object in the world'.

Subject destroys object

The repeated and uninhibited ruthless demand for the environment's adaptation amounts to a continual destruction of the object. The ongoing destruction is not intentional, but rather a necessary process of 'discovering' the externality of the object. Winnicott's use of the word 'destruction' here, I suggest, is akin to eating. We have to destroy the food we eat in order to metabolise its value. Destruction in this sense means a psychic eating which does affect the mother both physically and mentally. Her ability to survive physically and psychically is because of her maturity and her ability to appreciate that the infant has no other option than to destroy everything she offers.

Object survives destruction

The mother's sustained capacity to tolerate the baby's endless demands because of her state of primary maternal preoccupation offers the infant a sense of continuity and reliability. The mother's psychic survival involves her primary identification with the infant's position of dependency that includes mirroring, ego protection, processing and crucially, non-retaliation. The myriad aspects of the good enough mother's survival enables the baby to move from apperception to perception in the potential space between relating to subjective objects to perceiving objects objectively perceived. This phase of the baby's life takes him from absolute to relative dependence as he moves from total unawareness to a gradual awareness of the environment.

The baby is beginning to perceive that the mother is part of the Not-me world. As the baby starts to see the same person in a different way so the previous imago of the mother is destroyed. The previous merger of the environment mother and the object mother that made the baby feel he had two different mothers due to such extremely different experiences of both, emanating from his stage of development, begins to change and he becomes aware of one mother. It is at this point that the infant can start to feel concern about what s/he does to the object mother. Winnicott says that the baby puts one and one together and makes one (Winnicott 1958: 267–268).

Subject can use object

The monumental step has now been reached. The baby can now communicate with some awareness of what he does to his mother. He has reached the capacity to play because of having a sense that the object has survived his ruthlessness. Now he can say with full meaning:

> 'Hullo object!' 'I destroyed you'. 'I love you'. 'You have value for me because of your survival of my destruction of you'. 'While I am loving you I am all the time destroying you in (unconscious) fantasy'
>
> (Winnicott [1968a] 1969: 713)

Here Winnicott, again implicitly, highlights two interlinked processes. The capacity to love comes about because the object survives. This surely suggests that the object's non retaliation and survival mean that whatever the subject makes the mother go through she does not stop loving her infant. And this is not masochistic. It is her (mature) love that survives the ruthless demands/attacks. This adds to the meaning of psychic *survival-of-the-object*.

Moreover, Winnicott's work on the destructive drive concludes that it is a process of loving emanating from what he describes as the 'combined love-strife' drive related to the 'natural maturational process' (Winnicott [1969] 1989: 245). Therefore, the process of loving another, whomsoever, means that there is always a process of destruction that inevitably occurs. This is based on the notion of an imago that is continually destroyed in unconscious fantasy. The act of loving, starting in a ruthless way but evolving into a concerned way, means that the internal imago has to change. In this sense the previous imago is destroyed because it is replaced by another imago. This depicts a normal process of getting to know the Other.

The first version of this paper was published in 2003. Since then, Thomas Ogden has published his reflections on 'The use of an object' (Ogden 2016). His central argument in that paper is that the mother really suffers the infant's destruction and inevitably communicates this to her infant. In principle I agree with this position and it reminds me of Winnicott's paper 'What Irks?' in which he describes how much the mother suffers along the lines that Ogden depicts (Winnicott [1960] 1993). So, I believe that Ogden's position is in line with Winnicott's appreciation of what a mother has to go through for her infant.

However, what Winnicott makes clear is that the mother's suffering should not be 'known' or, rather, 'felt' before the infant has reached a capacity to recognise what they did to the mother during the earliest stage. Winnicott's emphasis in relation to the infant's 'destruction' therefore, is that the mother should suffer silently because she must not convey how much she suffers… yet. Acknowledgment of the mother's suffering can only emerge when the infant reaches a stage of development in which the discernment of Me and Not-me are clarified. At that point the infant is able to say, 'I was ruthless then', referring to the past stage of immaturity. At this point a development of the capacity for concern is beginning to be reached. Until that point the infant should not be aware of the sacrifices mother has to make and therefore, according to Winnicott, she must protect the infant from knowing the 'whole' truth until reaching the capacity to understand that once the infant really was ruthless. This recognition of immaturity applies to the analytic setting when the analyst should 'allow for' a certain amount of acting out until the patient is able to recognise their destructiveness (see Chapter 3).

The external object (mother/analyst) sustains her integrity and a sense of difference and continues to survive through and because of her non-retaliation. In other words, the mother is able to tolerate the projections, fears and anxieties in her infant as well as herself. It is her empathy and understanding of how the baby must feel through her deep identity (primary maternal preoccupation) based on her own experience as a baby. The same mother, because of her maturity, is aware of the reality principle so that she is able to help the baby with the transition from merger to separateness.

Father's role is crucial here because he must separate the two from each other and the mother has to allow for this intervention in order to facilitate disillusionment from the illusion of omnipotence. That sequence of psychic events is an essential stage of development. The capacity to feel sad initiates, and is intrinsically a crucial aspect of, mourning for the lost object. But, as we will see in Chapter 7, father has a crucial role to play at the very beginning of the infant's life but only through the 'mind of the mother'.

Essential to Winnicott's theory in the use of an object is that 'There is no anger in the destruction of the object… though there could be said to be joy at the object's survival' (Winnicott [1968a] 1969: 715). It is this joy that relieves instinct tension and assists the development of the ego's ability to distinguish between inside and outside, i.e. 'internal reality' as distinct from 'shared reality'. This will lead on to the consolidation and shaping of the intrapsychic surviving object.

These five stages, as outlined above, are a condensed description of the forming of an object relationship from the beginning in the phase of merger. I suggest that they are in constant dynamic relationship throughout each interaction, throughout each stage of development, throughout life. But the dynamic sequence is initiated from the beginning before object relations exist. It is due to this process that object relations can start to evolve. And each stage of growing will have its specific tasks concerning the way in which the surviving object develops inside. I suggest that it is with the establishment and consolidation of the surviving object that desire is allowed full reign.

A word on 'desire'

The English word 'desire' is important as it evokes the emotions of sensuality, passion, longing and sexuality. I suggest there is an implicit theory of desire in Winnicott's work which I develop in Chapter 4. As early as 1945 in 'Primitive Emotional Development', Winnicott writes in a footnote that a satisfactory feed could spell disaster for the baby because he could feel 'fobbed off'. The facilitating environment adapts to needs, but the mother has to recognise the signs that the baby is developing and is increasingly able to think for himself. This is the period when the mother starts to de-adapt. This 'failure' assists the infant to move from the 'illusion' (of omnipotence) towards 'disillusionment' (Abram 2007: 200–216). This occurs as the mother ordinarily fails during the phase of de-adaptation as she recovers from her primary maternal preoccupation. This enables the baby to feel that his effort is rewarded. The roots of the capacity to feel desire, I suggest, are initiated during this period and are a precursor to the capacity to action desire. The surviving object is required to be fairly well established for the individual to feel free enough to desire. In Chapter 4, I examine Winnicott's implicit concept of desire in more detail.

Destruction and adolescence

Adolescence is another crucial stage of development in which the evolving surviving object may or may not reach its potential and Winnicott pointed out that '…if in fantasy of early growth, there is contained death, then at adolescence there is contained murder' (Winnicott [1968b] 1971).

It is a time of processing all that has occurred in childhood as the transition towards adulthood takes place. It is so manifestly physical, and the adolescent is really involved with destruction on all levels – interpersonally and intrapsychically. Hate and rejection are normal features at this stage as the adolescent struggles with the anxieties related to destruction and murder. The parents and family need to survive and the more they survive the more necessarily they will be tested for their resilience. The adolescent's negotiation of inner and outer worlds requires an external object that survives in a parallel way to the baby who needed an object to survive at the beginning. And yet it is also a kind of survival that is completely different from any stage that has occurred before or will occur in the future.

Destruction in fantasy is a crucial aspect of all mature interpersonal relationships and the more destructive the subject, in unconscious fantasy, the more the object is objectively perceived. This results in more intrapsychic integration and consequently less need to project in interpersonal relationships. The ruthlessness involved in mature relationships is not the same as the ruthlessness in the infant at the beginning, although it is akin and does have its roots in the early feeding situation. For example, a baby whose mother survives the passionate hunger of her ruthless baby by not feeling afraid of the attack and rage of her baby's hunger, will be facilitating the shaping of the baby's surviving object. But ruthlessness in maturity means that the individual is able to take responsibility for her own feelings and is able to distinguish between the Me and Not-me world. The consequence of this process leads to the subject's growing capacity to resist pressure from the Other to comply. This is the mark of integrity and the capacity to know one's Self. This refers to Winnicott's work on compliancy in the context of a true and false self (Winnicott 1960).

As I hope to have made clear, *survival-of-the-object* is required at each stage of development from childhood to adulthood and is part of the provision of a stable environment that contributes to the internalised continuity-of-being that facilitates the tasks facing each stage of development. I am proposing that the (internal) surviving object depends for its development on the interpsychic (external) *survival-of-the-object*, and that this essentially occurs right from the start of life. I suggest that adolescence is the last stage in which the surviving object can become whole – related to the achievement of all the complex tasks involved in a true separation which, as Winnicott has pointed out, amounts to an intrapsychic union in his 'Concept of a Healthy Individual' (Winnicott [1967b] 1986: 36).

When Winnicott names the first moment of integration the 'theoretical first feed' the inference is that there will be subsequent theoretical feeds, leading up to a theoretical final feed at the end of the stage of adolescence. This perhaps would constitute the true moment of separation through a complete, whole experience having been achieved.

I want to emphasise that the surviving object is not simply a developmental object steadily going along a line of development. The surviving object carries a history of the dynamic process of the sequence of object relating to object usage at each stage of development. The intrapsychic constellations and configurations are the sets of subject and object relationships that relate to each stage of development and are caught up with memories and achieved capacities. The 'whole surviving object' is a theoretical object that the subject works towards attaining, but can never really be attained, just as independence cannot be truly attained. The human condition is de facto a position of inter-dependence.

The notion of a surviving object can be applied to several psychoanalytic theories. For example, the resolution of the Oedipus complex I suggest requires a surviving object. Similarly, in Kleinian theory, the reaching of the depressive position is facilitated through a surviving object. And the capacity to kill the dead mother in Green's concept of the dead mother will also require a surviving object. The stage of development designated in the use of an object constitutes the pattern of development that is at the foundation of all future developmental tasks up until and including the moment of death.

The corollary to the notion of a surviving object is a non surviving object. The cumulative reactions to gross impingements will bring about a non surviving object, based on an external object that has not survived the subject's destructive impulse. This amounts to psychic trauma. A non surviving object often dominates the internal picture of the analysand and overwhelms, in some cases eclipses, the undeveloped surviving object. And this is where clinical work is relevant.

My clinical work alongside my study of Winnicott has fed my reflections on these concepts. In the analysis of men and women, especially between the ages of 22 and 40, I came to see that adolescent breakdown was often a feature that indicated a recapitulation of a breakdown that had occurred much earlier, as Winnicott describes in his paper 'Fear of Breakdown' (see Chapter 8). The analytic setting is perhaps the only setting that offers an opportunity for an undeveloped surviving object to start to grow and constitutes, in many cases, a recovery from childhood and adolescence.

The clinical picture

In a letter to a correspondent written at some point in his last two years Winnicott wrote that '…everything boils down in the end to… survival of the analyst'. He added that it may take years for the patient to feel confident enough to 'take the risk' of relating without protecting the analyst (Winnicott [1969] in Rodman 1987: 181).

Each analysis will go through its various phases where 'survival' is paramount, and the analyst is always engaged in psychic 'survival' as the patient moves from object relating to object use. With some patients, the quality of urgency may keep the analyst on the countertransferential edge. Jill was one such patient with whom it was necessary to go through several stages of non survival that tested my own intrapsychic surviving object.

Jill, in her early twenties, approached me for treatment because she had suffered a breakdown sometime before, related to an abortion she had felt forced to go through by her parents. Her main symptoms were panic attacks. A short course of behavioural therapy had worked for some time but now she was terrified that the techniques she'd learnt were beginning to fail. She felt clear that there was something else beneath her symptoms – something she felt she needed help with to understand. She told me that although she felt terribly ill at times, she always had a sense of herself deep inside like something as strong as steel that she could cling to. I felt this remote but deep sense of strength indicated an undeveloped surviving object and that this augured well for Jill making good use of the analytic space.

The course of analysis

I will now outline the course of the analysis up to the point that Jill created the scene that showed how '…a thing that has not been understood inevitably reappears; like an unlaid ghost, it cannot rest until the mystery has been solved and the spell broken' (Freud 1909: 122).

When Jill started the treatment, she was living in a shared house, and had a network of friends and colleagues. Meanwhile she was very dependent on her parents, and in phone contact with them every day. They seemed to wish to keep her in a state of fragility, like an ill child, who had no choice but to carry the family's sickness. However, Jill's psychological mindedness and capacity to make good use of the analytic setting meant that the symptoms began to decrease so that by the end of the first year they had almost disappeared.

In the second year of our work together Jill made significant progress. She changed careers to be more financially independent as well as to have a more regular way of life that fitted in with her boyfriend. She recognised how much she needed a regular structure in her life. They were planning to set up home together which, while being exciting, was also causing huge anxiety and it was at this time that the symptoms of panic reappeared. We came to understand Jill's profound anxieties related to the meaning for her of becoming a woman. She was sure that her parents would not be able to bear her growing up – surely it would kill them. Our work bore fruit as Jill moved in with her boyfriend and found to her astonishment that her parents did not kill her, nor collapse, and as she changed so she observed their capacity to change. This was one of the first developmental steps achieved in the analysis and suggested that the undeveloped surviving object was beginning to grow. The consolidation of this moment increased as the two couples of different generations could enjoy visiting each other and enjoying going out together.

By the beginning of the third year Jill was living happily with her boyfriend, and her new career was taking shape successfully. Her relationship with her parents and her siblings had changed significantly. At each new stage of development towards adult maturity,

Jill's anxieties increased, and there would be something of a negative therapeutic reaction[4] as she had to let go of old defences. But her ability to make use of the analytic space enabled her to understand and thus work through her anxieties.

Breaks were always difficult for Jill, as at these times the symptom of panic would reappear. In the early years there was often an acting out around holiday breaks of her not returning when the sessions resumed or cancelling the final session or two before my break. We came to understand this as her need to do to me what she felt I was doing to her. This was repeating the pattern she felt so strongly inside of there always having to be one left lonely whilst the other goes off with an Other.

The details of this dynamic emerged in a dramatic way when Jill made a mistake about a holiday break. It coincided with the anniversary of her first breakdown which made it a difficult time anyway, but this year Jill was planning to get married in early summer. Her anxieties about breaking down came into sharp relief as she realised how far she'd progressed in our work together and how well she felt and yet, as already stated, this progress brought about a negative therapeutic reaction. Plans for an elaborate wedding all contributed to the regression. We worked on themes related to 'fear of envy' and 'those wrecked by success' (Freud 1916). Jill became aware of her need to be ill, that she was nostalgic for those days. This was a far more comfortable position than the thought of being envied or hated.

The transference was dominated by me as the witch mother who was envious and angry and ready to kill her if she didn't swear total devotion to me, by remaining a child. There were times when it seemed we were on a tightrope; I wondered if the transference would tip over to a delusional transference. We parted for the break.

Jill had been away for the first week of the break and had enjoyed herself with her family finalising the arrangements for the wedding. She (mistakenly) arrived the next week for her sessions, although I had always taken a two-week break at that time of year. She arrived and said she had a feeling that someone was in the house but when I didn't answer the door, she felt frantic. That day she rang me and (because of an electricity cut) the message of the answer machine had defaulted to the computerised voice. This very much alarmed her, although she left a message saying, 'Where are you?' Her boyfriend (an ally of her analysis) told her that she must have made a mistake as 'it had never happened before'. Somewhere in her mind Jill knew that he was right, but she was 'taken over with something else' – a powerful conviction that I had been whipped away from her – as if the Martians had landed and simply taken me away. The second time she arrived, and I was not there again, she felt even more panicked and by the third time her feelings of murderous rage towards me were at full height as she was sure I was tantalising her and had been in the house all along. On that occasion, she spoke to someone in the house who told her I was away and would be starting back to work next week.

Jill now realised her mistake on the reality level, but she had been on an emotional roller coaster in which she experienced me as the abandoning mother. But Jill's creating this scene came to be very useful as we started back to work because it helped her to start working on areas of her emotional life that were buried deep within. Gradually, we could focus on Jill's rage and her need for revenge. What were the fantasies behind this rage? What did she imagine when I was absent? Jill felt embarrassed to admit how she was convinced that I was on holiday with my husband. She imagined I was in a wonderful place and was having an amazing time – with him and without her. She felt so left out. This brought up further associations and memories of how very excluded she always felt from the parents' relationship. Jill started to contact the memory of her feelings of triumph when her parents suffered because of not knowing where she was in her adolescence. Now there was no panic to defend her Jill began to see the part her feelings had played in relation to her parents.

The analysis of the paradoxical, conflicting and intense emotions contained in the event made it possible for Jill, for the first time, to acknowledge her rage, envy and jealousy towards her parents. She felt abandoned and didn't want them to be happy together. Fundamentally, she did not want them to be together. Why had her mother been so dismissive of Jill when she was little? She seemed so preoccupied all the time. And yet when the father came home, she was happy and attentive to him and ready to go out and have fun, leaving her children behind. As long as the parents rescued Jill from her panic attacks, Jill felt that her vengeful feelings on her mother succeeded. This action masked how much Jill longed for her mother's lively attention and love.

Thus, the couple became the object to divide and destroy. This meant, of course, that getting married would make Jill the target of the other's destructive and violent wishes. She thought that if she was radiant on her wedding day she would surely be hated. What she really ought to show was how much she suffered, so as to avert the envy. Her mistake about my break dates brought all these repressed feelings towards her parents intensely towards me in the transference. The whole experience of coming to my house for the sessions when I was not there confirmed her image of me as the fun-loving neglectful mother abandoning children at home alone.

Meeting the 'unlaid ghost' that had pushed its way through at the time of the break had provided us with the opportunity for forward development as the spell was broken through further working through. This enabled Jill to enjoy her wedding day and the subsequent honeymoon. But the ghosts were not properly laid to rest; further consolidation and working through continued as Jill's increasing development regularly caused a negative therapeutic reaction[5] and stressful phases.

This particularly came to the fore as, a year or so after the wedding, Jill and her husband began to think about having their own family. Jill was extremely ambivalent related to the earlier abortion. Month after month, Jill suffered the disappointment of not conceiving and interpreted the failure as a punishment by me who was condemning her to be a girl/daughter forever. After several months, while Jill struggled with her conviction that both her mother and me were the envious attackers, she had a positive pregnancy test. A few weeks later, however, she suffered a serious miscarriage and had to be hospitalised. This felt disastrous and confirmed Jill's conviction that she was not allowed to have a baby. She can only go so far. Survival came to the fore. The fact of the miscarriage made Jill feel completely identified with the fetus.

The trauma forced further work, mostly taking Jill back to her memories of her first pregnancy that was terminated. Retrospectively, she reflected that she had given her body to her mother as if to say, 'This is your body not mine' Jill came to recognise that her passivity at that time of her development when she did not take responsibility for her body was a way of taking revenge. She came to see that the pregnancy was a vengeful act towards her mother and came to understand that after the abortion she was in shock and felt as if she had been killed and punished for daring to prove that her body had the potential to replace her mother. She remembered the story of the Queen in *Snow White* who cannot bear the mirror to tell her that Snow White is the fairest in the land and who, disguised as an old woman, went out to poison Snow White at the point of her reaching early womanhood. And in the transference, at this layer of experience, Jill was convinced that I was the older woman/witch who could not tolerate the fact of her fecundity and ability to produce.

This is a layer where there is only one winner and one loser. It is either her or me. After the miscarriage Jill was gripped by her identification with a young boy in a novel she was reading at the time, who was trapped on a lifeboat with a Bengal tiger. How could he survive? To get off the lifeboat into a deep ocean full of sharks would end in death. But on the lifeboat, there was a hungry Bengal tiger. Jill saw this as depicting her experience of analysis – she could not leave for certain death, but equally, to stay on the lifeboat meant that she had to find a way of keeping me, the Bengal tiger, at bay and prevent me from eating her up. How could she possibly survive my immense power?

Jill was aware of how her unbearable envy and jealousy of her friends who were having babies was eating her up inside, and these excruciating feelings also related to me who, in her fantasy, had had lots of babies and led a perfect life. Like the survivor in the novel, she believed his first story of survival rather than the second. The second was too horrific to imagine – murder of a father and sibling, decapitation of a mother. His body survived but not his mind. This is not *survival-of-the-object* but rather non *survival-of-the-object*.

The events around the miscarriage forced Jill to re-visit her exasperation with her mother who she felt continually let her down by not being emotionally available. Meanwhile, Jill felt panicked that when she left a message for me to ring her, after being taken into hospital, she was sure I would not ring her back. Significantly she did not leave the right number for me to contact her. This moment made my heart sink with a sense of helplessness. This feeling, that I identify as one of non survival, was characteristic of the countertransference edge of survival or non survival that Jill's projective actualisations mobilised in me. But her husband reassured her that I would ring. He had more faith in me than Jill. In fact, he rang me himself and left the correct number. When I did ring her, she felt surprised as this is not what she had anticipated. But because of the phone call she was able to return to a sense of me as her analyst rather than the archaïc object of her psyche (cf. Chapter 7).

This is where I leave Jill's story. This is where we were, struggling to work through the primitive layer of actual survival represented by the boy on the lifeboat with the Bengal tiger which depicted the analysis during that phase. This represented the layer of infantile anxieties related to aggression and appetite. During that phase of the analysis, the Bengal tiger was experienced by Jill as her analyst in the transference. Gradually, following several more years of analysis, Jill came to be able to acknowledge her ferocious hunger caught up with her murderous wishes meant that she was the Bengal tiger as well as the witch mother. Both represented something powerfully destructive inside her. This overwhelming feeling of violent destructivity, I suggest, emanated from Jill's experience of psychic non *survival-of-the-object*.

Discussion

André Green discusses the difference between recovered memories in analysis and the 'witnessing of something historical' and deep within the psyche. He describes what he means by historical by saying that it is a combination of '…what has happened, what hasn't happened, what could have happened, what has happened to someone else but not me, what could not have happened, and finally… what one would not have dreamed of as a representation of what really happened' (Green 1987 in Abram 2016: 2).

In other words, there is no such thing as the real event because it is always imbued with the above variables that conglomerate at various developmental stages in our minds as a multilayered construction. Some will be conscious, but many will be memory traces forcibly repressed in the unconscious. Green says that a screen memory may be all that is left. Actualisation occurs all the time in all analyses and '…it is a thing that is entirely new and is created by the analytic situation, and which does not and could not exist, apart from the situation' (Green 1987). But when the memory traces push through in the form of a screen memory transformed into a scene, a piece of theatre, then we have what Green refers to as 'actualised projection'. This term refers to a 'process through which the projection not only rids the subject of his inner tensions by projecting them onto the objects, but also constitutes a revivifying and not a reminiscence, an actual traumatic and dramatic repetition' (Green 1980: 159).

The scene that Jill created by her mistake about my holiday dates constituted such a projected actualisation that was 'vivifying an actual traumatic repetition'. She vividly felt this in the visits to my house.

It was as if I was there – the house represented me – but I was not available and could not be engaged with because I would not open the door. This also had its tantalising feature that enraged Jill intensely. The tantalising mother[6] is the worst mother according to Winnicott, and the erratic environment produces the defence of over-intellectualisation (Winnicott [1949] 1958c) 1949: 246).

This projected actualisation yielded further development as Jill became painfully aware about the meaning of her mistake. Her terror of falling forever she said felt worse than death. This was depicted by her once witnessing a suicide from a great height. This is reminiscent of Winnicott's description of primitive agony; an unthinkable anxiety which is far worse than death. Death implies that there has been life and so there has been something; but an unthinkable anxiety is a catalogued trauma where nothing could be assimilated because there was no self to take it in.

This emotional memory associates to Green's blank anxiety of the dead mother complex (Green 1980). The main characteristic of the dead mother complex is the mother's depression and her sudden lack of cathexis in her child. The result is that the baby does not understand. This is similar to Winnicott's notion of unthinkable anxiety, although Winnicott dates that much earlier in development. From the observer's point of view there is a loss, but the subject does not feel it so much as a loss but rather as a loss of meaning. The trauma occurs because the holding environment suddenly, and with no warning, turns into a nothingness. And the subject is full of terror and confusion. This is what causes the narcissistic wound that constitutes a premature disillusionment associated with no love and therefore no meaning. This is what seemed to have been revivified for Jill on the occasions she visited my office. She said she just could not understand what had happened. She felt I was there, but not there for her, and she lost all sense of meaning in our work together over the previous years despite the positive support from her boyfriend.

Green points out that the narcissistic wound activates different defences and relevant to Jill's scenes I will mention two. Firstly, there is the releasing of secondary hatred. It is not fundamental, but the subject wishes to take revenge. Secondly, there is the quest for lost meaning. These defences serve to structure the early development of the phantasmic and the intellectual capacities of the ego and activate the compulsion to imagine as well as the compulsion to think. These themes are linked to Winnicott's concept of the intellectual false self that comes about as a consequence of a premature ego development as a protective device caused by violation of the self (Winnicott [1960] 1965). Jill's main symptom when she had originally broken down were her panic attacks. In the analysis, she had the tendency to use her intellect as a defence against psychic pain.

At the core of the dead mother complex there exists a fundamental fantasy of the prototype of the Oedipus Complex:

> The dead mother complex delivers its secret: it is the fantasy of the primal scene.
>
> (Green 1980: 158)

According to Green, contemporary psychoanalysis attests to the fact that if the Oedipus complex is the structural reference of the psyche 'the determining conditions for it are to be seen… in the isomorphic fantasy of the Oedipus complex: the primal scene' (Green 1980: 159). But there is a significant twist to Green's contention that is relevant to Jill's case. He states that the core primal scene in the dead mother complex matrix is not that the child has witnessed the scene (like the Wolf man), but exactly the opposite. It is the fact that the primal scene has taken place without the child present.

The memory traces of the earlier reactions to impingement, which constitutes the dead mother complex, are forcibly repressed. He says that a screen memory may be all that is left. But the fantasy of the primal scene at a later developmental date will '…set fire to the structure which gives the complex of the dead mother retrospective significance' (ibid.). The fire that gets set IS the 'projective actualisation', as already stated. So that although this scene took Jill through a primitive agony that related to an early developmental stage, it was the fantasy of the primal scene at the later developmental date that provided the retrospective significance within the analysis. And this was the area of psychic work Jill had to face.

I started to question whether the miscarriage could be viewed as a projective actualisation that took Jill back to the trauma of her first pregnancy, in order to give meaning to what happened then. This was an intense quest for her. But this time round, was Jill's pregnancy not only a projective actualisation but also an act of honesty? In a short note Winnicott wrote that if a woman becomes pregnant during the course of an analysis and the analyst is not able to interpret the patient's fantasies of her inside 'the patient may have a miscarriage almost as an act of honesty' (Winnicott 1989: 161–162).

In that same note Winnicott wrote that what needs interpreting is 'the fantasy of orgiastic functioning that is chiefly oral' (ibid.) in the transference. It seemed to me that the Bengal tiger invoked this violent orality level of Jill's infantile fantasies related to the early dyadic relationship.

In contrast, the Oedipal layer was invoked by the narrative of the narcissistic Queen, in the story of *Snow White*, who becomes full of murderous hate and jealousy when the mirror tells her that there is another in the land who is fairer than her, a young woman ripe and fecund. This is how Jill experienced me like the dead mother depicted by Green who demands loyalty which stifles development and inhibits the capacity to love. 'The lesson of the dead mother', Green asserts, 'is that she too must die one day so that another may be loved.' He warns, though, that the death 'must be slow and gentle so that the memory of her love does not perish but may nourish the love that she will generously offer to her who takes her place' (Green 1980: 172).

Jill's task in the analysis during that phase was to find a way of bringing this about, so that as her capacity to love grew she was able to love her baby and not fear him. This needed to be achieved within the analytic dyad in which Jill had the potential to discover meaning about the catalogued traumata to increase her capacity to tolerate psychic pain. In turn, this experience in the transference relationship helped her to go through a process of mourning. This was a way of exorcising the ghosts. The surviving object needed to grow towards full maturity to make this possible. The process helped dispel her alliance to the dead mother. It required my psychic survival in the transference alongside the fact of my death as the dead mother in the transference. We both had to work through the dynamics of destruction and survival before Jill could safely leave the lifeboat.

Notes

1 For a more detailed account of the way in which some of Winnicott's concepts emanate from his dialogue with Klein, see Abram & Hinshelwood (2018).
2 The main aim of *Donald Winnicott Today* was to demonstrate that Winnicott's work constitutes a Kuhnian revolution in psychoanalysis.

This project is still in the process of being developed and this book is a contribution to that process.
3 These chronological time spans are not rigidly set and vary from baby to baby.
4 See Chapter 1 endnote 8. In Chapter 8, there is an investigation of Winnicott's concept of madness in the context of the negative therapeutic reaction.
5 See Chapter 8 for my perspective on the negative therapeutic reaction.
6 This theme was elaborated in a paper commissioned in 2015 on a patient with a psychosomatic complaint (Abram 2015).

References

Abram, J. (2007) *The Language of Winnicott: A Dictionary of Winnicott's Use of Words*, 2nd edition. Karnac Books.

Abram, J. ([2012] 2013) D.W.W. Notes for the Vienna Congress 1971: a consideration of Winnicott's theory of aggression and an interpretation of the clinical implications. Chapter 14 in Abram 2013.

Abram, J. (ed) (2013) *Donald Winnicott Today New Library of Psychoanalysis*. London: Routledge and The Institute of Psychoanalysis.

Abram, J. (2014) De la communication et de la non-communication, recherche d'un objet qui survivra, *Revue Belge de Psychanalyse*, no. 64.

Abram, J. (2015) La Mère tentatrice. Réflexions concernant un aspect de la théorie de Winnicott sur le psyché-soma Revue française de psychosomatique no. 47 (37–50).

Abram, J. (ed) (2016) *André Green at the Squiggle Foundation*, 2nd edition. Karnac Books.

Abram, J. & Hinshelwood, R.D. (2018) *The clinical paradigms of Melanie Klein and Donald Winnicott: comparisons and dialogues* (Routledge London & New York).

Birksted-Breen, D. & Flanders, S. & Gibeault, A. (2009) *Reading French Psychoanalysis* Education Section: New Library of Psychoanalysis Routledge.

Freud, S. (1909) Analysis of a phobia in a five year old boy (SE 10).

Freud, S. ([1915] 1917) Mourning and Melancholia (SE 14).

Freud, S. (1916) Some character types met with in Psychoanalytic Work (SE14).

Green, A. (1980) The Dead Mother in *On Private Madness* (reprint 1997 Maresfield).

Green, A. (1987) Experience and Thinking in Analytic Practice In: (ed) Abram 2016 *André Green at the Squiggle Foundation*, Karnac Books.

Green, A. ([1997] 2000) The Intuition of the Negative in *Playing and Reality* In: Abram, J. (ed) 2016.

Laplanche, J. & Pontalis, J-B. (1973) *The Language of Psychoanalysis*, The Hogarth Press Ltd.

Ogden, T. (1986) *The Matrix of the Mind: Object Relations and the Psychoanalytic Dialogue*, Jason Aronson.

Ogden, T.H. (2016) Destruction Reconceived: On Winnicott's 'The Use of an Object and Relating through Identifications. *Int J Psychoanal* 97 (5): 1243–1262.

Rodman, R. (ed) (1987) *The Spontaneous Gesture: Selected Letters of DW Winnicott*.

Winnicott DW (1945) Primitive emotional development. *Int J Psychoanal* 26:137–143.

Winnicott DW ([1949] 1958c) Mind and its relation to the psyche-soma. In: 1958a.

Winnicott DW ([1952] 1958b) Anxiety associated with insecurity. In: 1958a, 97–100.

Winnicott DW ([1953] 1988) *Human Nature*. Free Association Books.

Winnicott DW (1958). *Collected papers: Through Paediatrics to Psychoanalysis*, 1st edition. London: Tavistock.

Winnicott DW ([1960] 1965a) Ego distortion in terms of true and false self [1960]. In: *The maturational processes and the facilitating environment: Studies in the theory of emotional development*. London: Hogarth. (International Psycho-analytical Library, No. 64.) 140–52.

Winnicott DW (1967). The location of cultural experience. *Int J Psychoanal* 48: 368–372.

Winnicott DW ([1967a] 1989) Postscript: DWW on DWW In: *Psychoanalytic Explorations* 569–582. Karnac Books.

Winnicott DW ([1967b] 1986) *Home is where we start from* ed., R. Shepherd & M. Davis. Penguin, 1986. New York: W.W. Norton.

Winnicott DW ([1968a] 1969) The Use of an Object. *Int J Psychoanal* 50:711–716.

Winnicott DW ([1968b] 1971) Contemporary Concepts of Adolescent Development and their Implications for Higher Education In: Winnicott DW (1971) *Playing and Reality*. Chapter 11.

Winnicott DW ([1969] 1989) The Use of an Object in the Context of *Moses and Monotheism* in Winnicott DW *Psychoanalytic Explorations*. Winnicott C, Shepherd R, Davis M, editors. Cambridge, MA: Harvard UP.

Winnicott DW ([1970] 1986) Living Creatively In: *Home is where we start from* ed., R. Shepherd & M. Davis. Penguin, 1986. New York: W.W. Norton.

Winnicott DW (1988a [1967b]) Communication between Infant and Mother, and Mother and Infant, Compared and Contrasted [1967] (1988) in *Babies and their mothers*. Free Association Books.

Winnicott DW (1988b) *Human Nature*. Free Association Books.

Winnicott DW (1989) A Note on the Mother-Foetus Relationship In: *Psychoanalytic Explorations*, 161–162 (eds) Winnicott C, Shepherd R, Davis M, editors. Cambridge, MA: Harvard UP.

3

THE NON SURVIVING OBJECT
Some reflections on the roots of terror (2005)

Prelude

The focus on non survival was instigated by working with a patient with whom I very nearly did not survive. Rather than being on the countertransferential edge as I described with Jill (Chapter 2), with patient K. my anxiety grew to a sense of terror and paralysis. The real failure of the analysis at a crucial point in the work could have been disastrous for us both.

During the period I worked with K. I found myself reading some of the biographies of Mary Wollstonecraft and was particularly struck by her tragic premature death a few days after giving birth to her second daughter, also named Mary. The latter married Percy Bysshe Shelley when she was 16 and became Mary Shelley, the famous author of *Frankenstein*. I wondered about the fate of Mary Shelley's psyche to lose her mother at such an early stage of her psychic development and the terrors she must have suffered. That led me to think further about the compelling narrative of *Frankenstein*, written in 1818 when she was 18 and pregnant with her second baby. I have recently suggested that *Frankenstein* may be seen as an emotional autobiography of Mary Shelley's innermost phantasies related to her birth phantasies based on the fact that her mother, Mary Wollstonecraft, died as a result of giving birth to her (Abram 2019). The popularity of the story, I suggest in my argument, is related to a narrative of alienation and non survival that resonates with every one of us. I go on to suggest that Mary Shelley in her pregnant state was identified with the fetus

inside her womb as a creature who would kill her while being born.
This conviction emanated from the fact of the death of her mother.[1]
This narrative, applicable to all of us in various forms, associated with
a universal experience of non survival, was particularly resonant with
the patient K. and his early unconscious phantasies. Each one of us
has a fantasy of a 'birth story' that contains a narrative of what we did
to our mothers when she gave birth to us and subsequently. These
deep phantasies about the mother's body relate to Winnicott's fear of
WOMAN, which I elaborate in Chapter 4. In this chapter it was the
analysis of K. that mobilised Dr Frankenstein's creature in him – a
creature that related to K's birth story and his early psychic history.

There is a moment in the novel *Frankenstein* when the creature is
wandering through the woodland and comes across the woodcutter and his family going about their daily tasks in the woods where
they dwell. He watches them communicating with each other in a
kind and ordinarily loving way that makes him feel overwhelmed
with wretchedness. Shelley speaks for the creature when she writes,
'Miserable, unhappy wretch… I had never yet seen a being resembling me, or who claimed any intercourse with me. What was I? The
question again recurred, to be answered only with groans' (Mary
Shelley [1818] 2003:124).

★ ★ ★

'Terror is the right word', K. said, towards the end of a session. This
was his response to me saying that I thought he was telling me how
terrified he was of feeling dependent on me. We'd been through a
particularly difficult phase of the analysis when my sense of intense
dread before each session during the course of several weeks, had
led me to consider ending the treatment. In this aftermath session I
began to feel that I had managed to find the frame of mind to use the
words that meant something to K. and because he was a wordsmith,
I felt it a significant moment when he confirmed the interpretation.
At that moment, there was a glimmer of hope that the analysis could
continue, because at last a space for thinking promised to open up as
the atmosphere radically changed. I will return to this session later.

This difficult phase of K's analysis occurred at the beginning of the
second year and instigated my reflections on terror as an affect and its
place as a concept in psychoanalysis (Winnicott 1969). It led me to reflect
on the meaning of the analyst's psychic survival and the 'how' related to
the analyst's need to survive the patient's terror of psychoanalysis.

The word 'terror'

The Oxford English Dictionary aptly describes the word 'terror' as an intense fear, fright or dread whilst to terrorise is defined as: to fill or inspire with terror, reduce to a state of terror; *esp*. to coerce or deter by terror. The second definition states: to rule, or maintain power, by terrorism; to practice intimidation (O.E.D. online).

I wondered if terror was the apt word to describe my affective states of mind during this phase of the analysis. My consulting room is modest in size and K. was a tall man who, although ordinarily polite and respectful, became verbally abusive during that phase of the treatment in a threatening way that made me fear for my physical safety. And there was also the literal abuse of the setting, e.g. the slamming of the front door which caused the plaster to crack at the side of the door frame. It would be true to say that I did feel under siege from what could described as his emotional 'system of coercive intimidation'. To that extent, countertransferentially, I was at times feeling terrorised. Although K. had no psychiatric history and had reported no incident of physical abuse to anybody, there were times when I wondered whether the private setting was appropriate. However, as difficult as this period was, there were equally many sessions when K. brought dreams and associations and it was clear that there was something in him struggling to work in the analysis. While I was fairly sure that he would not in actuality attack me, I wondered if I was deluding myself. And when the rage and anger in him seemed to be worsening, I started to feel it might be more appropriate to terminate the analysis than to continue. I will say more about this later.

A sketch of terror and its place in psychoanalytic theory

Psychoanalytic theories cohere in agreement that extreme fear is incorporated in the conceptualisations of anxiety that start from Freud. To my surprise, I found that terror is not listed in the General Index of the *Standard Edition of the Complete Psychological Works of Sigmund Freud*. The word is also not present in the index of the most often used psychoanalytic dictionaries (Laplanche & Pontalis 1973; Rycroft 1968; Hinshelwood 1989; Abram 2007; Akhtar 2009). In Strachey's translation, the word 'terror' is used to emphasise anxiety and in relation to particular phases and types of development. For example, in Freud's case of Schreber, terror is associated with infantile anxieties, and in the Wolfman case it is applied to signify early castration anxiety. In *Studies on Hysteria*, it is associated with sexuality – 'terror of the snake' – and is used especially in Freud's short Medusa paper when he writes: 'The terror of Medusa is thus a terror of castration. The sight of Medusa's head makes the spectator stiff with terror, turning him to stone.' From this citation the affect of 'terror' causes the individual to be 'stiff with terror' as it 'turns him to stone' (Freud [1922] 1940 (SE 18: 273).

In essence, the above descriptions cover the three salient theories of anxiety in Freud's work: libido, birth and primary signal anxieties. What I found noteworthy in relation to the case of K. was that the last example, concerning signal anxiety, relates to the male's fear of women (see the Discussion at the end of this chapter and also Chapter 4, in which I link this primal fear with Winnicott's notion of the fear of WOMAN).

Melanie Klein uses the word 'terror' when she refers to the child's terror of faeces, the penis, the breast, related to the knowledge of the damage done to the mother's body and the terror therefore of what damage could be done to one's own body (Klein 1931: 24–25). Winnicott's use of the word 'terror' is mostly used in relation to children's 'night terrors', indicating the failure of the environment at the very early stages that result in 'primitive agony' and 'unthinkable anxieties.' It is striking that Winnicott only uses the word terror in relation to children, suggesting, like Klein, that it is an affect that is mostly experienced by children. If we turn to Bion's (1962) work, in particular his notion of 'nameless dread' in 'A Theory of Thinking', then we could imagine that terror is at the root of that kind of dread in the psychotic part of the personality. André Green's concept of 'angoisse blanche' and the dead mother complex seems to be intrinsically linked with the notion of 'terror' in which there is a paralysis and an inability to think. The Discussion in Chapter 2 relates Green's work to the patient Jill, who was overwhelmed with an inability to stay in the real world in the face of her analyst's absence. I suggest that she was also experiencing a terror at the roots of her rage and fear (see the Discussion in Chapter 2).

Perhaps it would be true to say that 'terror' is an affect that will be present predominantly in working with the psychotic and borderline patient, but I think that for all patients in analysis there is likely to be some sense of terror for each analysis. It is a symptom that indicates early trauma, i.e. non survival, and an experience in which there is no space to think or to symbolise before ego functioning evolves (cf. Abram 2021).

Following Winnicott's theory of 'use of an object', as I have explicated in Chapters 1 and 2, here I propose that terror as an affect is at the core of an intrapsychic non surviving object. The non surviving object occurs as a consequence of early psychic trauma and constitutes an element of psychic history that is waiting to be brought into relationship with an object that may be able to survive in the après coup of the transference–countertransference matrix. It is then and only then that the trauma of the past has a chance of being experienced by the Self. Following this, there arises a potential to work through the patient's early history and in doing so, relegate the trauma to the past.

Clinical picture

In the first meeting, K. told me about the incident that led him to seek psychoanalytical help. Speaking slowly, with his eyes cast down, he said, 'I had a deadline to meet – I'd been working on it all day, there was a lot of pressure – that's what it's like in my job – and I had to reach the office by 5.30 – they needed it by then. I finally did finish it – well I wasn't happy with it but I… well anyway, I put it in the pannier of my bike: I travel everywhere by bike; and I had to go as fast as I could. As usual I hadn't given myself enough time.' He shook his head berating himself. He continued: 'The office is down in the city and there are railings outside where I usually padlock my bike. I arrived in a hot sweat and I had very few minutes to reach the office in time and after padlocking the bike; in a rush as usual', he said with a large sigh. He paused, '…so as I bent down to retrieve the document I… I…', he raised the palm of his hand towards his eye and again with deep sighs of exasperation and despair he said, 'I spiked my eye on… on one of the spikes… of the railings'. I waited whilst he paused again. Now with his hand on his eye, K. said, 'I didn't think it was much at the time; it felt a bit sore but I did feel I should hold my eye', he laughed, incongruously I felt, 'and as I walked through the offices holding my hand to my eye I was telling everyone and they were all laughing at what I'd done.' He smiled, as if he liked the memory of people laughing at him whilst he was in pain and holding his eye. Later that day when he took himself to the hospital it turned out that the damage was serious; he was in danger of losing the eye that he'd spiked.

I was struck that, although hesitant, it seemed to me that K. was rather affectless during the account of his spiking his eye, whilst his analyst-to-be felt horror and shock that he could have done this to himself.

In this same first meeting K. complained of not having cried for 40 years. He said that he longed to be able to cry. The last time had been when he was 12 and a terrible thing had happened. It was a diving lesson and all the boys in his class had to dive from the diving board. He was the last one and for some reason he could not dive into the water. The swimming teacher made him stand on the edge of the diving board whilst the whole class watched. The more the teacher shouted, the more paralysed he became. The rest of the class were told to go on to the next lesson. Eventually, he thought he probably just jumped in after a very long time, shivering on the board. By the time he got to the next lesson the other boys were getting on with their work and he remembered sitting at the back of the classroom in a terrible state and just crying throughout the whole lesson. He was grateful to the teacher who quietly got on with the class and seemed to allow him to cry. Since that incident, K. said, he had never cried since and he feels it as a great loss to his emotional life. I was struck that K's reporting of this incident seemed more alive and terrible to him than the recent spiking of his eye.

Despite K's intense fear of analysis and his effort to break down the analytic boundaries during the early months (by arriving too early or leaving too late, trying to converse with other patients who were coming and going), through his dreams and responses to transferential comments and interpretations, he demonstrated a capacity to become a patient. In the assessment meetings K. had talked about what had brought him into analysis. He had tried several different kinds of therapy, but they had never lasted longer than six months. He had always left angrily. But now, from the advice of a friend to try psychoanalysis, he decided he must try because he was now rather desperate. He felt suicidally depressed and he was so enraged with his mother he felt he could murder her if he saw her. To avoid this, he had stopped visiting her.

So, as I had anticipated, the co-operation of the early months changed at the six-month mark. After the second break, K. returned and said he would now sit in the chair now as he felt he could no longer trust psychoanalysis. This was because of 'a brush with insanity' during the last break. His manner of sitting in the chair provided many clues to his states of mind.

The beginning of each session was accompanied by a fierce rubbing of his eyes with the palms of his hands so that I could hear his eyes sucking out of their sockets. Then he would close his eyes, and slump into the chair with his head bowed, while one hand remained as if to shield his eyes. As he began to talk, his hand played with his eyelashes and eyelids in an almost taunting way. It was such an evocative picture that I found myself quite mesmerised by the scene I think he was unconsciously creating. At the same time, I was aware of a reaction of feeling repulsed and pained. It was as if I was seeing the whole horrific scene of Oedipus pulling out his eyes and then falling into an abyss of painful despair and guilt.

K's account of his parents and home environment seemed mostly to concur with the evolving maternal and paternal transferences. There was a powerful layer in which he experienced his analyst as the hated, cold, frustrating, withholding mother, complying with, and oppressed by, psychoanalysis who was represented by Freud; the sadistic, volatile, violent father who abuses and humiliates. K. carried a deep grievance against both his parents, which he felt was absolutely justified. My sense of having to be vigilant to K's mood indicated a countertransference reaction to his family of origin. It was a sense of a foreboding that something terrible could erupt; perhaps like the volatile father and passive mother he described. And this brings me to the session that became a prelude to the difficult phase.

After eighteen months and after the fourth break, the violence in the transference increased. K. arrived for the first session in what seemed the usual way. He rang the doorbell a couple of minutes before time and I buzzed him in. I heard him blow his nose, a sort of trumpeting sound as if to alert me to his arrival in my house, and this was followed by a rather noisy opening of the door to the bathroom, situated off the waiting lobby. It was usual that when I opened the door to the consulting room on time, K. was almost always in the bathroom. Then I would go to my chair and wait. The waiting lobby is to one side of the entrance to my room so that when I am sitting in my chair, I cannot see the waiting area. K. would normally keep me waiting at the beginning of the session. He would come out of the bathroom, busy himself in the waiting area, which sounded as if he was rearranging things in his rucksack, before entering the consulting room and closing the door. There was something about the timing of that beginning that would inform me of what kind of frame of mind K. would bring to the session that day. However, after the sounds-off stopped, which was usually the point at which K. would slowly enter the room, on that cold January afternoon, nothing happened. That is to say, I heard him become silent and it was clear he was going to keep me waiting longer than had hitherto been usual. This dawning realisation that he was staying in the waiting area was accompanied by an increasing sense of fear and panic in me that was threatening to overwhelm my sense of self. Simultaneously, I felt immensely curious as to why I was feeling so afraid. Here I was sitting in my consulting room knowing that K. was in the waiting lobby, not having seen him for three weeks, and at that moment I was not able to hear him. There was an increasing deathlike silence from the waiting lobby, which became increasingly menacing in my mind. I tried first of all to calm myself in order to think. Why should I be so afraid? What could happen? Nothing was happening. I felt at sea to know what to do. I started to reflect on the previous term's work in an effort to work out how to deal with the situation. At that moment it seemed dangerous to leave my chair and go and fetch him. I felt paralysed and, in an effort to retain my analytic mind, I found myself reflecting on the previous term's work and the varying layers of the transference.

There were two significant narratives of the previous term. K. had told me how he felt very ashamed and guilty about something that happened once or twice with his dog when he was about nine or ten. He really liked the family dog and felt good friends with her; yet every now and then he would suddenly hit her, causing her to whimper, cower and tremble; then he would make up with her and stroke her again. He wondered what this was about. He shamefully admitted that what really shocked him was the sense of pleasure he would get out of this. It worried him. As I thought about this I wondered if I was like his dog waiting to be hit; or was it him cowering in the waiting area? This thought somehow kept me in my place and it felt of paramount importance to stay in my chair in my consulting room, as if it was the only way of staying safe. The other significant narrative was that when he was five, he had a gash on his knee that really repulsed him when it bled and; as it healed, he was terrified of looking at it. This memory had emerged after a first aid course when K. nearly fainted at the screening of an open wound. He said he thought it was the shape of a vagina.

I was in a kind of reverie with these associations which had calmed me, but then, noting the time, I was aware of having to decide what I should do if he remained in the waiting area until the end of the

The non surviving object

session. Then, five minutes or so before time I heard K. move. He then sort of sauntered[2] to the entrance of the door and at the threshold still outside the room, sheepishly told me that he'd decided to go but he thought he'd come and tell me why he hadn't been able to enter the room. He said, gesturing towards the couch, that he wasn't ready to sink into the chair let alone the couch yet, but it had been useful 'staying out there'. He'd felt a bit panicky, but then had done a lot of thinking and what he was reflecting on was that during the break he'd gone on a sea trip and on the boat there had been a violent storm. In his cabin, he had to hold on very tight as the boat was tossed in the sea. He said he was so terrified and convinced that he was going to die in this storm. He'd never experienced such a rough sea. After a pause, I said I thought he was telling me that entering the room today felt as if he would be entering that sea again and that his life would be threatened.

Following on from this, in almost every session, K. would sometimes stay in the lobby for chunks of the session. When he did manage to enter the room, he would always start the session by attacking Freud and psychoanalysis with intense contempt. It was as if he wanted to goad me into arguing the case for psychoanalysis and I sometimes interpreted how I thought he wanted to get me into an argument about the pros and cons of psychoanalysis. After some interpretations of this kind at the beginning of a session he would sometimes be able to make use of the remainder of the session and often brought many dreams. However, it seemed that the outcome of any element of constructive work was demolished in the subsequent session, by cancelling or staying out in the waiting area for much longer. Then there came a higher frequency of verbal abuse to me. He would tell me how, on his way to the session, he felt like 'smashing my face in', 'and pummelling me to a pulp'. He anxiously asked me if I was in fear of my life and whether analysts did get killed in sessions. He said he had to emphasise to me just how terrified he felt of what analysis would do to him and that he felt absolute terror about losing his sanity and he couldn't allow that to happen. While he was telling me how terrorised he felt by me, increasingly I was feeling that I was the one being terrorised. When the doorbell went at the time of his session, I became aware that I was at times filled with a sinking sense of dread, and was finding it hard not to feel afraid, intimidated, helpless, hopeless and certainly useless. The other telling countertransference reaction was that I began to question whether psychoanalysis really

The non surviving object

was the solution for him and perhaps he was right about its dangers. Should I continue to work with him? Was there a possibility of me being physically harmed, even though he had no history of having physically attacked anybody? At the peak of what felt like despair in myself and the whole analytic project there came a turning point.

As K. began a session saying he was going to leave and it was all a waste of time I noticed that I began to feel angry with him rather than afraid, and when he started to say he wanted to kick me in the face, I interrupted him and said that I thought he was trying to intimidate me, and I thought that he wanted to make me feel frightened. To my surprise, he seemed shocked and flustered by this statement and quickly denied it. But I continued, saying that I thought it may be because if he was able to frighten me there was a chance I would reject working with him and that it would be an easier way for him to leave the analysis. He paused, and I felt the atmosphere shifting. He lowered his head and muttered that it was so disrespectful this analysis. This stirred in me a sense of outrage that he could say this, considering how verbally abusive he had been towards me, particularly since he had recently confessed that he would not dare to speak to a male analyst the way he speaks to me. At that moment I felt like shouting abuse at him and saying something like, 'That's rich!' Instead I took a deep breath to gather my thoughts and then told him calmly that that was the reason he felt he could be as disrespectful to me as he liked. He was taking advantage of the fact that I'm a woman. He then became very still and silent. After a while he said, slumping in the chair and with what felt like a deep sense of sadness, 'I can't do this'. He seemed miserable, wretched, and humiliated, like Dr. Frankenstein's 'creature' who said, 'I am malicious because I am miserable'. My anger subsided and I started to feel anguished for him. I waited for a while and then said that I thought each day he travelled to the session he felt overwhelmed with a sense of humiliation; a sense that it was me who dragged him here every day, and it was this feeling of humiliation that enraged him and was preventing him from working here. He was quiet for a while and then conceded that he did feel I was 'rubbing his nose in it' every time he came here, and he found it punishing. I wondered aloud whether he thought that I even took pleasure in his sense of humiliation and shame, and that he felt I did not appreciate how much he had to go through to get here. Now there was a very long pause and as the session ended, he said that he could not stay in analysis for the rest of his life. This is the point when I said that I thought he was telling me he was terrified of feeling dependent on me. 'Terror' is the right word he said quietly, and it was time.

In the next session, to which he arrived on time, he reported a dream he'd had that night, where he was on his bike and feeling very positive as he glided through terrain that was unfamiliar, but very smooth, and he was feeling very positive and amazed at the distance he was able to travel. In the same session he talked about a woman whom he'd really liked; once, when she had visited him spontaneously, he had had to reject her because he felt so anxious that she was stealing his soul from him and that he could not afford to lose his sense of self, which was something he was so sure was going to happen with several women he had been close to in his life. But now he regretted all those missed opportunities and it was getting to be too late. The sense of lost opportunities and intense regret was palpable in this session and related to many other similar situations he'd told me about. I did not interpret in that session because it seemed to me that significant psychic work had taken place and K. needed some reflective space to breathe.

Things settled down for several weeks and then there came another session which happened to be just before I was going to take a week's break. He slouched on the threshold of the consulting room. I said that I thought he should come in for us to work.[3] Then, with intense contempt, he said, 'What work?' To my surprise, I found myself saying calmly but firmly that I imagined there were many things he may need to say or not, but sitting down was the minimum requirement. Almost immediately he went straight to the chair and got on with the session. In the following session he arrived on time and went straight to the couch. For the rest of his analysis, K. settled into the structures of the analysing situation and used words and the analytic space to air his grievances.

The intrapsychic non surviving object

In Chapters 1 and 2, I have set out my proposals concerning the intrapsychic surviving object. Its corollary is that of the development of a non surviving object. This object, I suggest, is an intrapsychic object that comes about as the result of the external object not surviving at the very crucial beginning. The infant's needs are not met, and therefore the baby's anxieties overwhelm the vulnerable psyche, causing a series of breaks in the continuity-of-being (Winnicott [1963b] 1965).

Depending on the vagaries of the not good enough environment at the beginning and subsequently, cumulative trauma will occur, and the development of an intrapsychic non surviving object will eclipse a stunted surviving object. The non surviving object corresponds to all psychopathologies and offers a relational perspective on the causes of mental illness. Here I suggest that at the core of a non surviving object lies a primitive terror that petrifies the sense of self and thus impedes the capacity for receptivity because the baby has had to insulate and protect the core self. The reader is re-directed to Winnicott's two early patterns of relating (as described in Chapter 1) and how in the not good enough environment the infant suffers violation of the self. Khan's paper on cumulative trauma is based on Winnicott's early theories of psychosis (cf. Khan 1964).

In theory, then, even if the non surviving object eclipses the surviving object it does follow that there exists a potential for a surviving object to grow if an opportunity arises in which a different psychic environment can be experienced. It is certain that the analytic relationship carries this potential and perhaps is the only method that could seriously change the inner dynamic. A theoretical feed in the analytic relationship constitutes the analyst's ability to receive the unconscious communications through listening and interpretation that constitutes the holding environment. Thus, the subject can feel s/he creates the object which, in turn, provides meaning. The ultimate result has the potential to lead on to the surviving object eclipsing the non surviving object. This requires a series of incremental symbolic feeds in which psychic change may occur and establish itself.

Discussion

Let us reflect on K's response to analysis in the context of a selection of early psychoanalytic theories that made sense to me in relation to K.'s transference. K's 'terror of dependency' was clearly associated with his intense murderous hatred of his mother. In 1932, Karen Horney, referred to the 'dread of woman' that she said was associated with the dread of the female genital (Horney quotes Groddek who said, '…of course men are afraid of women!').

> If the admixture of destructive impulses is really considerable, the mother's genital must, according to the talion principle, become an object of direct anxiety. Thus, if it is first made distasteful to

him by its association with wounded self-regard, it will by a secondary process (by way of frustration-anger) become an object of castration-anxiety. And probably this is very generally reinforced when the boy observes traces of menstruation.

(Horney 1932: 358)

When K. experienced horror when he saw the wound on his knee at the age of 4 or 5, his sister was about one year old. He often referred to losing his mother at 2 or 3 and yet never seemed to connect it with his mother's pregnancy and giving birth to her second child. Winnicott proposes that the fear of WOMAN is related to the fear of dependency and states that the denigration of woman in all societies is due to the fact that all of us owe a debt for our life to a woman. The original dependence is not remembered, and therefore the debt is not acknowledged, except in so far as the fear of WOMAN represents the first stage of this acknowledgement (Winnicott [1950] 1986). Although not directly stated by Winnicott, I previously suggested that this fear could be seen to be at the roots of misogyny (Abram [1996] 2007). This proposal is more fully developed in Chapter 4.

Another early author on female sexuality was Marie Bonaparte, who, inspired by Melanie Klein's work, referred to a primary anxiety related to the primal scene as an act of violence done by man to woman. She refers to the '…vital terror of the ripping up of the disembowelling violence done by man to woman' and proposed that the fantasies of this kind of violent primal scene could indicate a 'perforation complex' (Bonaparte 1938: 214–220) K's diving scene at the age of 12 shows a clear terror of penetration. Wrye, and I think her themes are most pertinent to K., has written on the 'erotic terror' associated with the early maternal erotic transference, which she states is a particular terror experienced by schizoid males who have a 'primal fear of intimacy' (Wrye & Welles 1989: 673). This perspective is complementary to Perelberg's thesis on the function of violence that is a defence against the analytic relationship. Perelberg goes on to say that this violence relates to a core phantasy about the primary relationship with mother as well as the primal scene (Perelberg et al. 1999).

K. often indicated that he had much to say about his sexuality and I had the impression he was deeply ashamed of his violent fantasies and feelings towards women. Following Perelberg's hypothesis, it is clear that this is how K's violence towards the analysis was functioning to keep a distance from the terror of the core phantasy. Fonagy and

Target suggested that 'the obstacle (for the violent patient's understanding of interpretations) is the patient's terror of a mind which offers understanding' (Fonagy & Target 1999) and they concur with Campbell that the father's absence in the patient's early infancy, and his inability to intervene and separate the mother and infant may often lead to the patient's violent pre-Oedipal relationship (Campbell 1999 in Perelberg 1999: 69). When K. started analysis, he was regularly banging his head against the wall, entirely connected, he said, with the murderous intentions he had towards his mother that were fused with his suicidal impulses.

The analyst's psychic survival constitutes the symbolic feed that will facilitate the possibility for the undeveloped surviving object to grow and thus enable the patient to reach a point of beginning to find 'les mots pour le dire' (the words to say it) (Cardinal 1975) instead of having to act out.

The notion of the non surviving object relates to how patients experience absence when the analyst has a break, as we saw with Jill in Chapter 2. K. found breaks difficult, but was initially out of touch with just how painful they felt. The constructive work that occurred before the breaks was often undone as a consequence of my absenting myself from him. I feel this related to his fear of breakdown (Winnicott 1963a?). The autumn before the second Christmas break had witnessed a gradual uncovering of memories and associations related to K's internal world and through his description of that break it seems very likely that the trip he decided to take did indeed cause him to revisit psychically dying and the 'fear of breakdown', and he blamed this on the analysis. In the transference it was true that the analysis had caused him to break down and in some ways this was true because he had no protection during the break and my absence seemed to repeat the unconscious memories of psychic neglect.

I came to see that my petrified state in that first session after the 2nd winter break was the result of a projective actualisation (Green 1987 in Abram 2016: 2), i.e., K's internal dynamic was mobilised in the transference and became an actualisation of a terrified petrification. It was also an intense unconscious communication of retaliation in quite a transparent way. While I was sitting in the consulting room and he was in the waiting lobby out of sight, I was being made to feel abandoned and confused. I almost lost a sense of my analytic mind and thus a sense of meaning. I reflected on the work of Bollas who commented on the analyst's countertransference, leading to becoming 'situationally ill', which he asserts is a state the analyst may often fall into with borderline patients (Bollas 1989). For several weeks subsequent to that session, we were both caught up in the dynamics of the non surviving object and subject. It was a terrifying place to inhabit because there was no space for thinking; all I felt I could do was, like him on that boat trip, hold on to anything to steady my body while a violent sea threatened to destroy the ship. The more sessions there were where I failed to survive, the more terrified (and consequently violent) K. became. But, paradoxically, I realised later, that while I was not surviving, I had the potential to survive by availing myself to surrender to being the object that the patient needed me to be so as to know what breakdown and non survival felt like. Being pulled into contact with the depths of his terrors that could not yet be put into words and could only be actualised, repeated the unconscious dynamic and history of his non surviving object. The analysis had to go through this crisis phase before I was in a position to metabolise the overwhelming nature of his projective actualisations.

My anger at the beginning of the session when his sadism had full reign was, at last, real. I recovered my sense of an analytic mind, in a way that his objects of the past probably never had, and I could confront him in the way his dog never could, or his mother never could with his father, or probably he never could with his mother or his father. It was this real boundary, from a different m/Other. When I found myself telling him that sitting down was a minimal requirement, something that I had not planned to say but that came quite spontaneously, it was clear from his reaction that this was something he had needed and longed for. I think this moment constituted the paternal function boundary, as I elaborate in Chapter 7. I also think about is as the analyst's act of freedom as conceptualised by Neville Symington (Symington 1983). For K. I think it could have constituted the first analytic theoretical feed because it was associated with an Oedipal couple working together. Several years later, I realised that the change in my response, from fear to anger, was related to a psychic change in me associated with the third. In Chapter 7, I propose the notion of an analytic 'paternal integrate' when the analyst has a third in mind parallel with the mother keeping the infant's father in mind. These formulations arose out of this clinical work and follow Winnicott's very late work on the early father, similar to, but not the same as, Green's concept of the 'other of the object' (Green [1991] in Abram 2016).

After this period the analytic work with K. was more 'normalised' in analytic terms. Some evidence of his increasing insight was demonstrated when he reported that his hatred and murderous feelings towards his mother had abated, alongside his violent suicidal urges which were fading away.

When he terminated the analysis, he said he felt confident that he would never be as depressed as he had been before starting the analysis, although, he added, he didn't know why and whether it had anything to do with the analysis. This could have been true at a conscious level; on the other hand, I wonder if it is a sign he found it difficult to feel grateful to the analysis for fear of entrapment. In terms of my formulations here I do consider it as evidence enough that he had received the first theoretical feed. Much psychic work had been achieved; for both of us. We had survived the storm intact, even though the development of an analytic intrapsychic surviving object in analysis had only just begun.

Notes

1 This argument was first presented in October 2019 for the European Psychoanalytic Conference for University Students (EPCUS) on the theme of Fears and Anxieties (Abram 2019). The paper is being revised for a forthcoming publication.
2 In many Victorian and early 20th century houses in London and the U.K. there is a hatch (a square opening in the wall) between the kitchen and the dining room through which the plates of food can be passed. This derived from the Victorian era and earlier, because the kitchen was not the usual place for members of the family to eat. Of course, this referred solely to upper- and middle-class families. In the lower classes and rural communities, everybody ate in the kitchen.
3 This reminded me of Nina Coltart's paper 'Slouching towards Bethlehem', which I found inspiring at the beginning of my work as a clinician. The title is taken from a poem by W.B. Yeats – 'The Second Coming'. Coltart cites the verse that ends with: 'And what rough beast, its hour come round at last, Slouches towards Bethlehem to be born?' For Coltart, the 'rough beast' is a metaphor for the 'analyst in embryo' (Coltart [1988] 1992).

References

Abram, J. (1994) Review of *How to Survive as a Psychotherapist* by Nina Coltart in Brit. *J Psychother* 11 (2): 31.

Abram, J. (1996) *The language of Winnicott a dictionary of Winnicott's use of words* London: Karnac Books.

Abram, J. (ed.) (2000) *André Green at the Squiggle Foundation*, Winnicott Studies, London: Karnac Books.

Abram, J. (2005) L'objet qui survit, trad. D. Alcorn, *Journal de la psychanalyse de l'enfant*, 36, 139–174.

Abram, J. (2007) *The language of Winnicott a dictionary of Winnicott's use of words*, 2nd edition. London: Karnac Books.

Abram, J. (ed.) (2016) *André Green at the Squiggle Foundation*, 2nd edition. Winnicott Studies, London: Karnac Books.

Abram, J. (2019) The Frankenstein Complex: on birth terrors – Annual Conference European Psychoanalytic Conference for University Students, Brussels, Belgium.

Akhtar, S. (2009) *Comprehensive Dictionary of Psychoanalysis*. London: Karnac Books.

Bion, W.R. (1962) The psychoanalytic theory of thinking. *Int J Psychoanal* 43: 306–310.

Bollas, C. (1989) *The forces of destiny*, Free Association Books.

Bonaparte, M. (1938) Some Palaeobiological & Biopsychical Reflections *Int J Psychoanal* 19: 214–220.

Campbell, D. (1999) The role of the father in pre suicide states in Perelberg, R. (1999) *Psychoanalytic understanding of violence and suicide*, Routledge.

Cardinal M. (1975) *Les mots pour le dire*, Paris, Grasset.

Coltart, N. (1988) Slouching towards Bethlehem in *Slouching towards Bethlehem and further psychoanalytic explorations*, Free Association Books.

Freud, S. ([1922] 1940 Medusa's Head SE 18: 273.

Fonagy, P. & Target, M. (1999) Towards understanding violence: the use of the body and the role of the father in Perelberg, R. (1999) *Psychoanalytic understanding of violence and suicide*, Routledge.

Green, A. (1991) On Thirdness In: Abram 2016.

Hinshelwood, R.D. (1989) *A Dictionary of Kleinian Thought*, Free Association Books.

Horney, K. (1932) Observations on a specific difference in the dread felt by men and by women respectively for the opposite sex. *Int J Psychoanal* 13: 348–360. Oxford English Dictionary Second Edition on CD-ROM Version 3.1.

Khan, M.R. (1964) Ego distortion, cumulative trauma, and the role of reconstruction in the analytic situation. *Int J Psychoanal* 45: 272–279.

Klein, M. (1931) The psychoanalysis of children. *Int Psychoanal Lib* 22: 1–379.

Laplanche, J., Pontalis, J.B. (1973) The language of psycho-analysis: Translated by Donald Nicholson-Smith. The International Psycho-Analytical Library, 94: 1–497. London: The Hogarth Press and the Institute of Psycho-Analysis.

Perelberg, R. et al. (ed) (1999) *Psychoanalytic understanding of violence and suicide*, Routledge

Rycroft, C. (1968) *A critical dictionary of psychoanalysis*, 1st edition. Nelson.

Shelley, M. ([1818] 2003) *Frankenstein*, Penguin Classics.

Symington, N. (1983) The analyst's act of freedom as Agent of therapeutic change. *Int Review Psychoanal* 10: 283–291.

Winnicott DW ([1950] 1986) Some Thoughts on the meaning of the word Democracy In: *Home is where we start From* ed. Winnicott, C., Shepherd, R. & Davis, M. Harmondsworth: Penguin.

Winnicott DW (1958) Primary maternal preoccupation [1956] In: 1958a, 300–305.

Winnicott DW ([1963a?] 1989) Fear of Breakdown In: *Psychoanalytic explorations psychoanalytic explorations* Winnicott C, Shepherd R, Davis M, editors. Cambridge, MA: Harvard University Press.

Winnicott DW ([1963b] 1965) Communicating and not communicating leading to a study of certain opposites in *Maturational Processes and the facilitating environment*, Hogarth Press 1965.

Winnicott DW (1969) The use of an object. *Int J Psychoanal* 50: 711–716

Winnicott DW (1975) Fear of breakdown.

Wrye, H.K. & Welles, J.K. (1989) The maternal erotic transference *Int J Psychoanal* 70: 673–684.

4

THE FEAR OF WOMAN/ANALYSIS

Reflections on desire, infantile sexuality and psychic *survival-of-the-object* (2010)

Prelude

In this chapter, based on clinical work with Lisa in the latter part of her fertile years, I propose there is an implied theory of desire in Winnicott's work that is based on the early parent–infant relationship. The fear of WOMAN, in both men and women, was a concept proposed by Winnicott in 1950 that highlighted a universal fear of dependency. This notion, as I have suggested, elaborates Freud's formulations on hilflosikeit (helplessness).

Analysis stirs up the fear of dependency for all patients. For Lisa, as I show here, her fear of dependency was inextricably caught up with a fear of becoming a woman. This clinical experience drew my attention to the psychosexual dimension of a surviving object and psychic survival which I explore here.

Freud pointed out that the phase of attachment to the mother was 'intimately related to the aetiology of hysteria…'. He noted that this was because the phase and the neurosis were characteristically feminine'. He considered that dependency on the mother held the 'germ of later paranoia in women' (Freud 1931: 227). We might wonder why he excluded men. Winnicott wrote, 26 years later, that if 'traced to its root in the history of each individual, this fear of WOMAN turns out to be a fear of recognising the fact of dependence' (Winnicott 1957: 125). This universal fear of WOMAN, for Winnicott, applied to men and women and was rooted in the fact that we were all once dependent on a woman for our life. I have previously suggested that this fear is at the roots of misogyny in both men and women (Abram 1996, 2007a: 135).

★ ★ ★

During a pause in the session, when I felt unsure that I'd managed to say anything that resonated with Lisa, unexpectedly, she said, slowly and with deliberation, 'What you said just now, I think is right. I hadn't really thought about it quite like that before.' I felt puzzled about what she meant. She continued, 'It's not just knowing what you really want that's so important – I mean of course it helps… but it's the act of getting it – it just really terrifies me – even the thought of getting what I really want terrifies me.' I then remembered that I'd made a comment that had addressed Lisa's inhibitions about 'having it all'. After another pause Lisa said, 'And I think that is why I can't ask for the fifth session despite really wanting it. Everything about it terrifies me in a way that asking for the third and fourth sessions didn't.' In the pause that followed I found myself reflecting back on Lisa's anxieties about psychoanalysis in our first meeting several years previously.

Lisa was a successful musician, highly intellectual, and desperate for some help with her panic attacks. Her problem was that while she knew she needed emotional help she was at the same time deeply suspicious of all psychological treatments, particularly psychoanalysis. Simultaneously, she longed to be in analysis. But, in the first consultation it was clear she was not ready to start an open-ended treatment and so I found myself offering her 1x weekly sessions for a period of six weeks. The time limit seemed to relieve her, and she attended the six sessions conscientiously. By the end of that time Lisa said she had found the sessions helpful and so we agreed to another six sessions that took us up to a break. We arranged one more session after the break. Lisa returned and discussed her wish to continue and to 'see how things would go'. This was the way she embarked on once-weekly sessions on an open-ended basis.

Gradually, over the course of several years, Lisa increased to four sessions a week. Each extra session was instated just after a significant life event. Just before asking for the second session, she had met a man whom she started seeing romantically. About a year later she started to live with this same man and asked for the third session. When she began the three weekly sessions, she began to use the couch for the first time. Just before moving to the fourth session she became engaged and was in the process of planning her wedding. This progress was highly surprising for Lisa as she'd been sure that she would never meet a man who would love her; furthermore, she had always argued against the institution of marriage.

Shortly after the wedding and in the lead-up to a summer break, she mooted the (wish for a) fifth session associated with her strong wish to have a baby. This was something she was certain she would never wish for. Lisa maintained that she could not identify with being an adult – a woman – and that this stage of development instigated terrifying phantasies associated with violence and murder.

Lisa's fear of (a full) analysis was inextricably linked with the fear related to her desire to become a woman. Of course, with Freud's work in mind, this fear was clearly reminiscent of the hysteric with her repressed sexuality that had to be disavowed. This was certainly a powerful layer in Lisa's pathology. In addition to the obvious Oedipal themes, however, the issue of becoming a woman is also related to the 'fear of WOMAN' and its corollary, the fear of desire. This essay is an attempt to explore these themes in Winnicott's work in the context of the analysing situation with Lisa.

In relation to the formulations of the surviving and non surviving objects, I suggest that many patients across the psychopathological spectrum turn to analysis because a non surviving object wields its power internally and overwhelms them to such an extent that they feel ill. For some patients, particularly the hysteric, a resistance to development is unusually intense, and the more analysis works, the more the resistance intensifies. Freud's 'negative therapeutic reaction' may constitute the anxiety in the transference that mobilises the 'fear of breakdown' related to the original catastrophe (Riviere 1936; Winnicott [1963?] 1974) (see Chapter 8 and Appendix). In so many cases of hysteria, analysis reveals the 'fear of desire' so that the fear of 'attaining the object of desire' becomes a dangerous aim. Winnicott indicates that this fear, paradoxically, may stem from too much satiation – '…the baby is not satisfied with satisfaction. He feels fobbed off. He intended, one might say, to make a cannibalistic attack and he has been put off by an opiate, the feed. At best he can postpone the attack' (Winnicott 1945: 154). It is this sort of fobbing off that amounts to one kind of maternal failure that constitutes non *survival-of-the-object* and may indicate that the baby has experienced psychic breakdown very early on (see Chapter 8).

Winnicott's implied theory of desire

Winnicott's theoretical matrix emphasises the distinction between needs and wishes (Abram 2007a: 84 & 290) and there are several authors who have concurred with this perspective, i.e. that desire is a developmental achievement arising out of the infant's experience of satisfaction (Akhtar 1999). I propose there is an inferred theory of desire in Winnicott's work that relates to his concept of psychic *survival-of-the-object* (Abram 2007b: 15–40).

As I have referred to in Chapters 1, 2 and 3, the evolution of both intrapsychic surviving and non surviving objects will depend on the inter-psychic *survival-of-the-object* at each developmental phase. Needs that are met on a consistent basis will instigate a capacity to feel desire. This relates to Freud's mnemic trace in his early theory of desire related to dreaming and dreams (Freud 1900). But, if the non surviving object overwhelms the internal landscape, then an awareness of desire will be negated. As we saw in Chapter 2, I suggested that terror is at the core of the non surviving object, so that a desire that becomes conscious will feel terrifying because the subject has had no experience of the Other having survived their desire related to appetite (Winnicott 1931).

Winnicott's concept of the first theoretical feed means that the baby creates the object through the paradox of finding what he needed and 'that what he found is created' (Winnicott [1954] 1988: 111).

Let us summarise the emerging developmental sequence that leads to the subject's capacity to feel desire and, more importantly, action it:

1. The newborn is in a state of physical need.
2. The consequence of the infant's needs being met, by a m/Other in a state of primary maternal preoccupation, brings about a sense of satisfaction which is pleasurable.
3. The next time the need arises (depending on the effect of an accumulation of needs being met), the baby will have internalised a sense of satisfaction (Freud's mnemic trace), and this will instigate desire, i.e. the urge to repeat the sense of satisfaction which we could think about as akin to self-survival.
4. Desire emanates from the experience of satisfaction, which is pleasurable, and it is located in the body. The feeling of desire is object-related in that the satisfaction has come about (or not) through the m/Other's ability to meet the need. This has to

include her pleasure and enjoyment in having the ability to meet the need.
5. The psyche evolves in relation to the infant–parent relationship and the baby experiences both survival and non survival of the object inter-psychically. This experience leads to an intrapsychic surviving and a non surviving object that are in the process of establishing themselves with meaning. This is what Winnicott refers to as the first theoretical feed that constitutes the threshold of the capacity to symbolise.
6. The quality and quantity of desire is related to an intrapsychic surviving and non surviving object being fed by the infant's inter-psychic experience of the m/Other.
7. Following Winnicott's notion of the first theoretical feed I have proposed that there are a series of subsequent theoretical feeds at each developmental stage. At the threshold of adulthood, the subject is in the process of reaching a 'final theoretical feed'. This final symbolic feed is related to negotiating the tasks of adolescence when a whole intrapsychic surviving object is internalised. This will depend on the previous *survival-of-the-object* during this final crucial phase. This constitutes the establishment of the capacity to symbolise and a move into a mature mode of being. The surviving and non surviving objects will continue to impact on the psyche which will develop at each subsequent stage of development, equipping the psyche with a capacity to manage both intrapsychic and interpsychic relationships.

Thus, desire, based on Winnicott's matrix, has two possible trajectories fuelled by either the surviving object or the non surviving object. Where the surviving object dominates the internal world desire will evolve and grow feeding the development of the capacity for concern and love (Winnicott 1963). In contrast, where the non surviving object dominates the internal world, desire will be cut off (either denied, disavowed, repressed or split off), and in an unconscious domain it will feed hate, contempt and especially envy. Therefore, the developing awareness of desire (for the analysand) may be terrifying because at the core of the non surviving object is the very real experience of terror. While this sense of terror has its roots in the infant's experience of non *survival-of-the-object*, by this time it belongs to the subject, i.e. it is the internalisation of the cumulative non *survival-of-the-object*, which has distorted development, as I proposed in Chapter 3.

Psychoanalytic treatment therefore offers a new opportunity for the stunted surviving object to grow. Everything that the analyst has to offer the analysand – the setting, holding, interpretation, continuity, listening, reliability – constitutes psychic *survival-of-the-object*, so that in the transference and the après coup of the analytic relationship the analysand's surviving object has the potential to be fed and to grow in a new way, thus catching up, as it were, from its hitherto stunted development. This will lead to a significant mitigation of the super-ego's corrosive inner attacks on the self and an increasing capacity to reach out for what is desired. While satisfaction is necessary, related to the 'illusion of omnipotence', disillusion is necessarily a crucial stage of maturity (Winnicott 1971; Abram 2007a: 200–212).

The clinical picture

Here I shall focus on a selection of some of the key exchanges of Lisa's analysis that occurred over the course of several weeks in the 4x weekly analysis during that period, which was Tuesday to Friday. The exchanges illustrate how Lisa was struggling between survival and non survival in the transference as she moved towards what I will call 'actioning' her desire. Taking up the 5th session was her conscious attempt at working on her anxieties related to 'conceiving a baby'. But, as we shall see, her wish to conceive was caught up with unconscious Oedipal terrors related to me in the transference.

After the summer break Lisa returned ambivalent and disconnected from her analysis. This was something she named as her 'oblivious' part and we had come to see that it was the way in which she defended herself at breaks. It was a rather manic and superior attitude that she managed to get into but one from which she usually crashed, as we will see. The possibility of a fifth session was hanging around in each session following on from her raising it as a possibility long before the summer break. As already stated, Lisa acknowledged that there was something about having the full analysis – five sessions – that terrified her. Where would it lead? She would subsequently want a sixth and seventh session, live next to me, want to live with me. And as she knew that she wouldn't be able to have that, why not stick to four?

Lisa's experience of prevaricating about the fifth session was like 'keeping the best thing on the plate till last'. The waiting was almost more delicious than the eating of the best thing, because once you had it, that was that; it was gone. But this led to a return of the original anxieties, albeit at a much more tolerable level. The emerging themes highlighted her anxieties about desire and stealing, love and hate, rivalry and envy. After a certain amount of working through she found a way of asking for the fifth session during the Friday session. I offered a Monday time to start in five weeks' time. However, Lisa did not confirm that this was something she could take up.

When Lisa returned for the Tuesday session, she said she had felt better that weekend, but now, in the session, she began to prevaricate again about the session on offer. She said it didn't feel like the right time. After a pause, she asked, 'What would anybody think watching from the outside?' This was followed by her telling me that she'd been completely obsessed all weekend about a play she'd seen on Saturday which took place in a train signal box (the stationmaster's room where he changed the signals). In the play, the stationmaster was so caught up with his sexual interest in a woman with whom he flirts, that he did not hear the warning bell that means he should change the signal for the oncoming train. As a consequence, the train crashes and he causes the death of 18 people. Lisa feels she is just like that. She will get wrapped up with something and a disaster will occur.

I said that I thought she was terrified of getting so engaged with me, like a love affair, that she feels she will miss a warning bell and this will cause a disaster.

She said she feels exactly like this and she doesn't know why.

After this session she lost her house keys and thought she'd left them in the waiting room. She still felt distracted about the train crash (as if it had really happened). When she reported this in the following session I said she felt lost – as if to take responsibility for having the fifth session felt so difficult with the phantasies of being caught up with me. She feigned feeling shocked that I was indicating that she hadn't yet confirmed she would take up the fifth session. She said she thought that it had all been agreed. There was a pause in which I felt it was clear that she knew she had not confirmed that she would take up the fifth session and that she was playing the familiar teasing game of leaving the best thing till last.

The silence went on for some time and felt uncomfortable. But it was fruitful as it led to her association to another play about Mary Queen of Scots and Elizabeth I. She hates this play, but she feels like Elizabeth, who did not want to sign the death warrant for the execution of Mary. In fact, Lisa said, Elizabeth wanted Mary dead, but she was disingenuous about her wish to kill her cousin and did not want to be seen as responsible for her death.

After a pause, I said that Lisa was feeling disingenuous here. She wanted the fifth session, but did not want to take responsibility for signing up for it as she felt it was like signing a death warrant. She felt paralysed like Elizabeth.

She tentatively agreed. Then she said, 'One of them had to go and that's what Elizabeth knew.'

I said, 'It's not possible to have two Queens.' She said, 'One of them had to die.' By now it was the end of the session and I found myself saying, 'The virgin Queen could not allow herself to be replaced by the sexy Queen of Scots.' Lisa replied, 'It's full of sex and the power of sex. I think that's why I hate that play so much.'

In the following week Lisa reported a dream she'd had in the summer. In the dream she had to do a prestigious lecture about Faust (she said she hated Faust), and she had not prepared properly and there was only five minutes to go. Then a man came in and said, 'You're leaving it all too late!' There were many associations to this dream, mostly related to her hatred of the oppression of women and the sexist, cruel Faust. What seemed core to Lisa's associations was that she felt so sorry for the woman that Faust had made pregnant. This woman had felt so ashamed that she killed her baby by Faust. She had 'suffered as a consequence of sex'.

Lisa started the next week telling me about the cat she and her husband were looking after for a neighbour. She was astonished at her intense feelings of jealousy towards the cat. Her jealous feelings terrified her. The cat had been crying all night outside the bedroom door. She thought the cat's owners take the cat into bed with them and she felt she was definitely not going to allow that! There were further associations with this event.

I said that this is how she had felt all weekend. She was crying to come into my bedroom and get into my bed. But she feels that I am like her; strict, and will not allow this. She sighed and said she could see that and even felt it now. Then she suddenly asked, 'What if I do have a baby and continue the analysis?' She feels she'd have to continue. But how could she bring her baby to the sessions? She would be so jealous of my feelings for the baby. She'd feel like a rival with her own baby.

Towards the end of the session, quietly, she said that she has to have the fifth session because she is not 'developed enough'.

The themes related to the queens Mary and Elizabeth continued and Lisa's associations led to her feeling convinced that one of us would have to die. Even though she could see this was a picture of her internal world, it nevertheless had a powerful grip on her. She could hardly make a distinction between internal and external realities.

At work, she felt resistant to being promoted, although she longed for it. She did not want anything to change. I said I thought that she was terrified of becoming a mother (represented by Mary Queen of Scots), and that it was much safer to remain a daughter. This reminded her that her mother made it quite clear to both her and her sister that they should never become women, let alone mothers. The most miserable years of her life were between 7 and 13. Her mother wanted her to remain a little girl forever.

I said that she feels that here too – that I could not bear her to make me the grandmother and that she is sure that I would feel as rivalrous of her as she feels towards me.

Lisa arrived in a great state of panic at the beginning of the last week before the fifth session was on offer. Completing a piece of work at the weekend had instigated it. She was feeling good about it and this was followed, 'out of the blue', by terrible panic that a colleague would accuse her of stealing her tune. This led to her feeling desperate despair and a wish to destroy all her good work.

I said that at the weekend, when she had finally finished her piece of work, there was a blur between her situation with her colleague and the situation with me. She is sure I will accuse her of stealing from me if she stakes her claim to become a woman in her own right. Her hesitation about the fifth session is because she is sure that it is me who cannot tolerate her desire to become a mother because she feels it will lead to a deadly competition. In her mind there can't be two queens.

At the beginning of the next session Lisa said that yesterday she had felt better for the rest of the day, but now, in this room, she's beginning to feel worse again. All she can think about is the colleague who accused her of stealing. She feels she has done something wrong. And today she has to meet her senior colleague who cannot understand why it has taken Lisa so long to complete this composition. Lisa wishes so much she could be like her senior colleague.

I said that she feels at some level that she does indeed steal and this is what feels wrong. After a pause she said quietly 'It's envy, I feel so envious everywhere.'

The fear of WOMAN/analysis

The following session began with Lisa telling me, sheepishly, that she and her husband had been trying for a baby already and she had been afraid of telling me. This seemed to explain her intense anxiety. She had thought she could be pregnant. When she turned out not to be, she felt relieved, because her desire to triumph over me was contaminated with a dreadful anxiety that I would take revenge or collapse and die.

We had reached the final session before the weekend break and Lisa had still not confirmed that she would take up the fifth session. It was clear that she felt trapped between staying the daughter – the four sessions – and moving forwards to becoming a woman and conceiving – the five sessions. She felt she couldn't go back, but it felt impossible to go forward.

She then, rather suddenly, confirmed that she did want the fifth session and felt ready to start. Then very quickly, in a little girl's voice, she said, 'Oh, do you think it will be all right? Won't it make things worse? I have not felt the anxiety so badly for all these years until this summer. Will it ever go away?'

After a pause I said that she wanted to stay small where it felt safe – that she wants me to reassure her that it will be all right to become an adult woman – even a queen – and that I can tolerate that. She said she didn't want to go backwards. There was an uncomfortable silence for a while, followed by Lisa remembering a photograph she'd seen that week at an exhibition.

It was of a mother in a war zone carrying her two children across a river because the bridge had been destroyed. There was harsh criticism of the photographer; it was felt that he should have saved her instead of just taking the photo and that he was accused of being a murderer. Lisa hadn't interpreted the photo like that, however. She felt it showed a strong woman who was surviving and looked like she would survive. And the true story, she went on to say, is that the woman did indeed survive. The critic had got it wrong. And there's another photo of the photographer with the woman and her children a year later.

I said it seems that she is portraying how she feels today, oscillating between the strong, surviving woman and the accusing critic. I'm the photographer.

'Yes, I do see that. It is how it feels', she said with conviction. Then quickly she asked again, in her little girl voice, whether it would work and pleaded, 'There's no going back', as if she was warning us of some pending disaster.

It was time.

Discussion

The incremental increase in sessions I came to see as illustrating a manifest developmental move towards maturity: from early adolescence (the second session), late adolescence (the third session and move to the couch), early adulthood (the fourth session) and, finally, fully-fledged womanhood (queen) (the crowning fifth session). Coinciding with her developing relationship with her man meant she could gradually allow herself to move closer to me. This was evidence of an increasing trust in psychoanalysis as a method of assisting understanding and developing insight. Lisa was feeling sure that without the analysis she would have been unable to sustain the relationship and was grateful she had experienced such a successful wedding.

Related to the notion of a surviving object, I came to think that this move towards the fifth session emanated from an intrapsychic surviving object that had been in the process of developing since Lisa had taken the decision to attend a brief course (six sessions) in our very first meeting. This could be seen as a sign that the undeveloped surviving object had a chance to grow in the analysing situation. However, the question that remained in her full analysis related to her psychosexuality and wish to become a mother. *Survival-of-the-object* makes it possible to work through the Oedipal death wishes. But if the patient is libidinally invested in retaining the status quo, this working through may be impossible and the painful predicament of an 'analysis interminable' may arise (Freud 1937).

Transference and infantile sexuality

The manifest content of the transference in the clinical picture I have presented illustrates that Lisa's core unconscious anxieties in analysis demonstrate the classical Oedipal dynamics. But what I am aiming to suggest here is that the issue of dependency in what Freud described as the feminine phase of development refers back to the earliest psychic development when the establishment of psychic survival or non survival takes root, as I propose in Chapter 2 and throughout the chapters of this book.

As will be gathered, Lisa's way of being in the sessions was often akin to a performance and I was struck how she consigned me to the audience position. Danckwardt and Wegner have developed the notion of performance as a form of the transference related to what has not been quite realised psychically and it works on a pre-symbolic level. 'In a performance, a one-person psychology and a monologue in action prevail' (Danckwardt & Wegner 2007: 1121). Accordingly, although Lisa seemed to be working at the symbolic level, with her rich content, simultaneously she kept me in the role of audience to avoid engagement and penetration. Her defensive cutting off at breaks was what she referred to as the 'oblivious' part of herself which she was only able to recognise in the latter part of the analysis. It was something she found herself doing and it anaesthetised psychic pain in an effective way. The problem was that it prevented mourning for the lost object and its manic quality meant that it didn't last and the intense anxieties returned. This 'fear of breakdown', which had brought her into the treatment in the first place, was a strong feature throughout the treatment (Winnicott [1963?] 1970).

This difficulty with symbolising was experienced by me in the countertransference as I could often feel as if I wasn't quite present, as shown at the beginning. Before her taking up the fourth session we had gone through many months of what seemed an impossibly negative transference that made me despair that anything could change. I found that taking the projections she assigned me, of an object that was giving up on her, and interpreting this, (a teacher who had given up on her ever understanding a certain subject), brought us through and led to her taking up a fourth session. I thought that not interpreting her envious attacks had helped her experience psychic *survival-of-the-object*. But after the fourth session was instated, I wondered whether I was right about that, and began to feel manipulated. This quality of the countertransference edge made me feel despair rather than panic or fear.

The tantalising way in which she hesitated about the fifth session, however, suggested a deferred-gratification way of being which coloured so much of how Lisa lived her life and was a way she felt she was in control of her objects. There is a strong sense that she hides a lot of good things that happen to her from the sessions. When I made an observational remark about keeping the best thing on the plate till last, Lisa felt surprised. I think she felt I'd understood her, but at the same time I think she may also have felt I had an X-ray kind of understanding which may have felt too magical and close. But it was fruitful in that it led to her disclosure of this very striking difficulty of taking good things in and keeping them there. Once she'd had the 'best thing on the plate' it had gone. The loss was traumatising, and it was as if there was nothing good to hold on to inside, i.e., good symbolic feeds that, in turn, nourish and help develop the surviving object. It raises the question of what happens, in her mind, when she gets the best thing. Does she enviously destroy the good object so that she is left focused on the sense of loss and trauma as in melancholia? (Freud 1917). But there may well have been an unconscious masochistic pleasure in not getting what she appeared to want. As Kohon has pointed out, deprivation for the hysteric is libidinally invested and this is where sexuality resides (Kohon 1986).

The experience of watching the play showed a clear anxiety about the passionate homoerotic transference. She felt overwhelmed by the thought that erotic and Oedipal feelings could cause the death of so many people in the train crash and I think there was something about this scene which made her feel on the verge of breaking down. This confused her so much she misplaced her keys and thought she'd left them in the waiting room. This links with the issues of responsibility: who makes her lose her sense of Self? Like the stationmaster in the play: was it his responsibility or the woman with whom he was flirting? Actually, for Lisa it was sexual desire that made him lose his sense of responsibility. There is much of relevance to Lisa's case here. In fact, she discovered that the keys were in her bag all the time. She had the key to her own destiny if she could only realise it (cf. Bollas 1989).

There were many associations to the story of Mary Stuart and Elizabeth Tudor, and she felt (hysterically) identified with both queens. The narrative illustrated the powerful sense of envy and fear of envy and the relevance of sibling rivalry in the transference (Mitchell 2000, 2003). Elizabeth may have lived, but in relation to these themes she did not survive psychically by signing the death warrant for Mary's execution. The comment I made at the end of the session, about the 'sexy Queen of Scots', was one of those moments when I found myself articulating the unsaid element and it seemed to mobilise Lisa's memory of her dream during the summer break about Faust. The focus of her associations to this dream led to her association about a woman's murder of her own baby. This was another frightening identification. And the man in the dream was certainly echoing a reality, i.e. that she was leaving things too late. Lisa was only too aware that her chronological age was increasingly lessening her chances of ever conceiving. The references to violence and destruction of creativity are all too transparent.

The fear of WOMAN/analysis

The Oedipal issues were always lurking and came to consciousness when Lisa looked after her neighbour's cat. She had long been aware that she could not bear the thought of three and can only deal with two. This is why she is so possessive. She knows she is not 'developed enough'. But this led to her seeing that it was 'miserable' to stay young and it was her (internal) mother, not her, who wanted her to stay little forever. That's why it was so dangerous to attain what she desired, i.e. to eliminate her mother and become the queen herself. This death-wish desire had to stay secret from everybody, including herself.

The oscillating between the little girl who needed reassurance from me, in the final session, moved me and I felt her sense of anxiety. Was the fifth session really a good idea? Did it indicate progress? For a moment, I felt persuaded by her intense fear that one or other of us would break down – non survival – a murdered analytic baby (Faust). There was a moment in the session that made it difficult to stay with before Lisa's last narrative of the surviving mother. This suggested a move away from the après coup moment of non survival to a new sense (and hope) of survival. I had the impression that she had indeed achieved a significant amount of psychic work during these particular weeks. Not being promoted, yet, by her senior colleague, seemed to help her feel safe enough to risk having the full analysis – with a view of working towards the bigger project, i.e. getting pregnant and becoming a mother. And although there was still a destroyed bridge to be repaired, there was hope that in the next year, the analytic baby/analysis would survive. The question was whether it would be enough for her to conceive a real baby.

Like Freud's hysteric patient Dora, Lisa was also overwhelmed by an unconscious desire for the mother she'd never had and this was played out in the transference-resistance. Dora was convinced that her primary passion had annihilated her m/other. The multiple layers of early non *survival-of-the-object* are blurred in the hysteric's psyche due to powerful forces of repression where desire is associated with the Oedipal death wish and to imagine participating in the primal scene is terrifying. This terror comes about because the infantile wishes and attacks towards the m/Other have not been survived at the earliest and subsequent stages of development. This indicates that terror of the object is at the core of a non surviving intrapsychic object, as I argue in Chapter 3. Dora's longing and desire for her mother/Frau K. related to her overwhelming non surviving object, was why her desire had to be repressed. It is the non surviving object that is at the core of the transference-resistance. Let us now turn to Winnicott's thesis about the fear of WOMAN and my proposal at the beginning of this essay in relation to the roots of misogyny.

I suggest that a sense of desire is inevitable in everybody who is alive and that it emerges out of the experience of satisfaction. Depending on the quality and quantity of satisfaction, related to the m/Other's capacities at the beginning, desire in the subject will be connected to both the intrapsychic surviving object and the non surviving object. The subject's desire that is related to non survival instigates a pathological malice, envy and jealousy. This may drive the individual towards power for power's sake and dominance. Desire becomes an insatiable greed that devours the Self. Conversely, desire is inhibited and kept hidden because the subject is convinced the Other will retaliate as in the case of Lisa. This also applied to the case of Jill in Chapter 2.

The corollary is a desire related to a surviving object that has potential to grow and blossom because the fear of reprisal is significantly mitigated by a trust that it can be survived by the m/Other. Like Freud's case of Dora, Lisa's foremost anxieties were concerned with her Oedipal & sibling rivalries.

Throughout the course of analysis, the analyst's capacity to tolerate and understand the vicissitudes of infantile sexuality and murderous passion associated with desire in each patient can incrementally lead to the development of a surviving object which, depending on the analytic setting, will hopefully start to eclipse the non surviving object. Every single aspect of analysis – holding and interpretation – contributes to the patient's internalising of an object that is alive and able to survive, i.e. remain intact despite the aggressive and passionate onslaughts from the patient.

Gradually, the patient's internal landscape can shift and the apprehension of the repressed aspects of unconscious desire can move to preconscious and subsequently conscious desire. Due to the increasing strength of the intrapsychic surviving object, which has evolved through the analyst's interpsychic survival of the attacks, the analysand is able to separate out her death wishes and infantile sexuality from the more mature adult position. This, in turn, diminishes the fear of moving into the adult world in which the capacity to give life, through survival of one's own primitive desires, offers a sense of freedom and satisfaction. This would indicate that the adolescent's psychic tasks are complete by the 'final theoretical feed' (Abram 2007a: 209). This is not to say that the struggle with infantile desires and death wishes are over. They will continue to disturb, but with a stronger surviving object there is more of chance they are kept under control.

A sense of satisfaction is achieved through the first and subsequent theoretical feeds that have led to the final theoretical feed. In maturity, once a whole surviving object has established itself, the subsequent part of the journey towards wisdom is that of disillusionment. The paradox is that the object of desire can be attained – in a good theoretical feed and ego orgasm – but it follows that it cannot last in reality. Thus, the sense of satisfaction, physically and emotionally, is dictated by the reality principle in which a process of mourning and working through must occur. These processes enrich the inner surviving object, leading to further growth up until and including death. In mature love, this must be accompanied by the acknowledgement and toleration of the paradox. The capacity to become aware of one's own desire will simultaneously carry a realisation that unconscious desire involves a combination of the erotic longing for the unattainable mother alongside the necessary metaphorical murder of the father. The hope embedded in this terrible realisation is that the process of mourning and working through can begin (Perelberg 2009: 729). This has the potential to lead to discernment of the other and the capacity to love.

References

Abram, J. ([1996] 2003) Squiggles, clowns and Catherine wheels: reflexions sur le concept Winnicottien du 'violation du self' *Le Coq Heron* 173 2003 Chapter 1.

Abram, J. (2007a) *The language of Winnicott: A dictionary of Winnicott's use of words*, 2nd edition. London: Karnac.

Abram, J. (2007b) L'objet qui ne survit pas: Quelques réflexions sur les racines de la terreur, Houzel D, translator. *J Psychanal l'enfant* 39: 247–270. Paris: Bayard. Chapter 3.

Akhtar, S. (1999) The distinction between needs and wishes: implications for psychoanalytic theory and technique *J Am Psychoanal Assn* 47: 113–151.

Bion, W.R. (1962) A theory of thinking. In: *Second thoughts* (1967). London: William Heinemann Medical Books.

Bollas, C. (1989) *The destiny drive in Forces of destiny: psychoanalysis and human idiom*, Free Association Books.

Danckwardt, J. & Wegner, P. (2007) Performance as annihilation or integration? *Int J Psychoanal* 88: 1117–1133, p. 1121.

Freud, S. (1900) The interpretation of dreams. SE 4 1–626.

Freud, S. (1917) Mourning and melancholia. SE 14 243–59.

Freud, S. (1931) Female sexuality SE 21 225–243.

Freud, S. (1937) Analysis terminable and interminable SE 23 209–254.

Kohon, G. (1986) Reflections on Dora: the case of hysteria in *The British School of Psychoanalysis: The Independent Tradition*, Free Association Books.

Laplanche, J. & Pontalis, J.-B. (1973) *The Language of Psychoanalysis*. The Hogarth Press & The Institute of Psychoanalysis.

Mitchell, J. (2000) *Mad men and Medusas: Reclaiming hysteria and the effects of sibling relations on the human condition*, Allen Lane The Penguin Press.

Mitchell, J. (2003) *Siblings*, Polity Press.

Ogden, T. (1987) The transitional Oedipal relationship in female development. *Int J Psychoanal* 68: 485–498.

Oxford English Dictionary Second Edition Version 3.1 Oxford University Press 2004, 2005.

Perelberg, R. (2009) Murdered father; dead father: Revisiting the Oedipus complex. *Int J Psychoanal* 90: 713–732.

Riviere, J. (1936) A contribution to the analysis of the negative therapeutic reaction. *Int J Psychoanal* 17: 304–320.

Winnicott DW (1931) Appetite and emotional disorder In: *Collected papers: Through paediatrics to psychoanalysis*, 1st edition. London: Tavistock.

Winnicott DW (1945). Primitive emotional development. *Int J Psychoanal* 26: 137–143.

Winnicott DW (1957) The mother's contribution to society in *The child the family and the outside world*. London: Tavistock.

Winnicott DW (1963). The development of the capacity for concern [1960]. *Bull Menninger Clin* 27: 167–176.

Winnicott DW (1971). *Playing and reality*. London: Tavistock

Winnicott DW ([1954] 1988). *Human nature*, Bollas C, Davis M, Shepherd R, editors. London: Free Association Books.

5

ON WINNICOTT'S CLINICAL INNOVATIONS IN THE ANALYSIS OF ADULTS (2012)

Prelude

This chapter takes an overview of Winnicott's contribution and focuses on his clinical innovations to offer some further reflections on Winnicott's emphases on the infantile as distinct from Freud and Klein. Drawing on the comments of several of his contemporaries, such as William Gillespie, Marion Milner and Pearl King, I show how he was appreciated primarily as a dedicated clinician. With reference to Winnicott's early scientific education Loparic has long argued that Winnicott's work is scientific: something Winnicott emphasised to his colleague Ella Sharpe in the 1940s (Abram 2018 in Abram & Hinshelwood 2018: 143). In reference to the contemporary literature of today I highlight some of the specific innovations identified by contemporary authors, as seen in Abram 2013: co-thinking (Widlöcher 2006); creating a non-fiction literature (Ogden 2001); actualisation (Green 2000); the clinical advance of primary narcissism (Roussillon 2010); fear of breakdown as an example of nachträglichkeit (Faimberg 1998); and his way of interpreting 'countertransference madness' (Goldman 2012). This chapter also examines Winnicott's paper on the 'aims of psychoanalytic treatment' and comments on the controversial area of what he termed 'modifications' in any given analytic treatment (Winnicott [1962] 1965). The clinical example from Winnicott's late work highlights his way of working in the countertransference.

It should be borne in mind that the aim of this chapter can only begin the enumeration of Winnicott's clinical innovations because the corpus of Winnicott's writings amounts to well over 600 articles with further unpublished writings in the archives. A simple search on PEP shows that his work is cited in almost 12,000 articles and books. The second edition of *The Language of Winnicott* (2007) contains 23 major entries with 165 sub-entries. Each entry illustrates how Winnicott elaborated on Freud's work while in an ongoing discourse with the parallel Kleinian development. Thus, the scope of the task of examining Winnicott's clinical innovations has an enormous potential, but requires substantial research to give full credit to Winnicott's clinical innovations in the analysis of adults. Despite this limitation, this chapter will hopefully inspire others to take up the baton of research.

The clinical language of Winnicott

Winnicott was one of the major conceptual innovators in the history of psychoanalysis during the 20th century. The primacy of the environment–individual set-up is at the core of his formulations and provides psychoanalysis with a new symbolic matrix i.e., the early parent-infant relationship. This contribution extends and amplifies the original Freudian Oedipal symbolic matrix. For Winnicott, psychoanalysis constitutes a scientific theory of emotional development and human nature which is illuminated through the Freudian lens of psychoanalytic practice.

Winnicott's writings invoke the clinical situation and the day-to-day intrapsychic and inter-psychic struggle that is demanded of each analyst in clinical work. He is able to convey the ineffability of what it means to be in 'the continual process of becoming an analyst', due to being 'on excellent terms with his primary processes' (Milner 1972: 10). 'He was first and foremost a psychoanalyst' (Gillespie 1972: 1) who believed that it was essential to be '…firmly rooted in the spirit of the psychoanalytic tradition, rather than the letter of it, if a psychoanalyst wishes to work at the cutting-edge of psychoanalytic discovery' (King 1972: 28).

The emphasis on 'psychoanalytic discovery' and psychoanalysis as a science was founded on Winnicott's early education at The Leys School, Cambridge, a school well known for the teaching of the sciences. Loparic, drawing on Thomas Kuhn's theory of the 'structure of scientific revolutions', has argued that Winnicott's debt to Darwin, like Freud, showed him that '…living things could be studied scientifically, with the corollary that gaps in knowledge and understanding need not scare' (Winnicott [1945b] 1996): 7) and illustrates how Winnicott's new 'exemplar', Kuhn's term for model or paradigm, came about through his clinical discoveries (Loparic 2012 in Abram 2013). So, while it is true that Winnicott's prose may be described as 'poetic', this does not mean that his innovations are more art than science. Winnicott himself always maintained that he did not view the psychoanalytic method as an art. In 1946, in a letter to Ella Sharpe, he writes that he does not agree with her that psychoanalysis is an art. He emphasises that for him the technique of psychoanalysis is 'based on scientific considerations more' (Winnicott 1946 in Rodman 1987: 10).

Thomas Ogden, through a detailed analysis of Winnicott's seminal text, 'Primitive emotional development', observes that '…Winnicott does not use language to arrive at conclusions'; rather, he shares his process of discovery and creates a 'non-fiction literature'. When reading Winnicott, Ogden writes, there is a '…meeting of reader and writing [that] generates an imaginative experience in the medium of language' and proposes that the formulations in Winnicott's writings are inseparable from the man and the life of his ideas (Ogden 2001).

Winnicott argued that '…dependent or deeply regressed patients can teach the analyst more about early infancy than can be learnt from direct observation of infants, and more than can be learned from contact with mothers who are involved with infants' (Winnicott 1960: 141). This statement endorses Freud's original argument that innovations in psychoanalysis can only evolve in the context of Freudian clinical methodology, i.e. the analysand on the couch in high-frequency analysis. This is the tried and tested setting in which psychic work can be generated and in which new clinical discoveries can come to light with each different case study. André Green has argued that Winnicott's thought emerged from a close examination of his countertransference in the analytic situation rather than his paediatric work (Green 1975, 2000). A clinical innovation, therefore, only has value as an authentic psychoanalytic advance if it emerges out of the transference–countertransference matrix of the analytic situation.

As I have demonstrated elsewhere (Abram 2007), Winnicott's capacity to invoke clinical psychoanalytic experience, for both analyst and analysand, gave birth to a distinctive psychoanalytic language. I suggest that it constitutes a 'clinical language'[1] which has generated a new theoretical matrix. In other words, Winnicott's clinical innovations, based on scientific investigation and discovery within the analytic setting, are integrated with his conceptual advances. They are of a piece.

Darwin and Freud – Winnicott's cup of tea

Winnicott said that when he found Freud's method he felt 'in line with it' and it reminded him of when he read Darwin at school and he knew his work was his 'cup of tea' (Winnicott [1967] 1989: 574).

Winnicott 'found' Freud's work in 1919 at the age of 24. Four years later, after a consultation with Ernest Jones, the founder of the Institute of Psychoanalysis (in London), he started analysis with James Strachey, who had just returned from Vienna having had an analysis with Sigmund Freud. In 1929 Winnicott started the analytic training at the Institute of Psychoanalysis only three years after Melanie Klein had come to live and work in London from Berlin.

Freud's clinical method continued to be Winnicott's 'cup of tea', and he maintained that '…it's an objective way of looking at things… without preconceived notions, which… is science' (ibid.). After a ten year analysis with James Strachey (1923–1933), who was the General Editor of *The Standard Edition of the Complete Psychological Works of Sigmund Freud* it is hardly surprising that Winnicott said he always felt that 'Freud was in his bones' and, he protested that any original ideas he may have '…are only valuable as a growth of ordinary Freudian psychoanalytic theory… and would make no sense at all if planted on a world that had not been prepared for it by Freud' (Winnicott 1954 in Rodman 1987: 75). A close reading of Winnicott's texts shows how, throughout his life and work, he was continually in the process of finding and using Freudian objects and 'creating the object' (Winnicott 1969). For example, in one of Winnicott's key texts, 'The theory of the parent–infant relationship' ([1960] 1962), he acknowledges that Freud's concepts on infancy are derived from a study of adults in analysis and subsequently illustrates in a footnote how Freud, paid '…full credit to the function of maternal care':

> It will rightly be objected that an organization which was a slave to the pleasure-principle and neglected the reality of the external world could not maintain itself alive for the shortest time, so that it could not have come into existence at all. The employment of a

fiction like this is, however, justified when one considers that the infant – 'provided one includes with it the care it receives from its mother' – does almost realize a psychical system of this kind.
(Freud 1911 cited in Winnicott [1960] 1965: 39)

Winnicott points out that Freud did not develop the idea of the powerful influence of maternal care on the psyche beyond this observation, because 'he was not ready to discuss its implications' (ibid., 39).

Later in 1926, Freud will identify the infant's state of helplessness – hilflosigkeit – and focus on the instinctual tension brought about by infantile need. These notions anticipate Winnicott's theories of dependency and his distinction between needs and wishes – a distinction originally made by Freud in 'The Interpretation of Dreams' (Freud 1900). Winnicott (as well as Balint, Suttie and Fairbairn in different ways) did build on the distinction (Akhtar 1999), and, for Winnicott, infantile needs and a sense of helplessness in the adult patient were clinical facts. This area of conceptualising became pivotal to his clinical approach, as I have suggested in Chapters 2, 3 and 4.

The aims of psychoanalytical treatment

In 1962, after over thirty years work as an analyst, Winnicott substantiates his approach through an outline of his aims in clinical psychoanalysis. He begins by saying that he does analysis '…because that is what the patient needs to have done and have done with' (Winnicott [1962] 1965: 166) and identifies three phases of a 'standard analysis' in terms of how the analysis affects the patient's ego. In the first phase it is the analyst's ego support that will help develop the patient's ego-strength. The analyst in a 'standard analysis' functions like the good enough mother with her newborn baby whose ego needs are supported by the m/Other's ego. This is in line with classical analysis of the early days of Freudian analysis in which the aims of the treatment were to reinforce the patient's ego functions. But, adding to classical analysis, Winnicott parallels this process with another one derived from his recognition of the crucial impact on the psyche of the earliest parent–infant relationship. In the transference the analyst has to be prepared to be both the mother of the early phases of life as well as the mother and father of the later stages of development. In the second phase – the longest phase of the analysis '…the patient's confidence in the analytic process brings about all kinds of experimenting… in terms of ego independence'. And in the third and final phase the patient is able to '…gather all things into the area of personal omnipotence, even including the genuine traumata' (Winnicott [1962] 1965: 168). By this third and final stage the patient will have worked through a sufficient amount to be able to take back the projections and develop beyond the traumata of the original situation, i.e. the patient's family history. Winnicott follows this by stating: 'If the patient does not need analysis then I do something else' (ibid.: 168).

The 'something else' in this paper is referred to as 'modified analysis' (elsewhere it is sometimes referred to as psychotherapy), and Winnicott identifies five specific conditions which qualify for a modification of standard analysis.

(a) Where fear of madness dominates the scene.
(b) Where a false self has become successful, and a façade of success and even brilliance will be destroyed at some phase if analysis is to succeed.
(c) Where in a patient an antisocial tendency, either in the form of aggression or of stealing or of both, is the legacy of deprivation.
(d) Where there is no cultural life – only an inner psychic reality and a relationship to external reality – the two being relatively un-linked.
(e) Where an ill parental figure dominates the scene.

In the above conditions Winnicott states that he 'changes into being a psychoanalyst' who will 'meet the needs' of that 'special case'. And while he refers to this being 'non-analytic work' he asserts that it is '…usually best done by an analyst who is well versed in the standard psychoanalytic technique' (ibid.: 169).

So, for Winnicott, standard analysis is appropriate for the patient who is capable of developing ego strengths through the ordinary use of 'standard analysis', i.e. psychic work in the transference–interpretation matrix of the analytic setting. This category of patient, usually referred to as 'analysable', contrasts with the patient who may display any one of the five conditions above for which, Winnicott believes, require the psychoanalyst to do 'something else'. He finishes the paper by stating that aims in psychoanalysis do not need to change if we are verbalising the 'nascent conscious stages' of development. But if this is not possible then the analyst has to practice 'something else' which would be appropriate (ibid.: 170).

This approach is controversial and, as we can see from the above, it is based on Winnicott's clinical discoveries related to his understanding about the traumatised infant (whose needs had not been met) in the adult patient. The psychoanalytic setting mobilises infantile states of mind, which will mean that the adult's unmet infantile needs will come to the fore in the transference and the analyst must be able to recognise that in a regressed state the patient has needs rather than wishes.

> The regressed patient is near to a reliving of dream and memory situations; an acting out of a dream may be the only way the patient discovers what is urgent and talking about what was acted out follows the action but cannot precede it.
>
> (Winnicott 1955: 22)

It cannot precede it because the patient is not functioning in a symbolic mode. Winnicott also refers to the patient who has an 'observing ego' that identifies with the analyst while going through a state of helplessness and need during the analytic hour. This patient can recover from regression at the end of the hour. But for the patient who cannot enlist an 'observing ego' acting out is the only way to re-visit the original failure situation. Winnicott's proposed modifications in analytic technique are controversial because they led him to argue for a phase of 'acting out' as a necessary prerequisite to ordinary psychoanalytic work, i.e. 'standard analysis'. Once it is tolerated new understanding will follow.

Green and Sandler have referred to this kind of acting out as 'actualisation' linked with what Sandler termed 'role responsiveness' (Sandler 1976; Green 1996 in Abram 2016). This term conveys that patient and analyst are caught up with an actualisation process which has to be experienced before it can be thought through and subsequently worked through. This is the stuff of analysis and occurs in every analytic treatment. Each clinical illustration in this book highlights the way in which the actualisation process functions.

Winnicott's understanding was not controversial; it was the extent to which he enlisted modifications that became controversial. For example, as we can see in some of his published accounts, he would extend or shorten the session time frame; provide a drink and/or biscuits; and in one reported case he held the patient's head (Winnicott 1958b, 1971b). He considered these 'modifications' as non-analytic and his reasons for implementing these changes were certainly not on a whim, but on the basis of his confidence in the psychoanalytic setting and his conviction that the adult patient was in the process of reaching the traumatised infant inside within the context of the transference. In Chapter 6, as I reflected on the role of the father, I started to question Winnicott's implementation of extending the temporal frame of an analytic session. However, since the issue of 'modification' for each analyst is a controversial area since the beginning of psychoanalysis, each analyst with each case has to decide what constitutes 'modification' in analysis (see Chapter 6). For example in Chapter 2, was it a 'modification' when Faith used the chair instead of the couch? Or in Chapter 3 when K. stayed in the waiting lobby?

Meanwhile, in this chapter, in order to appreciate more fully why Winnicott considered it acceptable for a psychoanalyst to 'change' from practicing psychoanalysis to 'adapting to the patient's needs' for a small number of patients, it is important to understand the foundations of his approach which were evolving alongside his ideas on regression to dependence (Winnicott 1955).

Early psychic processes

If the reader has approached this book and read each chapter in chronological order you will be familiar with the main tenet of Winnicott's 'there's no such thing as a baby' ([1952] 1958c: 99) and my emphasis that his quest throughout his work was to understand and theorise the earliest stages of human development that preceded object relations (Abram 2007: 1189). He proposed that at the 'theoretical beginning' the baby lives in a subjective world and that the 'change from the primary state' requires, in addition to 'inherited growth processes', an 'environmental minimum' (Winnicott 1971a: 151).

The 'essential paradox' for Winnicott is inherent in the infant's predicament '…although the object was there to be found it was created by the baby' (Winnicott [1968b] 1989: 205). Elsewhere he said, '…it is only what you create that has meaning for you' (1968b: 101). From the early 1940s onwards, Winnicott's view of the individual always took account of the environment to which I add the term 'psychic' to emphasise Winnicott's meaning that is not behavioural but related to the Other's affects towards the subject (Winnicott 1958c: 99). The focus on the move from 'apperception' to 'perception' required a facilitating environment that would stimulate the maturational processes so that the baby could grow from 'dependence towards independence'.

Melanie Klein was also developing a theory of early psychic development in the late 1930s and 1940s, although the environment in her formulations did not have the same emphasis. For Klein, the newborn in the paranoid-schizoid position (Klein 1946) was in a state of inner persecutory anxieties which are caused by the innate death instinct. The infant's sense of feeling attacked, therefore, was internal. For Winnicott, the baby could potentially become terrified if there was not a good enough holding environment. As we will see more explicitly in his very late work as shown in Chapters 7 and 8, he did not agree with the concept of a death instinct and argued that innate aggression is not a manifestation of hate, sadism and envy as Klein had maintained. For Winnicott, these affects came later in the baby's development. So, the aggression in Winnicott's baby is benign and related to the need to survive. The instinct is one drive towards self-preservation – following early Freud before the introduction of the death instinct in 1920 (Freud 1911). Winnicott refers to this drive as primary psychic creativity and emphasises that the infant's need to survive is dependent on finding an object that will survive. The m/Other's capacity to adapt to the infant's needs, and tolerate the infant's inadvertent damage to her, means she will be the object who survives. Her emotional and actual psychic survival is an aspect of her capacity to adapt and will contribute to the infant feeling that he has created the world.

> The world is created anew by each human being, who starts on the task at least as early as… the time of birth and of the theoretical first feed.
>
> (Winnicott [1954] 1988: 110)

As I first indicated in Chapter 2, Winnicott's 'theoretical first feed' refers to a culmination of countless needs being met and, Winnicott stresses, this feed is both actual and symbolic. The mother has to be continually meeting the infant's needs in terms of general care, but it is her emotional approach towards her newborn that will make all the difference to the infant's experience of being fed by a mother who is alive to his human needs. The coming together of the mother's primary maternal identification with her baby's needs will amount to the theoretical first feed (Abram 2007: 210). Thus, Winnicott elaborates the details of a process of internalisation at the earliest stages and creates a concept to account for early symbolic processes, the potential in human nature, and the concept of health (Winnicott 1986, 1988).

Consequently, there are two distinct paradigms on early psychic development – as if there were two different infants and two different mothers. This is expounded in Chapter 4 of the Klein–Winnicott book with Hinshelwood (Abram & Hinshelwood 2018: 41–65). In contrast, Melanie Klein's mother mitigates the infant's innate death instinct to enable the infant to develop the good internal object. The good internal object will assist the infant to integrate the good and the bad breast of the paranoid-schizoid position rather than projecting either one or the other onto the mother. In contrast, Winnicott's baby does not yet have the (inner) material to split the object into good or bad and is even less able to project (also because of a lack of inner material at the earliest stages). For Winnicott, projection comes later in the baby's development. This is why the mother is so powerful at the beginning. Through her state of primary maternal preoccupation, she is able to prevent the infant from falling into 'primitive agonies' due to her capacity to hold and receive the infant's communications of near-terror. Winnicott's infant will only become terrified and suffer persecutory anxieties if s/he is not held, which simply means if the environment is not good enough. So, the early psychic environment is crucial for both theorists, but in Winnicott's conceptualisations, it is the mother's failure at the earliest stages that will cause severe mental illness (Winnicott 1953) and for Melanie Klein it will depend more on the endowment of the innate death instinct. I am aware that this simple statement requires more unpacking which is beyond the scope of this chapter. Hinshelwood maintains that Melanie Klein's 'death instinct' was more metaphorical than biological (see Abram & Hinshelwood 2018: 186–7).

Through the mother's capacity to identify with the infant's predicament she offers the infant total dedication which constitutes the ego support and ego coverage which would gradually be internalised by the infant. In this way it is the mother's 'adaptation to needs' that leads to the maternal inscription on the infant's psyche which will significantly influence Self development. Winnicott had introduced the term ego-relatedness in 1956 to describe the phase of absolute dependence when, in his terminology, the baby is merged with the mother and benefits from ego-coverage that emanates from the mother's primary maternal preoccupation (Abram 2007: 42). In his paper on 'The capacity to be alone' (1958d), he had stated that this capacity was based on the introjection of an 'ego-supportive environment' – a consequence of the early good enough mother's attention and adaptation, i.e. ego-coverage. He indicated that it links in with the existence of a good internal object in Klein's theory and an ability to tolerate the '…feelings aroused by the primal scene' in Freud's. Winnicott's emphasis is that the introjection of the good internal object and the resolution of the Oedipus complex could not occur, however, without the 'introjection of an ego-supportive environment' at the very beginning. The capacity to be alone is based on the paradox of being alone in the 'presence of mother' (Winnicott 1958d: 30), which starts from the beginning of life when the mother either succeeds or fails. Thus, for Winnicott the good internal object will emerge later in development and will be a consequence of the 'introjection of an ego-supportive environment'.[2]

This sequence has a direct bearing on Freud's concept of primary narcissism and has been clarified in the work of Roussillon who argues that Freud's 'shadow of the object' refers to the mother of the earliest stages as described by Winnicott, and '…if suffering involves the shadow of the object that has fallen on the ego, the analyst will have to help the patient give that shadow back to the object, break free of the blend brought about by her narcissistic defences and deconstruct the basic narcissistic postulate of the self-generation of the mind' (Roussillon 2010: 822). The main thrust of Roussillon's argument is that Winnicott's discovery of the mother's powerful inscription on the Self that occurs during early psychic processes, transformed Freud's concept of primary narcissism into a clinical concept because Winnicott's primary narcissism 'cannot be conceived of in a solipsistic way' (ibid.). Roussillon suggests that in primary narcissism there is a 'kind of primitive illusion' that 'tends to obliterate' the fact of the mother's inscription and that the analysis of primary narcissism reintroduces 'what the primary narcissistic illusion has erased' (ibid.).

This constitutes a significant clinical innovation and is an example of how, having 'Freud in his bones', Winnicott extended many of Freud's concepts through his focus on early psychic phenomenon. The question of technique, then, relates to how the analyst helps the patient 'give back the shadow of the object to the object' (ibid.). And if the 'shadow' relates to the maternal failures of the earliest stages then the analysand will have to return to the original failure situation within the safety of the analytic setting.

Impingement and trauma re-vivified in the analytic setting

Winnicott's focus on early psychic processes and the environment–individual set-up led him to transpose the notion of 'adaptation to need'[3] to the analytic setting. The ordinary formal regression that inevitably occurs during the course of an analysis was seen as a way of 're-living the not-yet-experienced trauma' (Abram 2007: 275). The trauma had happened at the time of an early environmental failure when the baby had suffered gross impingement and had no other option other than to withdraw (Winnicott 1953). The trauma was 'catalogued' or 'registered', but could not be integrated into the developing self because there was not yet a Self to process the shock. In his late work Winnicott referred to gross impingements as a 'violation of the self' and a 'sin against the self' as elaborated in Chapter 1 (Winnicott 1965c).

Haydée Faimberg, who developed the concept of the 'telescoping of generations' (1981/85 in 2005), has illustrated how Winnicott's fear of breakdown enlarges on Freud's concept of *Nachträglichkeit* (Faimberg [1998] 2013 in Abram 2013). Faimberg poignantly illustrates that, while never explicitly using the term 'Nachträglichkeit', Winnicott's concept of the 'fear of breakdown' offers psychoanalysis an 'excellent example of Nachträglichkeit'. Winnicott states that when the 'fear of breakdown' is felt by the patient in the present time of the session, the analyst should interpret that the fear of the future breakdown is based on the breakdown that has already happened. This, Faimberg asserts, constitutes a construction as Freud had originally suggested in his paper of 1937 'Constructions in analysis'. She shows how Winnicott offers a 'retroactive meaning to the patient's fear of breakdown in the present moment of the transference'. Thus, Faimberg shows how Winnicott's formulation of the fear of breakdown constitutes another significant clinical innovation (Faimberg 2013: 314).

The analytic setting, therefore, provides a holding environment that potentially offers the patient an opportunity to re-visit the early failure situation. These concepts related to infancy complement and enhance psychoanalytic technique. When Winnicott writes that 'changes come in an analysis when the traumatic factors enter the psychoanalytic material in the patient's own way, and within the patient's omnipotence' ([1960] 1962: 585), he is referring to his view that good (enough) psychoanalytic technique requires the analyst to 'adapt' to the patient's way of being in the analysis rather than imposing an interpretation that the patient may not be ready to hear. When the traumatised infant inside starts to emerge in the evolving transference the analyst should be ready to become the m/Other of the early failure situation. In standard analysis this comes about in the ordinary transference situation which is illusory. Let me add here that in the context of analysis the traumatised infant is 'clinical' and the m/Other of the early failure situation is a feature of the countertransference actualisation which is also 'clinical' or 'analytic'. As I have argued in Chapter 7 no analyst can literally compensate for the original object's deficiencies.

A clinical example from Winnicott's late work

A well-known clinical example of Winnicott's that highlights his particular transformation of the Freudian concepts of primary narcissism and nachträglichkeit is of the case he writes about in Chapter 6 of *Playing and Reality* (1971c). During the course of an ongoing analysis, he finds himself feeling that he is listening to a girl, although the patient on his couch is a middle-aged man. He tells the patient, 'I am listening to a girl. I know perfectly well that you are a man but I am listening to a girl, and I am talking to a girl. I am telling this girl: "You are talking about penis envy"' (Winnicott 1971c: 73).

We learn that in this analysis there was a pattern of good work that was followed by destruction and disillusionment because 'something fundamental had not changed' (ibid.). But at this moment, Winnicott reports, there seemed to be an 'immediate effect'. The patient responded: 'If I were to tell someone about this girl, I would be called mad' (ibid.). Winnicott surprised himself by responding, 'It was not that you told this to anyone; it is I who see the girl and hear a girl talking, when actually there is a man on my couch. The mad person is myself' (Winnicott 1971c: 73).

The patient claimed that Winnicott had spoken to both parts of him – the man who he knew he was and the girl who had felt hidden and 'mad'. Subsequently, both patient and analyst come to the conclusion that the patient's mother had seen him as a girl before seeing him as a boy. As a baby, therefore, he was sane in a mad environment that had been introjected by the patient and subsequently projected on to his analyst who had felt this through his countertransference. Although Winnicott says it was difficult to prove that the patient's mother really had seen him as a girl to begin with, we must assume that the evidence for this conjecture is manifested in the countertransference. This is what felt authentic to both patient and analyst at that moment and led on to further meaningful psychic work.

The above clinical example is used by Winnicott to illustrate his conceptualisations of dissociated male and female elements. Dodi Goldman has recently proposed that the vignette shows how '…a channel of communication' between Winnicott and his patient opens up between the previously dissociated male and female elements in the patient who had to resort to 'complete dissociation' as a defence against repeating the trauma of the original situation. This also links with the concept of recognition in Winnicott's conceptualisation of the mirror role of mother, i.e. the baby's need to be recognised for who s/he is otherwise the baby is traumatised through misrecognition, as in the case of Winnicott's patient, by a mad mother/environment. Goldman concludes that this clinical account is a 'striking and courageous clinical innovation' because it is an acknowledgement that the analyst has received the actualised projection, as we saw in the Discussion of Chapter 3, i.e. the analyst has become the patient's dissociated original object. By saying that he is mad and not the patient Winnicott 'owns the projection as his own' (Goldman 2013 in Abram 2013: 351). Goldman suggests that this is an exemplary clinical example of 'living through together' 'previously dissociated elements' that are embedded in the psyche that become 'symbolized in thought and language' (ibid.: 351).

The analyst's capacity to tolerate the patient's unconsciously transmitted communication of the failed early environment means that the patient is facilitated to re-live the (frozen or catalogued) trauma for the first time, as we can see in the above example. This experience in the temporally present situation of the transference will potentially lead to an un-freezing. When Winnicott says that changes can only come about 'within the patient's omnipotence' he is referring to his formulations on 'illusion of omnipotence' (Abram 2007: 200–216). If the baby's needs are met by the good enough mother, he feels he has created the world and that he is god. This is the basis of self-esteem and it is only from this place of 'omnipotence' that the infant can move on to a normal disillusionment and the capacity to mourn the lost object.[4] When Winnicott tells the patient that it is he, the analyst/mother, who is mad, the patient can feel that he is sane in a mad environment, i.e. he was sane as a baby but living in a mad environment because his mother treated him as if he were a girl. This re-visiting of an earlier failure situation in the transference has to be lived through together, as Goldman has emphasised, so that it can be articulated and is thus thinkable at the symbolic level of psychic functioning instead of dissociated.

The example also highlights Winnicott's capacity for psychic availability and openness which is something that Widlöcher has identified, in relation to Winnicott's influence on French psychoanalytic circles in the 1960s, as 'freedom of thought' through his 'deep feeling for the analytical processes' (Widlöcher [2006] 2013). In reference to the theoretical turning point in psychoanalysis concerning the concept of countertransference, Widlöcher observes how Winnicott played a 'highly significant role in that shift of emphasis' by illustrating that the origins of a 'mutual communication' in the transference–countertransference 'lie in the interaction between mother and baby'. Widlöcher proposes the term 'co-thinking to describe the impact on the analysand's associative process and representations' (Widlöcher [2006] 2013: 236). Co-thinking is what leads Winnicott to say to the patient, 'The mad person is myself' (Winnicott 1971c: 74).

There is an obvious link here between what Winnicott describes as the 'freezing of the failure situation' and Freud's 'fixation point'. The difference between the two is that the failure situation relates to the earliest stages of development when the environment was either good enough or not good enough. In other words when the newborn baby is going through the phase of absolute dependency the mother either meets the infant's needs or not. This is the fact of dependence (Abram 2007: 133), which makes the environment so powerful. In my view, as I hope to have illustrated above, this is at the heart of Winnicott's legacy to psychoanalytic practice today. It emphasises the analyst's task to be attuned to the countertransference in order to listen to the traumatised clinical infant/child/adolescent inside each analysand (cf. Green 2005). Thus, the transference–interpretation matrix can offer the patient the possibility of a 'new beginning' (Winnicott 1954).

Notes

1 Cf. Green on clinical thinking.
2 The difference between Klein's internal objects and Winnicott's evolution of subjective and internal objects requires further analysis in the future.
3 For a more in-depth discussion on the meaning of 'adaptation to need' in Winnicott's work the reader is directed to the index in Abram 2007.
4 For further discussion on Winnicott's use of the word 'omnipotent' see Abram 2007 (index) & Abram & Hinshelwood 2018: 170.

References

Abram, J. (2007) *The language of Winnicott: A dictionary of Winnicott's use of words*, 2nd edition. London: Karnac Books.

Abram, J. (ed) (2013) *Donald Winnicott Today* New Library of Psychoanalysis. London: Routledge and The Institute of Psychoanalysis.

Abram, J. (ed) (2016) *André Green at the Squiggle Foundation*, revised edition. London: Karnac Books.

Abram, J. & Hinshelwood, R.D. (2018) *The Clinical Paradigms of Melanie Klein and Donald Winnicott: comparisons and dialogues*, London & New York: Routledge.

Akhtar, S. (1999) The distinction between needs and wishes: implications for psychoanalytic theory and technique. *J Am Psychoanal Assn* 47: 113–151.

Faimberg, H. (1981/85) The telescoping of generations: a genealogy of alienated identifications. In: Faimberg 2005 Chapter 1.

Faimberg, H. (2013) *Nachträglichkeit* and Winnicott's Fear of Breakdown In: Abram, J. editor 2013 Chapter 8.

Freud, S. (1900) The Interpretation of Dreams SE 5.

Freud, S. (1911) Formulations on the two principles of mental functioning SE **12**, 213–226.

Gillespie, W. (1972) Commemorative Meeting for Dr. Donald Winnicott, 19 January 1972 in Scientific Bulletin of The British Psychoanalytical Society and The Institute of Psychoanalysis.

Goldman, D. (2012) Vital sparks and the form of things unknown In: Abram, J. editor 2013 Chapter 15.

Green, A. (1975) Potential space in psychoanalysis: the object in the setting in *Between Reality and Fantasy* ed. S. Grolnick and L. Barkin (1978, pp. 169–189) Jason Aronson Publishers Inc., an imprint of Rowman & Littlefield Publishers, Inc.

Green, A. (2000) The posthumous Winnicott: On Human nature. In: Abram J, editor. *Andre Green at the Squiggle Foundation* (pp. 69–83). London: Karnac.

Green, A. (2005) *Science and science fiction in infant research in Clinical and Observational Psychoanalytic Research Roots of a Controversy* ed. *Joseph Sandler, Anne-Marie Sandler & Rosemary Davies* Karnac Books.

King, P. (1972) Tribute to Donald Winnicott Commemorative Meeting for Dr. Donald Winnicott, January 19, 1972 in Scientific Bulletin of The British Psychoanalytical Society and The Institute of Psychoanalysis.

Klein, M. (1946) Notes on Some Schizoid Mechanisms. *Int J Psychoanal* 27: 99–110.

Loparic, Z. (2012) From Freud to Winnicott: aspects of a paradigm change in *Donald Winnicott Today* 2013 (ed. J. Abram) New Library of Psychoanalysis Routledge.

Milner, M. (1972) Commemorative Meeting for Dr. Donald Winnicott, January 19, 1972 in Scientific Bulletin of The British Psychoanalytical Society and The Institute of Psychoanalysis & Chapter 6 In: Abram 2013.

Ogden, T.H. (2001) Reading Winnicott. *Psychoanal Q* 70: 299–323.

Rodman, F.R. (ed) (1987). *The spontaneous gesture: Selected letters of DW Winnicott*, Cambridge, MA: Harvard UP.

Roussillon, R. (2010) The deconstruction of primary narcissism. *Int J Psychoanal* 91: 821–837.

Sandler, J. (1976) Countertransference and role responsiveness. *Int Rev Psychoanal* 3: 43–47.

Widlöcher, D. ([2006] 2013) Winnicott and the acquisition of freedom of thought In: Abram, J. editor 2013 Chapter 10.

Winnicott DW (1945a). Primitive emotional development. *Int J Psychoanal* 26: 137–143.

Winnicott DW ([1946] 1987) Letter to Ella Sharpe in *The Spontaneous Gesture, Selected Letters*, ed. F. Robert Rodman. Cambridge, MA: Harvard University Press.

Winnicott DW (1953). Psychoses and child care. *Br J Med Psychol* 26: 68–74.

Winnicott DW (1954) is Human Nature published posthumously in 1988 and in the references.

Winnicott DW (1955) Metapsychological and clinical aspects of regression within the psychoanalytical set-up. *Int J Psychoanal* 36: 16–26.

Winnicott DW (1958a) *Collected papers: Through paediatrics to psychoanalysis*, 1st edition. London: Tavistock.

Winnicott DW (1958b) Birth memories, birth trauma, and anxiety. In: *Through paediatrics to psychoanalysis* (pp. 174–193). London: Tavistock, 1958.

Winnicott DW (1958c) Anxiety associated with insecurity [1952]. In: 1958a, 97–100.

Winnicott DW (1958d) The capacity to be alone [1957]. *Int J Psychoanal* 39: 416–420.

Winnicott DW ([1960] 1962) The theory of the parent–infant relationship. *Int J Psychoanal* 41: 585–595 & In: Winnicott DW 1965.

Winnicott DW (1965). *The maturational processes and the facilitating environment: Studies in the theory of emotional development*, London: Hogarth. (International Psycho-analytical Library, No. 64.)

Winnicott DW ([1962] 1965) The aims of psychoanalytical treatment in *The Maturational Processes and the Facilitating Environment* (1965) London: The Hogarth Press and the Institute of Psychoanalysis.

Winnicott DW (1965c) Communicating and not communicating leading to a study of certain opposites [1963]. In: 1965b, 179–92.

Winnicott DW (1965d) Ego distortion in terms of true and false self [1960]. In: 1965a, 140–52.

Winnicott DW (1968a) Communication between infant and mother, and mother and infant, compared and contrasted. In: Walter G. Joffe (Ed.) *What is psychoanalysis?* London: The Institute of Psychoanalysis/Baillière, Tindall & Cassell.

Winnicott DW (1969) The use of an object and relating through identifications. *Int J Psychoanal* 50: 711–716.

Winnicott DW (1971a) *Playing and reality*, London: Tavistock.

Winnicott DW (1971b) Dreaming, fantasying and living a case-history describing a Primary Dissociation Chapter 2 In: Winnicott 1971a.

Winnicott DW (1971c) The split-off male and female elements to be found in men and women [1966]. In: 1971a, 72–85.

Winnicott DW (1986) The concept of a healthy individual In: *Home is where we start from: Essays by a psychoanalyst*, Winnicott C, Shepherd R.

Winnicott DW (1988) *Human nature*, Bollas C, Davis M, Shepherd R, editors. London: Free Association Books.

Winnicott DW (1989a) *Psychoanalytic explorations*, Winnicott C, Shepherd R, Davis M, editors. Cambridge, MA: Harvard UP.

Winnicott DW (1989b) Postscript: DWW on DWW [1967]. In: Winnicott C, Shepherd R, Davis M, editors. *Psychoanalytic explorations* (pp. 569–582). Cambridge, MA: Harvard UP.

Winnicott DW ([1968b] 1989) Playing and culture. *Psychoanalytic explorations*, 203–206.

Winnicott DW ([1945b] 1996) Towards an objective study of human nature in *Thinking about Children* eds. Ray Shepherd, Jennifer Johns, Helen Taylor Robinson Karnac Books.

6

ON WINNICOTT'S AREA OF FORMLESSNESS

The pure female element and the capacity to feel real (2013)

Prelude

The experience of formlessness was the way in which Winnicott identified the crucial early infantile experience of 'unintegration'. Without that early experience the infant will miss out on the vital early experience of being in the arms of a woman who is totally dedicated to her infant. 'Ordinary devotion'[1] in 1949 became 'primary maternal preoccupation' in 1956 and by 1969 unintegration was identified as 'formlessness' (Winnicott [1956] 1958; Winnicott [1969] 1971b). No adult can know what it means to 'be' without the experience of formlessness. Winnicott's patient, in the clinical example, has not had an experience of 'desultory formlessness' so Winnicott decides to find a way of offering this by modifying the analytic setting. In my discussion I start to question his 'modifications' related to paternal and maternal functions as intrinsic and necessary components of the analytic frame. The notion of an 'integrate' from Winnicott's very late paper, 'The use of an object in the context of *Moses and Monotheism*', leads to my proposal of a 'paternal integrate' elaborated further in Chapter 7.

★ ★ ★

Winnicott identifies formlessness as 'the experience of a non purposive state… a ticking over of the unintegrated personality' and he links this state of mind with Freud's concept of free association. Formlessness is a subjective phenomenon initiated in the context of the infant's early psychic development and the dyadic relationship between mother and infant. It is this area that constitutes the 'pure female element' and is fundamental to the capacity to feel real.

Following Freud, Winnicott proposed that the search for the Self can only come about from the 'desultory formlessness' in the analytic session, and in *Playing and Reality* (Winnicott 1971a) he offers two clinical examples to illustrate his application of these ideas.

As I have argued throughout the chapters in this book, especially Chapter 2, without the experience of psychic *survival-of-the-object* a search for the Self cannot truly be initiated because there is not yet an establishment of an intrapsychic surviving object. And, following Winnicott's very late concept of the 'father as a whole object', I will add my proposal that the 'paternal integrate' is an essential component of the surviving object. I suggest that it is the 'paternal integrate' that provides form and the capacity to feel real.

Formlessness in the clinical setting, therefore, acquires form through the existence of the paternal integrate represented by the varied and different aspects that go to make up the structures of the analytic setting. Following André Green, I will argue that, in health, the triadic dynamic is crucial for emotional development. But my meaning of triadic does not wholly concur with Green's argument. This is a point I elaborate in Chapter 7.

From the beginning of life, the infant in a good enough environment is offered a psychic environment ready and prepared to survive his destruction as I set out in Chapter 2. As I point out, 'destruction' from the infant's point of view is instinctual because it is the only way the infant can literally survive at the very beginning. The mother who knows this, because of her deep identification with her infant's predicament, is able to tolerate whatever the infant demands. To begin with she has no choice. It is her survival of the infant's so-called destruction that results in the intrapsychic surviving object. I now think of this as the definition of primary love. The infant knows, later on, that the mother has sacrificed much for her sake. This is why, at that moment of awareness of her destructivity, the infant can say: 'I love you. You have value for me because of your survival of my destruction of you' (Winnicott 1969: 713).

The specificity of the psychoanalytic setting offers optimal psychic conditions in which the subject's surviving object can evolve.

The maintenance of form, i.e. the analytic structure, is the essential frame in which the experience of formlessness, between analyst and patient, can occur, because the integrated components of the male and female elements in the analytic setting constitute potential psychic *survival-of-the-object*. The female element, associated with BEING, as I shall highlight below, emanates from the earliest psychic relationship which will always be female. This is related to Freud's work on the feminine phase as indicated in Chapter 4.

Formlessness and unintegration

Winnicott cites Marion Milner's observation about the 'original poet' in us all when we find the 'familiar in the unfamiliar' that will relate to a very early and deep experience (Milner 1950). Both Donald Winnicott and Marion Milner found innovative ways to elaborate and thus extend Freud's original concept of primary processes (which was specifically designated a characteristic of the 'system unconscious'). Their main conclusions, from their separate but related explorations on the deepest layers of the mind, led to an acknowledgement that the most primitive layers of the inner world made an enormous contribution to the outcome of the personality and the capacity to imagine. They had rather different ways to describe these early processes, but in the early 1940s they were both exploring the way in which the infant would be enabled to move from pre-symbolic thinking to symbolic thinking. There was an emphasis on a developmental sequence related to the evolution of capacities so that maturity, at its best, constituted an integration of different layers of processes. Living a meaningful life needs enrichment through the capacity to move between these layers and processes in order to discover and thus evolve one's own 'original poet' within who is able to 'live creatively'. And for Winnicott these processes could not be initiated without an 'environmental minimum' from the start.

In 1972 André Green, following Winnicott's ideas on transitionality, added to Freud's primary and secondary processes by proposing the term 'tertiary processes'. Later in 1991 he writes: '…tertiary processes function as a go-between and link primary and secondary processes' (Green 1991 in Abram 2016: 48). The important point here is that although Winnicott's theoretical matrix constitutes a sequential development, its overall emphasis is that each phase continues to have its value. This is why formlessness will hopefully be a resource in mature development as Milner argues in her book *On Not Being Able to Paint* (Milner 1950; cf. Abram 2012a).

'Formlessness' is a word that Winnicott added to his vocabulary in the final five years of his life and yet he had been exploring this aspect of early psychic development from the start of his work. The notion of the mother's sensitivity to the newborn's predicament and state of mind relates to a specific concept of infancy which always includes the object. 'There's no such thing as a baby' means that there's no such thing as a subject. Subjective phenomena are inscribed with the psychic environment of the primary object (Abram 2013: 1).

The term 'formlessness' is associated to Winnicott's earlier concept of 'unintegration', first proposed in 1945 (Winnicott 1945). The state of primary unintegration – during the phase of absolute dependence (primary narcissism) – refers to the infant's early states of sensory experience, i.e. the baby at the very beginning in the arms of a mother who is completely engaged with her infant through her profound identification with the state of helplessness. In the 1950s Winnicott designated the term 'primary maternal preoccupation' to depict this stage of maternity (Winnicott [1956] 1958). Without the mother's total preoccupation with her infant there is no possibility that the infant will experience the luxury of unintegration which, Winnicott states, is the precursor to relaxation. This is a state of mind without anxiety and it is the mother's reverie that creates the optimal condition in which the baby can 'be'. Unintegration, therefore, is a normal phenomenon of the infant's early psychic life but, as with the concept of 'formlessness', it depicts a state of mind that depends on the capacity of the m/Other who, like the analyst, is able to offer a psychic space or a psychic place in which to 'be'. True form, like true integration, can only emerge from formlessness and unintegration, and this can only occur in the context of relating. Each layer of these different processes nourishes the other through the operation of tertiary processes. By 1970 Winnicott suggested that each baby needed to have this early experience of formlessness in order to evolve a true-self personality. The 'illusion of omnipotence' at the start of life means that the infant will live from a core experience of 'being' a (true) Self.[2] From this foundation, the developing child could potentially tolerate and integrate the process of disillusionment in the later developmental stage of the reality principle.

If the infant did not experience the components that essentially make up the 'good enough environment', then s/he would be forced to enlist defences. For example, the patient described in Chapter 2 of *Playing and Reality* had been 'disturbed her whole life' because the quality of her daydreaming prevented her from 'living creatively'. In that chapter Winnicott examines the differences between dreaming, fantasying and living in this 'case of a primary dissociation' and shows how, despite false self living appearing to function for his patient, it was actually interrupting growth and Self-enrichment because it was essentially masturbatory, like thumb sucking. The 'pattern of relating', as he termed it in 1952, starts right from the start, and Winnicott suggested that, for this patient, it was because she had not been allowed to begin her life with formlessness. So, from the start she had had to comply with what the environment demanded of her. Winnicott comes to realise that '…fantasying interferes with action and with life in the real or external world, but much more so it interferes with dream and with the personal or inner psychic reality, the living core of the individual personality' (Winnicott 1971a: 31).

Clinical experience convinces Winnicott that formlessness is therefore an essential foundational experience of the personality, as it provides a sense of meaning in life. The patient, without this fundamental experience, is not truly living a life and has to enlist defences to avoid reaching a sense of futility and emptiness at the core of the Self. The defences are the patient's only way in which to deal with the trauma of not being truly recognised. The deficiencies of the early environment give rise to a non surviving object from which these defensive manoeuvres emanate.

The distilled female element

Examining the origins of creativity Winnicott locates the 'pure' female element at the very beginning when mother and infant are merged, and he is unequivocal that, '…no sense of self emerges except on the basis of this relating to the sense of Being… it antedates… being-at-one-with, because there has not yet been anything else except identity. Two separate persons can feel at one, but here at the place that I am examining the baby and the object are one' (Winnicott 1971d: 80).

The distilled female element is rooted in the merger between mother and infant and is located at the core of the environment–individual set-up. This is the place of the location of culture and creativity and the beginning is paramount to an authentic Self. From the 'object relating' of the pure female element comes the establishment of BEING.

> Here one finds a true continuity of generations… passed on from one generation to another, via the female element of men and women.
>
> (Winnicott 1971d)

Thus, formlessness is intrinsic to the female element.

Although Winnicott develops this notion around the same time as he is developing the ideas in the use of an object, that is, from 1968 onwards, it seems to me that in the conceptualisation of formlessness he does not include the crucial 'new feature' of psychic *survival-of-the-object*. I am also struck that in his application of these concepts in his clinical work he does not include the paternal factor. These are the areas I intend to develop later, but let us first turn to his notions of psychic creativity from which the first subjective objects are formed.

Creative apperception and subjective objects

Creative apperception depicts illusory states in the formless, unintegrated relating of mother and infant. Winnicott claims that this specific experience, more than any other experience, makes the individual feel that life is meaningful and worth living. The infant who evolves from the centre of gravity and whose early psychic Self is lodged in the kernel of the environment–individual set-up is in the process of apperceiving creatively and it is this very experience that will initiate a sense of feeling real. From creative apperception, in a good enough environment, the infant moves towards being able to perceive the object as separate and other. Winnicott's poem in Chapter 1 illustrates the sequence of looking and being seen that are the dual essentials constituting ordinary primary identification (Winnicott 1967: 114).

From the experience of being, through being seen, emerges a psychic space in which to dream and to play, i.e. the initiation of symbolic processes. This sequence relates to the process that overlaps with silent communicating and relating to subjective objects. This sort of Self-relating – that is not masturbatory or solipsistic – is a necessary aspect of healthy narcissism and enriches the sense of self, feeling real and living a life that feels meaningful as referred to in Chapter 5.

Subjective objects are a consequence of that early process of the infant's subjective experience of the external object. From the observer's point of view, there may seem to be object relating in the primary merged state, but for Winnicott at the beginning the object is a 'subjective object' (see Chapters 1 & 2 and the Index).

Subjective objects, therefore, pre-date internal objects and are the ancestors of internal object relations. The infant 'creates the object' through the mother's capacity to 'adapt to his needs'. Gradually, creative apperception moves into the infant being able to objectively perceive the object thanks to a 'good enough environmental provision'. It is creative apperception that will contribute to the capacity for imagination and 'creative living'.

All this was fairly well established in Winnicott's formulations during the 1950s and 1960s, but there was one question he could not yet answer: what had to happen between infant and mother, in the sequential movement from apperception to perception, for the infant to take the necessary developmental step towards a true capacity to discern? As I pointed out in my Introduction, it was this question that led to his formulations, as proposed in 'The Use of an Object', which he says (in a footnote written in 1970, in his book *Human Nature*) resolved this problem. I will return to this question later in this chapter, but let us first of all look at what happens when there is a failing early environment.

Deformation/psychosis: an environmental-deficiency disease

The mother's inability to offer 'ordinary devotion' has a catastrophic effect on the infant. This 'lack' constitutes a serious deficiency because the infant is unable to establish the foundations of the sense of self emanating from the 'illusion of omnipotence'. And the sense of feeling real is therefore unavailable to the infant, whose environment is deficient in the essential ingredients of facilitation. Deformations of character are thus initiated due to the failures at specific stages of development (Winnicott [1963] 1962). Psychotic anxiety occurs due to early trauma when the 'unthinkable' experience occurs because there is not yet a Self to integrate external psychic impingement. The result for the infant is the fact of annihilation which constitutes a violation of the core self. (This is one of the key themes already introduced in Chapter 1 of this book.) If the m/Other is not available to protect the infant's nascent self, then psychotic defences have to be enlisted by the infant. Winnicott lists a series of what he terms as 'primitive agonies'.

1. A return to an unintegrated state.
2. Falling forever.
3. Loss of psychosomatic collusion, failure of indwelling, depersonalisation.
4. Loss of sense of real (defence: exploitation of primary narcissism).
5. Loss of capacity to relate to objects (defence: autistic states, relating to only self-phenomena).

Thus, psychotic illness is an organized defence against unthinkable primitive agony

(Abram 2007a: 172)

The value of formlessness in the clinical setting – theory and technique

As I previously mentioned above, Winnicott saw that formlessness was a term redolent with Freud's 'free association'. In many places in his late work, he shows how he observes a corrosion of the essential technique of free association in psychoanalytic clinical work. It seems clear that this statement constituted a criticism of his general view that British analysts often over-interpreted in their clinical work. But he was the first to admit that he felt he was also guilty of this in his early work. It appalled him 'to think how much deep change' he had prevented for the patient, due to his being too keen to make an interpretation as soon as he understood something in the session. Now, in 1968, he said he gave interpretations to show the patient the limits of his understanding. 'The principle is that it is the patient and only the patient who has the answers' (Winnicott 1969: 87)

In Chapters 2 and 4 of *Playing and Reality* Winnicott argues for the analyst to understand the need to offer the patient the experience of formlessness in the analytic setting and he describes how he applies this concept with two female patients. Winnicott's patient of Chapter 2, as already referred to above, is a middle-aged woman who is described as never having 'lived creatively' due to her defensive 'daydreaming' which constitutes a defence against primary dissociation. The distinctions between living and not living are examined and Winnicott states that the cause of her primary dissociation is due to the failure of her early environment because nobody had been there '…who understood that she had to begin in formlessness' (Winnicott 1971b). Therefore, the patient's primary dissociation amounts to a deformation which prevents her from evolving and feeling real.

Patients whose dreams do not contain symbolic value are perhaps the most difficult to treat because they have not developed a capacity to play in the psychoanalytic sense. If the patient cannot play (due to a deficiency in symbolic thinking) then the analyst has to wait until the patient is able to because '…interpretation out of the ripeness of the transference amounts to indoctrination' (Winnicott 1969).

Linked with the above statement on the analyst's need to wait for the patient's own process, Winnicott felt that a too early intervention of the analyst's results in a patient who is likely to become compliant. Compliancy is the death of creativity. Winnicott's great emphasis on the value of formlessness led him to believe that the analytic setting could offer a chance for the patient to have an experience of formlessness for the first time. If the conditions were facilitating enough then there was a chance the patient could be helped to discover something intrapsychically that her early environment had failed to offer, i.e. desultory formlessness.

In the clinical account in *Playing and Reality*, we see how the patient begins to appreciate the distinction between a dream that has no symbolic value from a dream that is related to 'living'. In Chapter 4, 'Playing: Creative activity and the search for the self', we see a patient given the opportunity to take her time to reach a sense of her Self, i.e. that her Self is evolving. In both chapters Winnicott describes how he decided it was necessary to modify the ordinary psychoanalytic setting. The time will be of 'indefinite' length; he will be writing notes; the patient is allowed to move around the room; milk and biscuits are available. Based on his psychoanalytic convictions we read about Winnicott's attempt to offer a psychic environment that aimed at replicating, as far as is possible, the early dyadic formlessness between mother and infant. For Winnicott, it was only '…from desultory formless functioning… that which we describe as creative can appear… but only if reflected back' (Winnicott 1971d: 64).

The clinical vignettes do illustrate how each patient arrives at a particular insight during the course of (up to) three hours. While

Winnicott is cautious about feeling too satisfied about any real progress made he is at the same time convinced that the work achieved in these reported sessions could not have been achieved if the session had been the usual length.

In the light of Winnicott's theory 'The use of an object', Chapter 6 of *Playing and Reality*, it seems to me that desultory formlessness (between analyst and patient) can only come about as a consequence of the object's psychic *survival-of-the-subject's* destruction. It is the internalised experience of the object's psychic survival that leads to the establishment of the intrapsychic surviving object that, in turn, facilitates Self-development. And for that to be realised the crucial factor is not only the analyst's interpretations but also the maintenance of the analytic setting with its firm boundaries. The patient can only start to search for the sense of self once an analytic rhythm and pace is established. From that basis the subject can start to search for an object who will survive which leads to the capacity to search for the self, i.e. the capacity to transform and evolve. The subject needs to continually experience destroying the object, in unconscious fantasy, until the object in the external world is gradually perceived as separate and different rather than a 'bundle of projections'.

Winnicott himself had previously highlighted that the 'analytic setting' came up in Freud's work because 'he took for granted the early mothering situation'. The setting parallels the holding environment and offers an opportunity for free association and regression. Winnicott adds to his list of 12 components of the analytic setting that 'for Freud there are three people, one of them excluded from the analytic room' (Winnicott 1955: 284–286).

Winnicott was indeed aware of the father and the importance of the father's role in development, but where is the father in early psychic development in Winnicott's matrix? Before attempting to answer this question let us go to Winnicott's late and very late concepts that I think pave the way to formulations that Winnicott was beginning to address towards the end of his life.

The object's psychic survival of the ruthless impulse

As I have argued in the chapters of this book, central to Winnicott's late work is the concept of psychic *survival-of-the-object* as seen in 'The use of an object' and the subsequent discussion papers, especially 'The use of an object in the context of *Moses and Monotheism*' (see

Abram 2013). Winnicott's concern was to locate how symbolic processes were initiated in relation to the 'primitive love impulse' without recourse to the idea of a 'death instinct'. The primitive impulse was, for the observer, ruthless but for the infant it was pre-ruth when the child is able to look back from a different developmental point (Winnicott 1969).

He goes on to state that he 'assumes there is a primary aggressive and destructive impulse that is indistinguishable from instinctual love appropriate to the very early stage…' and then adds a footnote saying that he could not publish his book *Human Nature* because he had not resolved this issue (i.e. what happens to the infant's primary aggressive impulse in order to make the move to an awareness of having been ruthless) before he wrote 'The use of an object'. What precisely was the discovery that he felt resolved this issue?

Always mindful of the role of the facilitating environment Winnicott's question was: what did the mother have to do to facilitate her infant's development of the capacity to move from creative apperception to objective perception of the object? For Winnicott, the answer was hidden in the intrapsychic processes that occurred between mother and infant at the beginning and he was motivated to study the intermediate area' …which is neither dream nor object relating'. The essential paradox is that the intermediate area is 'neither the one nor the other of these two, it is also both' (Winnicott 1971d).

The communication from subject to object is the key passage of that original paper, as I highlight in Chapter 2 when the subject says to the object: 'Hello object. I destroyed you. You have value for me because of your survival of my destruction. While I am loving you, I am all the time destroying you (in unconscious fantasy)' (Winnicott 1969).

This is the point at which (the capacity for) fantasy begins. I link this formulation of 1968 with the earlier notion of the 'theoretical first feed', as outlined in his posthumously published book *Human Nature*. It seems to me that the infant's real experience that his needs (which at that moment are part of the instinctual primitive impulses) are being met by the object, facilitates his sense of the object having survived his destruction.

Let us remind ourselves of the five stages of the sequence proposed by Winnicott that I examined in Chapter 2 of this book: (1) Subject relates to object; (2) Object is in the process of being found instead of placed by the subject in the world; (3) Subject destroys object; (4) Object survives destruction; (5) Subject can use object.

Due to the object surviving the subject's destructive primitive impulse, the subject can start to place the object outside in the world. For me this is the crucial element in the sequence and, as Winnicott stated, constitutes the 'new feature' in his theorising. *Survival-of-the-object* highlights the crucial nature of early object/subject relationships for the Self's evolution and developing capacities.

The newborn infant needed to be offered the desultory formlessness by the object before any other developmental achievement could occur. Winnicott was absolutely clear about this (Winnicott [1954] 1988: 104). The environment mother offers this 'background of safety' during the quiet times. The question is what needed to happen during the excited and potentially traumatic times, when the baby was not peacefully feeling unintegrated, but was rather in pain, hunger or near terror? The simple answer was that the object mother had to receive the communications and adapt to his needs. She could do this because of her identification with her baby's predicament of helplessness which felt close to annihilation. During these times a different kind of relating or technique was required. In other words, the task and function of the object mother is different from the environment mother and yet it is the same woman who is the m/Other who has to perform these different functions. Let us review this difference.

The sequence in 'The use of an object' refers to the way in which the environment mother alternates from being the facilitator of formlessness in the first stage when the subject is simply relating to the object. She then has to change her task when the infant's urgency increases. Then she becomes the object mother, who has to be able to receive the painful communication due to physical discomfort that merges with emotional pain. But this very special task is instigated by the infant needing to 'destroy' the object. When the inner calm is disrupted by a physiological need this can be experienced as a terrible attack from the object. But the infant's urgent cries can also be experienced by the object as an attack. The environment mother, which includes the support of the father and the extended family, in her mind, has to sustain a mutuality of attention and consistency in contrast to the object mother who is required to receive, translate and attend to the urgency of the communication from the infant in his excited and agitated states.

Both tasks, with their inevitable overlaps, mean that the good enough mother oscillates between the roles. Thus, *survival-of-the-object* means that the environment mother psychically survives through her consistent and developing investment in a recognition of her infant's needs and developing self. At the same time the same woman performing the task of the object mother survives by being able to appreciate and attend to the infant's communication of near terror. It is the good enough mother's response that will contribute to the infant being able to transform the near-overwhelming feeling of disruption. If the m/Other is not able to perform these complex tasks and is not finely attuned enough then the infant will be forced to retreat into a withdrawn state. Therefore, *survival-of-the-object* was the 'new feature' in Winnicott's formulations, and he felt 'that the issue of recognition of the destructive element in the crude primitive excited idea' was thus resolved for him in terms of his formulations (Abram 2012b in 2013: 308).

In the process of moving between the tasks of environment mother and object mother, the actual woman performing these tasks will oscillate between succeeding and failing in her extraordinary effort to stay infinitely tuned into her infant's communications. The experience of the object mother's ability to survive, i.e. NOT retaliate, is gradually internalised by the infant. While the moments when she is not able to survive, at either the environment or object level of interpsychic responsiveness, are also internalised. These interactions constitute a subjective experience of both survival and non survival, even in the case of a good enough experience. The oscillating between psychic survival and non survival by the object leads to two subjective objects that feature in the infant's internal world. Thus, I am suggesting throughout this book we have the birth of an intrapsychic surviving object as well as an intrapsychic non surviving object that emanate from the relationship with m/Other.

The theoretical first feed constitutes the initiation of symbolic processes, which is the outcome of the subject's experience of the object having survived. Due to this, as long as the object is able to sustain its continuity of psychic survival, the process will lead to subsequent theoretical feeds. I have proposed a 'final theoretical feed' to refer to the moment when the tasks of adolescence culminate in a final configuration of the sequence outlined in the use of an object. At that moment of development, the subject can then discern the Other as separate and different. This moment signifies the evolution of a whole intrapsychic surviving object which means the subject is now able to function in the three-body relationship.

Adolescence and the object's survival

Many patients are internally dominated by a non surviving object. This means that before they are able to start to search for the Self, it is necessary to discover the experience of an object who will survive in the new psychodynamics that are mobilised through the analysing situation. The capacity to search for the Self, therefore, is not possible without an intrapsychic surviving object which is growing in relation to the interpsychic dynamic survival of the external other. In Chapter 2 I elaborated this idea in relation to adolescence and the isolate, communicating and not communicating, destructivity and murder. Following Stern's notion of the 'clinical infant', I have proposed the notion of a 'clinical adolescent' that emerges at particular stages of the transference evolution (Abram 2014). Let me now attempt to amplify my previous interpretations of this area of Winnicott's formulations.

Psychic *survival-of-the-object* in relation to the female and male elements

As we have seen, Winnicott places the experience of 'being' with the female element in terms of his theory of 'the continuity-of-being', creativity and playing. Formlessness is facilitated by the mother's finely attuned sensitivity to the infant's immaturity and helplessness.

'The study of the pure distilled uncontaminated female element leads on to Being, and this forms the only basis for self-discovery and a sense of existing...', as we saw above. And later Winnicott emphasises that this is the essential ingredient that gives meaning to life. The male element comes into focus as the infant struggles to distinguish between Me and Not-me; it is part of the process related to intrapsychic separation and relates to the stage of concern, when the subject is able to integrate both the environment mother and the object mother together and see the m/Other as the same person of both the quiet times and the excited times. This is an important developmental achievement because the 'object relating of the male element to the object presupposes separateness'. It also means that the subject is increasingly able 'to be' and 'to do'. For Winnicott, there is a crucial sequence: 'After being – doing and being done to. But first, being' (1971e: 85).

In these formulations we are very aware of Winnicott's emphasis on the mother and her role in facilitating the infant to the stage designated the male element. In the clinical setting his modifications aimed at a replication of the earliest stages to facilitate a particular kind of regression. And while Winnicott never denied the importance of the father's role in emotional development as 'vital' in child development (see Abram 2007a entries Environment & Mother), it is clear that he privileges the pure distilled female element in the earliest phase of life. Significantly, the question that he latterly came to ask concerned the father's role at the beginning of life. Let us now reflect on this specific development of his very late work.

'The use of an object in the context of *Moses and Monotheism*' ([1970]1989)

In this short paper instigated by his New York discussants in late 1968, Winnicott began to formulate a new concept that concerned the father at the earliest stage of infantile life. He sets up his argument by saying that few people reach the stage of the Oedipus complex in their emotional development, which means that 'repression of the libidinised father figure has but little relevance.' In other words, few people have reached the capacity to appreciate a 'three-body relationship'. This is an important point he was trying to make in 'The use of an object' because, as I stated above, he was attempting to conceptualise the specific interpsychic dynamic between mother and infant that facilitated the infant's capacity to perceive the second and, subsequently, the third. To distinguish between Me and Not me leads on to distinguishing between Me and Not me with another Not me, i.e. the third. A year before he dies, he proposes that '…in a favourable case the father starts off whole (i.e. as father not mother surrogate)… that he starts off as an integrate in the ego's organisation and in the mental conceptualisation of the baby' (Winnicott [1970] 1989; Abram 2013: 297).

For the father to start off as an 'integrate' in the ego organisation of the infant, it follows that he must already be an 'integrate' in the mother's ego organisation. If we accept Winnicott's theory of primary maternal preoccupation, it is the mother's ego that constitutes the newborn's ego at the beginning of life. Following Winnicott, André Green suggested that the father in the mother's mind could be called 'the other of the object' (Green 1991 in Abram 2016). But it seems to me that Winnicott indicates that the proposed 'integrate' is paternal, thus I propose the notion of a 'paternal integrate'. Because even though the integrate contains a potential integrating force which amounts to constituting a third object (as Green emphasises), in Winnicott's theoretical matrix, I suggest, it is related to the male element which provides the capacity to do: but only after being and as a consequence of being. Consequently, it seems to me that it has to be paternal rather than simply 'other'. This inevitably leads to the notion that both female and male elements are essential from the start of life. Both are crucial because they constitute the seeds from which integrative processes can grow. But Winnicott emphasises a sequence which must be remembered. The distilled female element has to be established before the male element follows.

I have proposed that Winnicott's very late concept of an integrate advances the theory of 'primary maternal preoccupation' because the mother's capacity to provide ego-coverage means not only that she will transmit the father imago in her mind to her infant, i.e., through transgenerational transmission, but also that she is responsible for the inscription of the paternal integrate on her infant's psyche, as I argue in Chapter 7. In health, this constitutes her active engagement, intra-psychically with her paternal imago, and interpersonally with the third who facilitates her 'ordinary devotion' to her infant. At a later phase, the third separates the close intimacy of mother and infant, as in Freud's emphasis, all of which will aid the infant towards an evolution of symbolic thinking.

At the beginning, however, the father cannot be present for the infant because he, the infant, is not yet capable of perceiving the second let alone the third. And yet, as I am emphasising above, the father's presence and ongoing relationship with mother makes an essential contribution to the evolution of the infant's sense of self. Thus, the environment mother includes the fact of the parents' relationship and love, necessarily including their sexual relationship that influences the infant's psychosexuality. Thus, in the light of Winnicott's very late proposal of the father as whole object, there is no doubt he was edging towards the idea of there being no such thing as a dyadic relationship. The dyadic relationship is a subjective phenomenon at a particular stage of development, which is related to the early psychic merger. Conversely, it is a phenomenon related to psychopathology, i.e. the mother who disavows the infant's father which will lead to psychosis. The triadic relationship, as Green has identified, is an essential fact from the beginning of the infant's existence – psychically and physiologically (Green [1991] in Abram 2016: 46), but this is only true IF the mother allows the father to be in her mind: indeed, it is the mother who introduces the father to the infant, as we see in the Ukiyo-e print. These themes are elaborated in Chapter 7.

The intrapsychic surviving object is thus imbued with the dynamics of the triadic relationship. The paternal imago in the mother's mind and the father's reinforcing ego support makes an essential contribution to her capacity to survive the infant's ruthless demands. In fact, without the father in the mother's mind she is less able to function in the constellation of psychic *survival-of-the-object*. It follows, therefore, that the non surviving object emerges as a consequence of the denial of the father's contribution and is the outcome of paternal deficiency, which may be due to the mother's exclusion of his role. This may be the result of the parents' malfunctioning relationship which means that the subject's attempt to destroy the object is not survived. This leads to deformation and withdrawal from interpersonal relating. The real chance for ameliorating this kind of deficiency is the analytic setting.

The paternal integrate in the analytic setting

Green pointed out the transition from the object relating to object usage in a different language. He referred to the transition 'from the stage of potential thirdness… to effective thirdness' (Green [1991] in Abram 2016: 46).

Potential thirdness for the subject is the good enough mother's inscription on the Self. Effective thirdness means the subject has reached three-body relating. As I have suggested above, I consider that this was precisely what Winnicott was grappling with and felt was resolved when he proposed *survival-of-the-object*. When, at the last minute, he added the notion of the father as a whole object I suggest that his theories were in the process of advancing. The paternal integrate and the father's role were necessary to complete his theoretical matrix.

Transposed to the analytic setting the father's role, as Winnicott pointed out, is present in all the components that go to make up the structure of the analytic setting. I imagine it will be clear by now that my concern about Winnicott's 'modifications', as I indicated above, is because I have the impression that his modifications negated the paternal factor. To offer the patient an 'indefinite' amount of time, in my view, negated the necessary frame. Despite Winnicott's argument that his modifications were not analysis as I referred to in Chapter 5, was his sincere effort to provide what he believed had not hitherto been offered to his patients, I am convinced that without the analyst's maintenance of the frame and structure of the analytic setting the opportunity for the patient to experience formlessness in an authentic way cannot be facilitated. It is simply not possible for the analyst to compensate for the deficiencies of the original mother. The analyst can never offer that essential dedication that the 'ordinary devoted' mother of a newborn is able to offer.

The analyst's function is to offer a psychic frame (environment mother) and to receive the patient's transference projections (object mother). In addition, the intrapsychic female and male elements alongside the interpersonal maternal and paternal relationships constitute the setting, as is clear in Winnicott's final theories. The patient will be unable to search for form and the sense of self that will lead to the capacity to feel real, without the consistent experience of the dynamics involved in the sequence of destruction and *survival-of-the-object*. I argue that while the experience of analysis will hopefully be invaluable for each patient, it will never compensate for the early deficiencies. The latter are a fact of the patient's development. The best outcome of any given consistent analysis, therefore, is that the patient's intrapsychic surviving object has arrived at a place where it eclipses the non surviving object. This will augur well for a potentially satisfactory life. But the non surviving object will always be present and at times of crisis can threaten to eclipse the stronger analytic surviving object which, nevertheless, is still vulnerable.

Notes

1 In 1949 Winnicott gave nine talks for the BBC which were later published as *The Ordinary Devoted Mother and her Baby*. These talks can be listened to via *The Collected Works of DW Winnicott* published in 2015 by Oxford University Press.
2 See entries for Being and Self in Abram 2007 for the relevant Winnicott papers on these concepts.

References

Abram, J. (ed) (2000) *André Green at the Squiggle Foundation*, London & New York: Karnac Books.

Abram, J. (2007a) *The language of Winnicott: A dictionary of Winnicott's use of words*. 2nd edn. London: Karnac.

Abram, J. (2007b) L'objet qui ne survit pas: Quelques reflexions sur les racines de la terreur, Houzel D, translator. J psychanal de l'enfant 39:247–70. Paris: Bayard.

Abram, J. (2012a) Review of Marion Milner's *On not being able to paint* and *The hands of the living god*. Int J Psychoanal (2012) 93: 1340–1347.

Abram, J. (2013) (ed) *Donald Winnicott Today* New Library of Psychoanalysis Routledge.

Abram, J. ([2012b] 2013b) DWW's Notes for the Vienna Congress: a consideration of Winnicott's theory of aggression and an interpretation of the clinical implications In: 2013a.

Abram, J. (2014) De la communication et de la non-communication, recherche d'un objet qui survivra, *Revue Belge de Psychanalyse*, no. 64.

Abram, J. (ed.) (2016) *André Green at the Squiggle Foundation*, London & New York: Karnac Books.

Green, A. ([1991] 2000/2016) On thirdness In: *André Green at the Squiggle Foundation*, London & New York: Karnac Books.

Milner, M. (1950) *On not being able to paint*, London: Heinemann.

Winnicott DW (1945) Primitive emotional development. *Int J Psychoanal* 26:137–143.

Winnicott DW (1954 [1949]) Mind and its relation to the psycho-soma. *Br J Med Psychol* 1954: 27.

Winnicott DW (1955) Metapsychological and clinical aspects of regression within the psychoanalytical set-up. *Int J Psychoanal* 36:16–26.

Winnicott DW (1956 [1955]) Clinical varieties of transference. *Int J Psycho-Anal* 1956: 37: "On transference".

Winnicott DW (1963 [1962]) Dependence in infant-care, in child-care, and in the psychoanalytic setting. *Int J Psycho-Anal* 1963: 44.

Winnicott DW (1965a) *The aims of psycho-analytical treatment. In The maturational Processes and the Facilitating Environment*, London: Hogarth (166–170).

Winnicott DW (1965b) Communicating and not communicating leading to a study of certain opposites [1963]. In: 1965b, 179–92.

Winnicott DW (1965c) *Ego integration in child development in Maturational Processes and the Facilitating Environment*, London: Hogarth, 1969 (56–63).

Winnicott DW (1965d) From dependence towards independence in the development of the individual [1963].

Winnicott DW (1965e) Providing for the child in health and crisis [1962]. In: 1965b, 64–72.

Winnicott DW (1967) Mirror-role of mother and family in child development. In: Lomas P, editor. *The predicament of the family: A psychoanalytical symposium*, 26–33. London: Hogarth

Winnicott DW (1968) Playing: Its theoretical status in the clinical situation. *Int J Psychoanal* 49:591–597.

Winnicott DW (1969) The use of an object. *Int J Psychoanal* 50:711–716.

Winnicott DW (1970) Dependence in child care. *Your Child* 1970: 2.

Winnicott DW (1971a) *Playing and reality*. London: Tavistock. Winnicott DW (1971g). Creativity and its origins [1970]. In: 1971a, 65–85.

Winnicott DW (1971b) Dreaming, fantasying and living: A case history describing a primary dissociation [1970]. In: 1971a, 26–37.

Winnicott DW (1971c) Interrelating in terms of cross identifications In: 1971a.

Winnicott DW (1971d) Playing: Creative activity and the search for the self [1970]. In: 1971a, 53–64.

Winnicott DW (1971e) Creative and its Origins In: 1971a, 65–85.

7

THE PATERNAL INTEGRATE AND ITS ROLE IN THE ANALYSING SITUATION

(2013)

Prelude

Winnicott's very late preoccupations centred on the father as indicated in Chapter 6, and, for the first time in his writings, I suggest he develops an argument to counter Freud's concept of the death instinct more explicitly than hitherto. My reflections on the theme of the paternal led me to re-consider my clinical work with K., as presented in Chapter 3. For several years I had wondered about the significant turning point when I was able to move from non *survival-of-the-object* to *survival-of-the-object*. In dialogue with André Green, who proposed the 'other of the object' I propose the notion of a 'paternal integrate'[1] that takes up Winnicott's very late notion of the 'integrate'. In revisiting Strachey's early paper that identified the 'mutative interpretation' I explore aspects of the clinical encounter that I believe made all the difference to my ability to overcome non survival. This led me to suggest the 'analytic paternal integrate' that occurs as a result of the third in the analyst's mind.

★ ★ ★

Following his presentation 'The use of an object' to the New York Psychoanalytic Society in November 1968, Winnicott felt frustrated that he had not managed to convey the main thrust of his argument. At the same time, it became clear he was also inspired to engage with the points made about instinct theory and so he wrote several postscripts, including 'The use of an object in the context of *Moses and Monotheism*'. In the latter postscript Winnicott, for the first time, declares his disagreement with Freud's notion of the 'death instinct'. This was something he had not clarified when he wrote 'The use of an object'. My proposal, in 2012, as I have re-presented in the chapters of this book, was that Winnicott's thesis on the '*survival-of-the-object*' at the centre of 'The Use of an Object' is his alternative theory to Freud's concept of the death instinct. It is not an 'alternative' for the sake of creating an alternative, but rather it is the result of Winnicott's quest to conceptualise the fate of primary aggression or the so-called destructive drive without resorting to the notion of the death instinct (see Abram 2012 in Abram 2013). Perhaps the only concept of Freud's that Winnicott disagreed with was the concept of the death instinct. He felt it was an error and it is well known that Winnicott was not alone in his disagreement.

Let us consider how Winnicott argued against the duality of the life and death instincts inspired by the philosophy of Empedocles who proposed a love-strife drive. Winnicott enlists this idea to argue that the unity is primary, and he inevitably adds that 'The fate of this unity of drive cannot be stated without reference to the environment' (Winnicott 1969 in Abram 2013: 293–301).

Here, we see that Winnicott is referring in this citation to 'destruction' as a drive. It demonstrates that his focus was not on instincts, but rather on how the primary drive in the infant is received by the object. The reader will remember that the 'psychic' environment as I describe it '…is part and parcel of the child's development… and cannot be omitted' because 'there's no such thing as a baby' (Winnicott 1953 [1952]). In this theory psychosis is an environmental deficiency disease. The reader who has traversed the preceding chapters in this book will, by now, be familiar with my exploration of these themes in Winnicott's work.

In addition to this late clarification about his disagreement with the death instinct, Winnicott (almost inadvertently) advances his thinking on the role of the father and introduces a new concept in his work that, as I have proposed in Chapter 6, constitutes the earliest father in the infant's nascent psyche. Thus, I suggest, 'integrate' refers to the early father in the infant's nascent psyche.

In 1969, to clarify his position he proposes that 'in a favourable case' the father starts off as a whole object in the infant's psyche, not as a mother surrogate: '…he starts off as an integrate in the ego's organization and in the mental conceptualization of the baby' (Winnicott 1969 in Abram 2013: 297).

In this citation Winnicott creates a new concept by using this new term. The word 'integrate' is almost always used as a verb although, according to the O.E.D., its etymology suggests that its usage has been both as an adjective and a noun. Here, Winnicott finds himself enlisting the word as a noun. The 'integrate' refers to the 'whole father' in the mental conceptualisation of the baby.

If we accept Winnicott's theory of 'primary maternal preoccupation', it is the mother's ego that constitutes the newborn's ego at the beginning of life. Therefore, the (idea of the) father who starts off as an 'integrate' in the ego organisation of the infant means that he (the father) must already be a developed internal father imago in the mother's ego organisation. It would follow therefore that the mother's internal father imago stems from her original paternal integrate that, originally, had been psychically transmitted from her mother.

André Green, following both Freud and Winnicott, and strongly influenced by Lacan, had proposed the notions of tertiary processes and thirdness that, in my view, are based on Winnicott's concept of transitional phenomena. While appreciating the meaning of Winnicott's claim that 'there's no such thing as a baby', Green argued that 'there's no such thing as a mother and baby', in order to emphasise the crucial role of father in shaping the psyche from the start. In this way Green argued against the notion of a 'dual relationship' at the beginning of life and, influenced by Lacan's concept of the 'paternal metaphor', proposed the 'other of the object' (Green 1991 in Abram 2000, 2016: 45).

My inquiry in this essay concerns the question of the 'father in mother's mind' in relation to Green's assertion that it constitutes the 'other' in the infant's psyche. Following Winnicott's very late proposal of the father starting off whole in the infant's psyche I wish to propose that the integrate is therefore paternal.

My proposal, although at odds with Green's suggestion of the 'other' in the infant's psyche, at the same time concurs with his view that the mother can only be the infant's facilitator if she is psychically engaged with the actual father of her infant. Furthermore, I suggest that her capacity for intrapsychic intercourse has evolved from her original paternal integrate that, throughout her development, has grown into a paternal imago. It follows, therefore, that during the time she is in a state of primary maternal preoccupation and ordinarily devoted towards her infant, the father (as a whole object) will be psychically transmitted to her newborn. I suggest this is what Winnicott means when he proposes the father as a whole object in the newborn's psyche. The good enough mother psychically and unconsciously transmits her paternal imago who will become inscribed in the infant's psyche as a 'paternal integrate'.

The transition from 'potential thirdness' to 'effective thirdness'

Let us expand on some final thoughts presented in Chapter 6 concerning Green's work. Following Freud's idea of the father in mother's mind, and strongly influenced by Winnicott's late work, André Green proposed that the infant had to make the journey from 'potential thirdness' to 'effective thirdness'. His notion of 'potential thirdness' referred to the phase when the father was 'only' in mother's mind. 'Effective thirdness' meant the stage of development when the infant could perceive father as a 'distinct object by the child'. He was clear that this was a phase 'long before the so-called Oedipal phase' and emphasised that there were two independent sequences in this journey. The first was the issue of separation between mother and infant; the second related to the infant's awareness that the third was an obstacle to the first relationship (Green 1991 in Abram 2016: 46).

To my mind, Green's work on thirdness emphasises Winnicott's formulations in 'The use of an object', albeit in a different language and with the emphasis on the father. But essentially Green is describing what Winnicott had already proposed on the developmental move from apperception to perception; from being merged with the mother to seeing her as separate and Not me; from object relating to the use of an object. However, Green elaborates on the meaning of perception by showing how the infant is not only obliged to move from the stage of Me to Not me, but also has to subsequently move to the final stage of this sequence to perceiving the Not me with another Not me, i.e. the third. This is clearly the Oedipal stage of development that is so often, mistakenly I believe, a stage of development that is taken for granted. In Chapter 3 I suggest that this final stage of development emanates from a whole intrapsychic surviving object that marks the end of (a theoretical) adolescence (Abram 2013).

In defining the journey from potential thirdness to effective thirdness Green identifies something that I think is implicit in Winnicott's conceptualising in 'the use of an object' and highlights the importance of the father from the very beginning of life. But this does not mean that the earliest experience is triadic. In fact, it confirms, I believe, that the newborn, due to extreme immaturity can only relate in the dyadic frame of reference. That is why thirdness can only be a potential.

Green explains that when the father is (only) in the mother's mind he is 'the other of the object' (i.e. that which is not the subject), because the third element is not restricted to the person of the father; it is also symbolic. This position follows Lacan's concept of the paternal metaphor proposed in 1957 which Lacan designated as 'the metaphorical character of the Oedipus Complex' itself and claimed it stood for the 'fundamental metaphor on which all signification depends' (Evans 1996: 137).

This notion correlates with Winnicott's very late suggestion that the father is a whole object in the infant's psyche as an 'integrate in the ego's organisation'. Winnicott's use of this term suggests that the father functions intrapsychically as an integrating force, which potentially, depending on the facilitating environment (mother), will lead to (what Green describes as) 'effective thirdness'. Winnicott states that the father will be felt differently. 'In this way one can see that the father can be the first glimpse for the child of integration and of personal wholeness' (Winnicott 1969 in Abram 2013: 297). But as Green has pointed out and as Winnicott implies, this possibility can only occur if the mother is psychically engaged with the father. I believe this is what Winnicott means by 'a favourable case'. However, I suggest that if we agree with Winnicott's proposal that the 'integrate' emanates from the actual father, due to his good enough intercourse with mother, then it follows that the integrate is, at least to begin with, paternal. In other words, the integrate cannot be at its origins neutral. Later in development it will become symbolic for the developing infant.

This very late concept from Winnicott's final years advances his theory of 'primary maternal preoccupation', which constitutes the mother's capacity to provide ego-coverage to her newborn. In this way, as long as she is in a loving relationship with the father of the child, she will transmit the fact of this union to the infant's nascent psyche. This psychic transmission from the infant's third occurs through the mother's mind (as she nourishes the father in mind) will become, as Winnicott says, an integrate in the infant's psyche. My proposal here is that this integrate, following Winnicott's suggestion, is de facto a 'paternal integrate'. In health, this constitutes the mother's intrapsychic active engagement with her internal paternal imago, which is reinforced interpersonally with the infant's actual third who is the father.

Moreover, I suggest that the actual good enough father constitutes the third (who reinforces the mother's paternal imago as I mention below) and, in turn, facilitates her capacity for 'ordinary devotion' towards her infant. At the start the father's role is to support the mother's devotion and facilitate the dyad's mutuality. The good enough father is able to wait until the infant develops sufficiently so that s/he is able to tolerate father separating the close intimacy shared with mother and, as Green noted, this paradise, i.e. the merger between mother and infant, has to come to an end. It is at this point that he, the father, becomes an 'obstacle' as Green wrote, to the newborn, who by now is becoming a baby, as depicted in the Ukiyo-e where we see a baby of about three months old. This latter paternal function is more familiar in psychoanalytic theory.

The conceptualisation of the paternal integrate contributes, I suggest, to completing Winnicott's theoretical matrix because it accounts for the father in early psychic development. In addition, I think it offers psychoanalysis a way of making sense of the sequential steps towards the developmental achievement of the Oedipus Complex (cf. Parsons 2000).

The paternal integrate thus also adds to the notion of an intrapsychic surviving object. Indeed, without the third in mother's mind, the mother is less able to offer her infant a good enough experience of psychic *survival-of-the-object*. Therefore, the consistent non *survival-of-the-object* indicates early paternal (integrate) deficiency which comes about through the actuality of the mother's negation of the father in her mind. This negation by mother is what Green referred to as a closed dual relationship that 'paves the way for major psychic disorders' (Green 1991 in Abram 2016: 45).

Let us now turn to a chapter in *Donald Winnicott Today*, in which Christopher Reeves makes a philological examination of the role of the father in Winnicott's writings (Reeves 2013 in Abram 2013). He confirms, as I have previously stated, that the father is indeed integrated in Winnicott's theories. Reeves suggests that there are two distinct fathers present in Winnicott's work and he names the first the 'co-nurturant father' and the second the 'sire father'. The paternal integrate, I suggest, precedes the role of the co-nurturant father. But

I believe that the influence of the co-nurturant father, who is a man who loves the mother of his child and celebrates the fruit of their love making, will naturally reinforce the mother's paternal imago. Therefore, the transmission to her infant of her paternal imago and the father in her mind as she nurses her infant will make the infant's paternal integrate all the more powerful.

Let me now turn to the clinical situation in order to illustrate how the paternal integrate plays a significant role in the analysing situation. The case of K. was introduced in Chapter 3 to illustrate non *survival-of-the-object*, which causes an intrapsychic non surviving object. When I had initially written about the case back in 2005, I had not yet appreciated the ingredient that had instigated my affective change towards the patient. It was only later that I understood that moment as a genuine psychical turning point in the work. Instead of terminating the treatment due to my fear and paralysis, it meant that the work could continue as I narrate in Chapter 3. So, here, I return to discuss that turning point in the light of my reflections on the paternal that were initiated in 2012.

The non surviving object and the roots of terror

In my Discussion of Chapter 3 I refer to the intensity of an 'erotic maternal transference' linked with 'the fear of WOMAN'. I illustrate how necessary it is for the analyst to go through the experience of non survival in the transference as a prerequisite to the process of 'working through' of early trauma that has the potential to offer a real experience of *survival-of-the-object* for both the patient and the analyst. In the depths of the transference the analyst inevitably will become something like the original object, to a greater or lesser extent, while simultaneously remaining the analyst. This is the operation of Green's concept of actualised projection, as indicated in the Discussion of Chapter 2.

Let me remind the reader about the phase during which I felt terrorised by the patient K. The phase lasted several weeks in which we were both suffering because of a sense of terror of each other. K. did not and probably could not attend his five sessions during those weeks. Sometimes he cancelled; sometimes he simply did not attend; sometimes he came late; sometimes he stayed in the waiting lobby as he had done for the first session after the winter break as I describe in Chapter 3.

Then there came the session when, as he sat down in the chair opposite me and began to whip himself up into a frenzied attack towards me, I found myself becoming angry. I describe how this happened and what I found myself saying to him. But why had I not managed to feel that he was treating me badly before that particular moment? What had made the difference to my state of mind? What did that change in me signify? As I started to focus on the paternal, these specific questions began to be answered.

The third in the analyst's mind

As I have already stated during that phase of the analysis, I reached a point where I thought I should probably terminate the treatment. As I report in Chapter 3, I started to feel that the patient was right about psychoanalysis not being an appropriate treatment for him. The intensity of 5x weekly can be contraindicative for some people and not all analysts can help everyone. I felt it was clear that the transference was on the verge of becoming delusional. That tipping point, between illusion and delusion in the transference, as Campbell has pointed out, is a very dangerous phenomenon when working with some patients who are dominated by suicidal ideations (Campbell 1995).

I called on a trusted colleague with whom I had consulted for several years. I presented my work with K. and told him how afraid I felt and was thinking of terminating the treatment. He was thoughtful and silent. I then asked him directly what he thought about me terminating the treatment. I remember him taking some time to reflect on this question. He then responded dispassionately and carefully, saying that only I could make that decision. I left our meeting feeling somewhat perplexed because I had really wanted some direct advice. But little by little over some hours I gradually felt an increasing sense of freedom that, although it seemed counter-intuitive, it may be in the patient's best interest to terminate. I was then able to realise just how trapped I had been feeling. In retrospect, I believe this moment of realising that I could terminate the treatment if I decided to, released me from the sense of entrapment I felt. Subsequently, I began to realise that that specific feeling may be a countertransference reaction that was contributing to an internal psychic shift inside me from the feeling of terror and paralysis towards a sense of outrage and anger that belonged to the Me in the real world. I had reached a point where I really wanted to say to K. 'Stop it! Stop this tantrum and try to think about what you're feeling! Let's talk about it!' It is only in retrospect in the après coup of that phase in the context of the consultation with a trusted colleague that I am now able to articulate what I was feeling.

Holding and the mutative interpretation[2]

The analysing situation mobilises the patient's internal perspectives through holding and interpretation. The analyst offers the patient a psychic space through the analyst's specialised form of free-floating attention akin to primary maternal preoccupation. Thus, the holding environment is inextricably linked with interpretation; the analyst's ongoing internal subjectivity is caught up with the process of interpreting with or without words being spoken.

When K. was at the height of his anguish, I felt forced to undergo deep levels of psychic work as non *survival-of-the-object* was mobilised in the transference. It was several years later that I can see I had become an 'archaïc phantasy object' for K. in the transference towards whom he felt murderous. And it was his conscious murderous feelings towards his mother caught up with his suicidal ideations that had brought him to psychoanalysis in the first place. Reaching that state of mind in the transference was terrifying for him and for me as he could hardly distinguish between his internal archaïc object and his analyst. Later, I wondered whether my wish to get rid of him was indicative of his archaïc object which would have been retaliation on my part.

The 'uncanny' change in me – at the beginning of the session when my fear evaporated and I began to feel angry with him rather than terrorised – was a prelude to being able to give a series of interpretations (the minimal doses as Strachey depicts) that finally led up to what I now identify as a mutative interpretation. This had not been consciously planned, of course, but, at last, I found myself in a position to say something that would reach him. There were two main reasons for this: (a) I felt different (as a result of contact with an internal third instigated by an external third); and (b) because after my first intervention I felt K. was listening to me in a different way.

As I spoke more, I felt he was listening thoughtfully, and this made me more confident in being able to confront him with the truth. I think that truthful point was when I said to him that I thought he was taking advantage of the fact that I was a woman. A few weeks previously, he had told me that he would never treat a male analyst the way he was treating me. When I made that comment the change in him was visceral and I could see that he seemed to be breaking down when he responded, 'I can't do this'. This illicited a further shift in me as I felt genuinely moved by his sense of wretchedness. It reminded me of the creature in *Frankenstein*, as I reported, who said 'I am malicious because I am miserable' (Shelley [1818] 1985). Subsequently, I was able to re-gain my empathy and to be able to be technically neutral instead of being masochistically dominated by a terrifying and violent object.

Following Strachey, I think I can say with sincerity that my interpretation at that point was 'emotionally immediate'. I remember to this day feeling anxious and that I was taking a risk as I could not be sure how he would respond. But I think K. experienced my comment as authentic and he could not deny he had been taking advantage of the fact I was a woman. This is how Strachey identifies the 'mutative interpretation'.

> The patient… will become aware of a distinction between his archaïc phantasy object and the real external object. The 'interpretation' has now become a 'mutative one', since it has produced a breach in the neurotic vicious circle.
> (Strachey 1934: 138)

This is indeed what seemed to occur, and the rage K. had felt towards me never returned with such intensity. Strachey points out that the patient who becomes aware of the real external object's 'lack of aggressiveness will be able to diminish his own aggressiveness' (ibid.: 143).

From that session onwards K.'s acting out diminished significantly and he was subsequently able to make good use of the analytic situation. His suicidal ideations and murderous feelings towards his mother abated and while he did not understand the reason why at a manifest level, he told me in the final stages of analysis that he felt certain he could not imagine feeling like killing himself or his mother in the future. I felt this was authentic and that he had achieved a significant psychic change.

Some tentative conclusions

The analysing situation constitutes a specialised holding environment in which the early deficiencies of infancy can be experienced by the patient for the first time thanks to the fact of transference and the operation of nachträglichkeit. For all patients a certain degree of acting out has to be truly experienced in the countertransference before it can be worked through. As I've tried to show, this requires deep levels of psychic work for the analyst who has to hold the clinical infant and clinical adolescent in the adult and be prepared to receive the actualised projections that relate to the archaïc object. Strachey's formulation, which identifies the mutative interpretation, illuminates the analyst's task and the complex layers related to the act of making interpretations. He writes that '…the giving of a mutative interpretation is a crucial act for both the analyst and the patient'. He points out that it will be risky because the analyst's confrontation is '…deliberately evoking a quantity of the patient's id-energy while it is alive and actual and unambiguous and aimed directly at the analyst' (Strachey 1934: 159). Here, it seems to me, that Strachey's use of the term 'id-energy' is equivalent to the way in which Winnicott refers to 'destruction' and *survival-of-the-object*.

The analyst's internal third (that in origin must stem from the analyst's original paternal integrate) and has grown into a paternal imago, strengthens her ability to take such a risk in confronting the patient at the moment of heightened tension. Before that point in the work with K. I had cowered too much in the way I think his mother had probably cowered with K.'s father with whom he had identified (see Chapter 3). Thus, the analyst's capacity to hold the analysing situation, internally and externally, constitutes psychic *survival-of-the-object*.

The analytic paternal integrate

During the last few months of K.'s analysis he found ways of showing his gratitude, albeit indirectly. To his surprise he had re-found the capacity to cry. He left telling me that he felt confident he would never be as depressed as he had been before starting the analysis, and he could not imagine ever feeling suicidal again or feeling that intense hate and repulsion towards his mother who, he now realised, was a rather vulnerable old lady. He added that he didn't really understand why this had happened, or, indeed, whether it had anything to do with the analysis. In terms of my formulations here, I felt the final stages of analysis showed evidence of an intrapsychic surviving object eclipsing a non surviving object. This psychic change, I suggest, was initiated by the major turning point, when the third in his analyst's mind activated paternal functioning manifested through holding and interpretation.

Strachey says that the 'mutative interpretation' is not something that will occur in every session and it is not something the analyst should be aiming for in any conscious way. I suggest that when the analyst's psychic work leads to a 'mutative interpretation' it is due to the analyst's third (paternal imago) that is transmitted and internalised by the analysand. At that moment, the patient's original paternal integrate at the heart of the un-evolved surviving object is revivified. This produces what I propose to call an 'analytic paternal integrate' because it is revived through and because of the analysing situation. This inter-psychic event that impacts on the intrapsychic domain marks an emotional developmental achievement for both patient and analyst. This is why and how the analytic relationship facilitates the growth of the surviving object and leads towards what Green refers to as 'effective thirdness'. Thus, the patient has reached object usage and can make use of the analysis in a more meaningful way that has the potential to lead to psychic change.

Notes

1 The idea of a 'paternal integrate' was first presented in French on the invitation of Haydée Faimberg (2013) to present in her atelier for the French Speaking Congress (CPLF) in 2013 on the subject of Le Paternel.
2 I use this title in Chapter 10 of the book I co-authored with R.D. Hinshelwood. I am grateful for the dialogue with Hinshelwood in that book that sharpened my thinking on Strachey's work.

References

Abram, J. (ed.) (2000) *André Green at the Squiggle Foundation*, 1st edition. London: Karnac.
Abram, J. (ed.) (2013) *Donald Winnicott Today*, New Library of Psychoanalysis. Routledge.
Abram, J. (ed.) (2016) *André. Green at the Squiggle Foundation*, 2nd edition. London: Karnac.
Campbell, D. (1995) The role of the Father in a pre-suicide state. *Int J Psychoanal* 76: 315–323.
Evans, D. (1996) *Dictionary of Lacanian psychoanalysis*, Routledge.

Faimberg, H. (2013) The "As-yet situation" in Winnicott's "Fragment of an analysis": Your father never did you the honour of"...YET The Psychoanalytic Quarterly 2013 Volume LXXXII Number 4.

Green, A. ([1991] 2000). On thirdness. In: Abram, J. (editor) *André Green at the Squiggle Foundation*, 69–83. London: Karnac.

Parsons, M. (2000) The Oedipus Complex as a lifelong developmental process: Sophocles'Trichinae in *The Dove That Returns, The Dove that Vanishes: Paradox and creativity in psychoanalysis*, The New Library of Psychoanalysis Routledge.

Reeves, C. (2013) On the Margins: the role of the father in Winnicott's writings Chapter 16 In: Abram 2013a.

Shelley, M. (1818) *Frankenstein*, Penguin Classics.

Strachey, J. (1934) The Nature of the Therapeutic Action of Psychoanalysis. *In J Psychoanal* 15: 127–159

Winnicott DW (1953 [1952]) Psychoses and child care. *Br J Med Psychol* 1953: 26.

Winnicott DW (1969) The use of an object. *Int J Psychoanal* 50: 711–716.

8

FEAR OF MADNESS IN THE CONTEXT OF NACHTRÄGLICHKEIT AND THE NEGATIVE THERAPEUTIC REACTION (2018)

Prelude

For the final chapter of this book, I examine how, towards the end of his life, Winnicott formulated a theory of madness. Firmly located in the earliest psychic environment, madness means the infant suffered unthinkable anxiety due to the deficient ego protection from the m/Other. This is the 'fact' of the patient's history and it this fact that has to emerge and be lived through in the transference of the analysing situation. Winnicott's term 'breakdown' essentially refers to the deconstruction of a fragile defence that has been enlisted by the traumatised infant that only thinly covers the underlying 'madness'. Madness is a state of mind in which nothing can be comprehended because there is no ego functioning in the subject and no ego protection from the psychic environment. This is how Winnicott distinguishes between psychosis – which is madness – and psychotic defences – which signify a layer of ego functioning which is, nevertheless, not good enough.

Emanating from work with a patient whose manifest fear of death, murder and madness was a predominant feature of his symptoms, the psychoanalytic notions of nachträglichkeit and the negative therapeutic reaction were invoked. Drawing on Freud, Riviere and Faimberg's plea for a broader conceptualisation of nachträglichkeit, this chapter offers my perspective on Winnicott's late theory of madness. While Winnicott's thesis has its roots in Freudian thought his specific psychoanalytic advances concerning the 'psychology of madness' argue, once more, against the notion of a death instinct.

Thus, my proposal here is that Winnicott's contribution to the concept of breakdown and madness in psychoanalysis offers a significant dimension that constitutes the essential hallmark of his work, i.e. the vicissitudes of the parent–infant relationship. I also point out how I believe he was influenced by Joan Riviere's paper on the negative therapeutic reaction which she presented at a scientific meeting of the British Psychoanalytical Society when it is highly likely that Winnicott was in analysis with her. As I show here, however, Winnicott argues that the fear of going back to the past in analysis is not because of the intrapsychic horrors due to what many analysts consider a 'death instinct', but rather due to the deficiency of the early psychic environment. Deficiency at the beginning of life amounts to a catastrophic trauma (see Abram 2021).

★ ★ ★

A close reading of Winnicott's late papers 'The psychology of madness' (1965a) and 'Fear of Breakdown' (1963?) brought a patient of mine immediately to mind. The main clinical feature, though not obvious from the start of analysis, was a fear of an agonising death in which he would lose his mind. This was initially manifested and articulated as a fear of abandonment in which he would be utterly alone, falling forever, as he floated away in outer space – infinitely. It was a terrifying fantasy of utter helplessness. He could not save himself or be saved as he fell further away from the spaceship that had cut him off. This was an agony that would last forever because nobody would hear him – simply because nobody was there. The thought of this event made him feel he would be going mad.

Over the course of several years of a full analysis (5x weekly), it became clear that this fear of the future agony, mobilised by analysis and the evolving transference, was equal to his terror of emotional contact, as he felt increasingly dependent on the analysis. Dr Z was a conscientious patient with a highly functioning intellectual defence. While his conscious aims were increasingly fulfilled, from month to month and year to year, he wanted to reassure us both that the analysis was working. But any sign of progress always led to a serious backlash when the symptoms would return so as to prove that analysis did not work and, in fact, made things worse. It followed then that I was to blame for ruining his life. Over the course of several years this pattern established itself and yet, despite this oscillating pattern, Dr Z's quality of life out of the consulting room seemed to be improving. However, the closer he came to live the normal life that he felt everybody else could lead, the more intensely he felt the backlash. He came to recognise, on an intellectual level, that he needed the suffering. It functioned for him. At the same time, it made him feel terrified because he was convinced the symptoms were killing him and would cause his death. Although there were phases in which he realised he was capable of living an ordinary life – enjoying work and relationships – this did not change or even mitigate his fundamental belief that he would die in some kind of horrific scenario – always alone and unloved.

It will be clear to many readers that this clinical picture of Dr Z fits well with Freud's description of the 'negative therapeutic reaction' (Freud 1923). I realise now that this clinical phenomenon fits with many of the patients I have written about in these chapters. And this phenomenon is common in most analyses, to a greater or lesser extent. Freud conceptualised that this common feature in analytic practice indicated an unconscious sense of guilt related to the 'economic problem of masochism' (Freud 1924). In one of his late papers Freud discussed this clinical phenomenon in economic terms related to analyses both terminable and interminable (Freud 1937a). Freud identified that the patient is not in emotional contact with an unconscious sense of guilt: '…he does not feel guilty; he feels ill' (Freud 1923: 50). This was a major reason why Dr Z sought analysis. While it was clear he suffered from an unconscious sense of guilt his conscious complaint was that he was ill. For Freud, the basis of this particular psychopathology was caused by the death instinct.

Joan Riviere added to Freud's concept by including Melanie Klein's evolving ideas on internal objects and the Kleinian development of the 'depressive position'. In that paper she stated that the patient's fear of losing the manic defence during the course of analysis is related to the fact that '…the worst disasters have actually taken place' (Riviere 1936: 312). Although this paper was written ten years before Klein had formulated the concept of the paranoid-schizoid position,[1] Riviere was presumably referring to the patient's early psychic development (which she argues has actually taken place). The notion of returning to an infantile state of mind is not new in psychoanalysis, but the clinical feature of Riviere's 'refractory case' is closely related to Winnicott's axiom concerning the 'fear of breakdown'.[2] However, while the clinical observations of both Riviere and Winnicott concur, their respective clinical paradigms are decisively different. Joan Riviere's proposal is based on Klein's notion of the adult patient re-experiencing the terrifying disasters associated with the 'depressive position' while for Winnicott the patient's fear of the future breakdown is related to regressing to a state of mind that has been 'catalogued' (rather than experienced), due to the failure of the early psychic environment. I will elaborate on these points later.

Haydée Faimberg's contribution to the notion of nachträglichkeit (inspired by both Lacan and Laplanche) led her to propose that Winnicott's 'fear of breakdown' was an excellent example of Freud's 'constructions' in psychoanalytic technique (Faimberg [1998] in Abram 2013). I referred to Faimberg's work in Chapter 5 on Winnicott's clinical innovations. Freud emphasises that the analyst's timing of the construction should occur when the patient was affectively re-calling the repressed memory. Winnicott's proposed technique amplifies Freud's concept of 'constructions' and I suggest he was likely to have been influenced by Strachey, when he emphasises that both patient and analyst have to live through the experience of madness in the present situation of the transference. As I indicated in Chapter 7, Winnicott must have been well acquainted with Strachey's 1934 paper on the therapeutic action of analysis. Within the structures of analysis, the analyst will inevitably 'fail' the patient. This is highlighted especially in my work with K. in Chapter 2. The 'failure' is related to the original object in the patient's psyche that the analyst 'becomes' in the transference–countertransference dynamic. Becoming aware of this fact is the only route to offering the patient a very different experience.

In my attempt to discuss Winnicott's theory of madness, I find myself drawn to the above classical Freudian concepts, which seem to be inextricably linked with Winnicott's formulations. My aim in tracing the way in which I think both nachträglichkeit and the negative therapeutic reaction are related has been stimulated by my clinical experience. My aim here is to illustrate how Winnicott's contribution to an understanding of madness creates a powerful extra dimension that contains the essential hallmark of his work, i.e. the vicissitudes of the parent–infant relationship. And it is this hallmark that highlights why I believe his contributions are radical for psychoanalysis – in practice and in theory.

The case of Dr Z

After almost five years of Dr Z's 5x weekly analysis I came to the realisation that the analytic task was impossible. Hitherto, I had always resisted the notion of unanalysability, but with Dr Z I began to change my mind. Paradoxically, this was a relieving thought and was helpful in retaining a sense of neutrality in listening to his complaints and even staying thoughtful on the occasions he tore into me. The neutral position had been difficult to retain in the early years when I had either felt overwhelmed by his rages or, in contrast, very often indifferent. My sense of feeling overwhelmed when he was enraged was quite different from working with K. I did not feel afraid and terrorised as I had done with K. Instead, I felt mad. At times, I felt I was being pulled quite literally into a world in which nothing made sense. So, when I recognised that the analysis could not achieve what it was intended to achieve, i.e. to offer him a sense of freedom from his crippling symptoms because Dr Z needed to suffer, then I could begin to find a different stance. This does not mean that I had given up on the task of analysis; rather, I felt it important to face the facts related to an interminable analysis due to the patient's unanalysability. This reminds me of Winnicott reporting that one of his patients told him that the only time he had felt hopeful for a good outcome in analysis with Winnicott was when Winnicott told him the analysis was hopeless (1960). I was not in a position to say that to Dr Z feeling intimidated by his sensitivity to being unanalysable.

One of the major findings that contributed to my realisation (of the impossibility of analysis) was that Dr Z gradually came to see that he had made a pact with his mother that he should never supersede her on a professional level. This meant he was in a permanent bind because, although in a different profession, Dr Z's main conscious aim for his analysis was to succeed beyond his mother's professional success. This, of course, also related to me in the transference. Dr Z sought analysis with me because of an unconscious transference that fitted with his maternal imago and the powerful narrative connected with it.

As he neared completion of the project he had started when commencing the analysis (between the sixth and seventh years) the pending rupture of the pact was imminent. This thought filled him with a terror of retaliation and revenge from his mother. But the crippling symptoms played out the revenge and pre-empted the anticipated fantasied external attack. It became clear, over and over again, that he was indeed his own worst enemy. His internal(ised) attacking mother was efficient in retaliating to such an extent that Dr Z's illness meant he was unable to work. He felt out of control of what happened to him and while he understood on an intellectual level that he was responsible this awareness made no difference.

In the final stages of his project, he made a conscious decision to deal with his symptoms through medication. This made a difference, and the work was going well. Meanwhile, he became increasingly aware of his love for his mother and felt pained that he had disappointed and betrayed his mother. This was the reason, he surmised, that his mother had rejected him. The only way he could really feel loved and cared for was for me to be permanently available. He hated the structures of analysis and experienced the boundaries as cruel and punishing in the same way he had experienced his mother in the past.

This increasing awareness developed alongside his memories of feeling that as a young child he had to put others before him. Any problem he had did not matter. And this was because he felt he had all the resources to make everybody else well and that therefore his task was to put everybody else first and his own needs last. In this scenario then he was obliged to suffer for others. These memories arose as he started to feel good and even enjoy aspects of his life. Punishment had to follow because enjoying life meant he was neglecting his responsibilities and his true role in life.

Saying all this aloud in the course of our analytic conversations evoked a Jesus scenario for Dr Z, i.e. that his destiny was to suffer for others. He felt embarrassed by becoming aware that he might have some sort of Jesus complex and derided himself. Nevertheless, he remembered that in his late adolescence he decided to ask the philosophical question: to what limits was he obliged to care for others before he was allowed to think of himself? Although this question felt like a conviction – something he had to live by – on an intellectual level he thought it couldn't be right. This problem, then, was behind the motivation to study a specific branch of human interaction and to come into analysis.

I interpreted that these aspects of his inner life were an undercurrent of the transference in which he felt that he had to stay in analysis to save me. Now the pact existed between himself and his analyst. If the pact was broken (success of analytic insight) then actual murder was bound to follow. A foreclosed battle to the death felt visceral in some sessions, as if there was no escape from the inevitable horrific slaughter or, worse, a painful, lonely and lingering death.

These emerging insights were in distinct contrast to his conscious need for the world to feel sorry for him because he was treated so badly by his family – namely, by his mother and sister who were both successful professionals. It was impossible for him to see how he had instigated their rejection of him over the years. And while he accused them of envy towards him it was transparent that it was Dr Z who felt envious, which he totally disavowed. This illuminated the underlying reasons for his unconscious sense of guilt and his need to be punished. Suffering functioned for Dr Z and relieved him of his murderous and violent hatred towards his mother and sister.

The so-called 'negative therapeutic reaction' and the 'refractory' case

Dr Z's difficulties resonate strongly with the description of Freud's cases of the negative therapeutic reaction associated with masochism that leads to an interminable analysis. These pathological symptoms, for Freud, could only be explained by the innate death instinct that was responsible for destroying any psychical improvement. Joan Riviere's contribution to Freud's concept illuminated the strength of the resistance – which is why she refers to the patients as 'refractory'. This term depicts an intense resistance to psychic change.

However, Riviere's aim in her 1936 paper was to illustrate that the patient had already experienced the terrors, and this is why they were so afraid in the transference, because they carry a deep unconscious memory of what it will feel like when their manic defence dissolves as a result of analysis. Joan Riviere suggested that the underlying force makes the patient feel that death or madness is inevitable

> …his own and others is ever before the eyes of his unconscious mind. He cannot possibly regenerate and recreate all the losses and destruction he has caused, and if he cannot pay this price, his own death is the only alternative.
>
> (Riviere 1936: 152)

Riviere emphasised how crucial it was that the analyst understand this internal predicament and recommended that the main technical issue should be to analyse the love and guilt associated with depressive anxiety. Moreover, Riviere seemed to be pleading with her colleagues, to recognise the difference between psychic truth and a 'false' transference (Riviere 1936: 153).

While Freud's basic assumption, underlying his theory of the negative therapeutic reaction, is based on the death instinct concept, Riviere's argumentation is based on Melanie Klein's concept of the 'depressive position'.[3] Nevertheless, Riviere's basic assumptions included the notion of the death instinct and the theoretical position that the 'worst disasters have actually taken place' indicates Klein's theory of a universal intrapsychic infantile depressive position. Thus, for Riviere, the terror of returning to that infantile state of mind could be seen to underlie the resistance of all patients. Riviere's paper is passionate and compelling. As already indicated above, I feel sure that Winnicott would have been familiar with its argument and probably even heard this paper when it was first given. I suggest that many aspects of Riviere's argumentation influenced him when he came to formulate his own ideas about the fear of breakdown and the psychology of madness.

However, it should be borne in mind, as I emphasise throughout this book, that Winnicott never accepted Freud's formulation of the death instinct – let alone Klein's – and, as already stated, it was in his late work that he was able to formulate an alternative theory in 'The use of an object'. For Winnicott, the variable strength of the patient's resistance was due more to the emotional vicissitudes in the early parent–infant relationship than constitutional and instinctual factors. The stronger the resistance the more indication, therefore, of non survival of the object. The infant's healthy constitution completely depended on the m/Other's capacity to respond to the infant's primitive needs.

Joan Riviere was Winnicott's second analyst after James Strachey. In a talk he gave to a small group (known as the 1952 Club), Winnicott said that when he talked to Riviere about 'classifying the environment' she responded by telling him she would turn him into a frog (Winnicott [1968] 1989, 2013). His joke related to the fact that as a Kleinian her focus was entirely on the patient's internal world. And while her paper on the negative therapeutic reaction offers a vivid depiction of a particularly powerful resistance shown by a certain category of patients to psychoanalytic treatment, the specifics of her proposals on technique suggests a divergence from Klein's aims in technique. For Riviere, the analyst should focus on love and guilt instead of aggression, hate and envy. Nevertheless, I believe the theoretical foundations of her argument do not take the role of the early environment into account in understanding the patient's psychical predicament in their fear of breakdown. And this is precisely what Winnicott addressed in his theory of fear of breakdown. When Riviere states that the terrors have occurred before (in early psychic development), she is referring to the state of mind that all infants go through rather than the problem of the refractory case depicting a drastic failure of the early psychic environment, as Winnicott proposed.

'The psychology of madness' in the context of Winnicott's theoretical matrix

In the Appendix to this book, I outline my reasons for considering that 'The psychology of madness' was written in 1965, two years after 'Fear of breakdown'. The 1965 paper was prepared for Winnicott's colleagues at the British Psychoanalytical Society but was never given and remained unpublished until 1989.[4] But it clearly follows the themes already set out since 1952, as we shall see, and outlined in the 'Fear of breakdown'.[5]

In order to appreciate Winnicott's theory of madness, let us examine the way in which his theory focuses on what I believe is core to his conceptual preoccupations in the third phase of his work (1960–1971) – *survival-of-the-object*. The whole of his conceptual scaffold is fundamentally based on how the 'psychic' environment is totally responsible for the infant's psychopathology. This means that the cause of a state of madness emanates from the psychic events of the early psychic environment. This has been his main message since the early 1940s when he stood up in a scientific meeting and said 'There's no such thing as a baby!' (Winnicott 1952: 99). From then on it was not possible for Winnicott to conceptualise without taking account of the emotional environment in which the individual was nurtured. Nature also had its part to play – Winnicott refers to 'inherited tendencies' – but these tendencies would not evolve along healthy lines unless the individual was in the context of a facilitating environment.

Winnicott tells us that he began to conceptualise the notion of psychosis in 1952. In that paper he produced diagrams to illustrate the 'two patterns of development' which are referred to in Chapter 1. He writes in the 1965 paper that previously, in 1952 in his paper 'Psychosis and Child Care', he surprised himself by referring to schizophrenia as an 'environmental deficiency disease' and that he was getting near to a statement about madness that he would elaborate in 1965 (Winnicott [1965] 1989: 123–124). For Winnicott, the infant who suffers as a consequence of a lack of holding has to enlist certain defences depending on the stage at which the failure took place. In his 1960 paper 'Ego distortion in terms of true and false self' he classifies five different false selves (Winnicott 1960b: 143–144); there is a 'healthy' false self, but there are at least three types of false self that are inauthentic and disassociated from the true self.[6] In 1962 he identifies six stages of infantile dependency to illustrate the outcome of a deficient environment at each distinct stage. At the stage of extreme dependency, for example, the failure of the environment causes schizophrenia, which is why he refers to schizophrenia as an 'environmental-deficiency disease' (Winnicott 1962).

Winnicott was very clear until the end of his life that there were two categories of people: those who had been held and those who had not. It is striking that in this 1965 paper he concedes, a little, that 'some experience of madness… is universal' because no first environment can protect the infant entirely and perfectly. But he continues in his late work to draw a line between all the variations of one kind of human being on the not good enough side of the environment from all the variations of another kind of human being on the good enough side. It is the 'borderline' or 'psychotic' patient who carries around a 'significant experience of mental breakdown' (ibid.). This indicates that the clinical phenomenon of 'fear of breakdown' refers to the category of patients who had suffered in their early psychic development due to the failure of the early environment.

Now the question of the false self defence in Winnicott's theory has come about because the infant has suffered something unthinkable, i.e. a sudden loss of the holding environment or lack of a good enough holding. Early deficiency of ego coverage results in the break in the continuity of being. This constitutes early psychic trauma before the infant has achieved a strong enough functioning ego. But the borderline patient has achieved a degree of ego functioning – a false self is akin to ego functioning – and Winnicott was clear that the 'false self is built up on a basis of compliance' (Winnicott 1960b). So, if there is no inter-connection between the (healthy) false self and the true self then the individual is doomed to a compliant sort of living which Winnicott said was no life at all (Winnicott [1947] 1949).

The patient's fear of losing his defences as analysis progresses is linked to his unconscious memory of the trauma caused by the break in the continuity of being. In other words, at a profound level the patient's fear – like panic – protects them from re-visiting the psychic pain of trauma. The memory is 'catalogued' – it was a psychic event that occurred, but there was no Self to experience it and comprehend what happened. This tallies with Faimberg's plea for a broadening of the concept of nachträglichkeit (see Chapters 5 and 6). As ego functioning increases in strength, due to the good enough holding of the psychoanalytic setting, how can the patient trust that what happened before will not happen again? Why should the analyst (as the new environment) be any safer than the earlier environment which had caused unthinkable pain? These questions resonated profoundly in the analysis of Dr Z. Primitive agony and a falling forever was going on all the time in the deep recesses of his mind, as illustrated by the scene he presented early on in the analysis of being cut off from the spaceship falling through space in which there was no boundary, no Self, no body. But in relation to Winnicott's theory of madness the fantasies of his pending death in the future indicated that early environmental damage was a fact; he had already suffered a psychic death and a falling forever.

When Winnicott refers to 'madness' he is referring to an infant who is absolutely dependent on the m/Other, but has lacked consistent experience of his needs being met. This condition of utter isolation causes a trauma that overwhelms the nascent psyche. This constitutes madness. It does not mean that all babies are mad at the beginning, as Winnicott asserts in this paper. For him, the paranoid-schizoid position that Klein formulated in 1946 was an apt description of what occurred to the infant's state of mind due to the failure of the early psychic environment. For Winnicott, it was not a universal phenomenon as Klein proposed. Madness equals psychosis whereas psychotic defences in Winnicott's language are set up to tolerate the unthinkable anxiety. In 1949 Winnicott referred to the notion of cataloguing that refers to an unconscious memory of a reaction to trauma. Madness, therefore, is an accumulation of reactions to trauma that have been catalogued in the mind/memory without having been processed or digested. The patient cannot conceive of the possibility of re-visiting traumatic affects without losing his mind again and becoming mad, i.e. with nobody there to help process the feelings. From a treatment point of view the patient does not comprehend the meaning of 'working through' because it has never happened before. In Dr Z's case the only way he had dealt with psychic trauma was to self-hold and omnipotently take care of others before himself. Thus, he could disavow his position of being utterly dependent because that would mean a repetition of the terror of abandonment. As he came to acknowledge his dependency on the analysis his pathological omnipotent defences began to breakdown.

Winnicott's Axiom

Winnicott had identified the crucial nature of time and space since Phase One of his work when he distinguished '…three processes that start very early: integration, personalization and the appreciation of time and space and other properties of reality' (Winnicott 1945: 149). Later, in his paper 'Metapsychological and clinical aspects of regression within the psychoanalytic set-up' (Winnicott 1954: 288), he emphasised the importance of the analyst's time keeping with the regressed patient because of their extreme vulnerability to the analyst's errors that would repeat the earlier object's unreliability. By Phase Three of his work, the notion of time and continuity in the clinical encounter are more clearly defined. For example, if we turn to his paper on the capacity for concern, he states:

> Time is kept going by the mother, and this is one aspect of her auxiliary ego-functioning; but the infant comes to have a personal time-sense, one that lasts at first only over a short span.
> (Winnicott [1960a] 1963b: 77)

This point will be elaborated a few years later in his paper on the 'Location of cultural experience' in 1967 in which he describes how the infant's 'continuity of being' can be ruptured by the mother's absence that constitutes a clear failure of the holding environment. So, once again, the issue of temporality for Winnicott is entirely related to the early psychic relationship – 'time is kept going by the mother' – and this is one of the analyst's tasks in the context of the analysing situation and why timekeeping for the borderline patient is crucial.

Temporality and the parent–infant relationship are core to Winnicott's 'Axiom' in his brief note of 1963 (see Appendix) and developed further in 1964 as a Postscript to the paper on Classification (Winnicott 1959–64). Let us enumerate the main points of the Axiom:

- The breakdown that is feared has already occurred at the stage of absolute dependence
- The patient's 'illness pattern' constitutes the 'new' defences enlisted after the original breakdown, e.g. a false self
- The patient gradually 'remembers' the breakdown in the therapeutic setting 'because of ego growth'
- One root of the 'fear of breakdown' is the patient's need to remember, i.e. bring into consciousness
- A later version of the breakdown may be highlighted in the transference, but always relates to the original early breakdown
- The environmental factor is not a single trauma, but a pattern of distorting influences

Nachträglichkeit and constructions

It was Lacan who originally drew attention to the notion of nachträgchlikeit as both Laplanche and Pontalis highlight in their *Vocabulaire de Psychanalyse* (Laplanche & Pontalis 1967). They pointed out that while Freud had used this notion implicitly, he had not outlined a theory. Later Laplanche went on to conceptualise 'afterwardness' (Laplanche 1989). Faimberg's work on the 'telescoping of generations' enlarges further on temporality in psychoanalysis and in several publications, she writes about recognising in her work, retrospectively, that she had used 'the concept of après coup in a much broader sense than Freud' (Faimberg ([1998] 2013 in Abram 2013: 206). As I have already referenced in Chapters 5 and 6, in arguing for the 'broader conceptualization of nachträglichkeit' Faimberg proposes that 'Winnicott's 'Fear of breakdown' is paradigmatic of this broader conceptualization' (Faimberg 2007: 1221). When the patient feels the 'fear of breakdown' in the present time of the session, the analyst should interpret that the fear of the future breakdown is based on the breakdown that has already happened. This, Faimberg asserts, constitutes a construction, as Freud had originally suggested in his paper of 1937 'Constructions in analysis'. Faimberg writes about the patient in analysis undergoing a sense of helplessness that '…the breakdown he is now experiencing for the first time, already took place at a moment when the patient was not yet there to have the experience' (Faimberg [1998] 2013 in Abram 2013: 207). The past, therefore, can only be constructed in the present time of analysis, i.e. in the transference.

This observation of Faimberg's is another way of defining the concept of early psychic deficiency of the environment and the psychic trauma that occurs as a result. If there is not a Self who is capable of dealing with the 'thing' (event and/or lack of holding), then the psyche can only 'catalogue' rather than 'process' the experience (Winnicott 1954). This indicates that the infant was unprotected at a crucial moment of development and 'catalogues' (what can only be described as) 'primitive agony,' a 'falling forever,' and 'unthinkable anxiety'.

Faimberg's emphasis in her 'broader conceptualization' warrants closer examination. Following Freud, she proposes that there are two phases in the operation of nachträgchlikeit in the course of the analytic treatment. The first is the phase of anticipation relating to the patient's increasing sense of a fear that something terrible is about to happen. The evolving transference mobilises this anticipation, and it is founded on the patient's 'need to remember'. The second phase, at the moment the patient is ready to listen, due to ego growth, involves the analyst's construction to the patient. This means that the past can be constructed for the first time in the present tense of the transference situation.

Faimberg's appreciation of Winnicott's implicit use of nachträglichkeit illuminates the Freudian roots of Winnicott's proposed technique. This has the potential to change the patient's fear of impending disaster because in the context of the present analysing situation the past event can be placed in the past in the organisation of the mind. This occurs because of ego growth, reinforced by the analyst's ego holding function, that allows the patient to risk remembering while feeling dependent on the analyst. In this way, Winnicott's formulations in his theory of madness constitute a clinical concept that contributes to theory and practice. And while he 'stretches'[7] the Freudian notion of temporality he simultaneously holds the psychic environment of the past responsible for the patient's madness in the present analysing situation. By inference, therefore, the analyst avails herself to become the early archaïc object mother who had originally failed. This is why 'changes come in an analysis when the traumatic factors enter the psychoanalytic material' (Winnicott 1960a: 37) and also why 'interpretations that are alterative are those made in terms of projection'

Fear of madness

(ibid.), as illustrated in the clinical examples of Chapters 2 and 4. Winnicott concludes:

> So in the end we succeed by failing – failing the patient's way... In this way regression can be in the service of the ego if it is met by the analyst and turned into a new dependence...
>
> (Winnicott 1963a: 258)

Thus, the structure of the analysing situation offers the patient a safe setting in which early traumata will be unconsciously anticipated by the patient. While Faimberg's identification of the anticipatory phase in the operation of nachträglichkeit is the same as Winnicott's fear of breakdown there is also a strong resonance with Joan Riviere's observations of patients who are caught up in the 'negative therapeutic reaction'.[8] The difference in the formulations, however, as stated above, suggest that for Riviere the fear of breakdown is wholly to do with internal factors whereas for Winnicott, following Freud, there has been a psychic event, i.e. trauma to a Self who was not there (due to immaturity) in the context of an environment that was also not there (unavailable for whatever reason). This suggests that Winnicott's emphasis on the environment's responsibility for traumatising the newborn and his suggestions on technique correlate with Freud's late work as seen in 'Constructions'. And, strikingly, towards the end of that paper Freud anticipates both Winnicott's concept of 'fear of breakdown' as well as Faimberg's plea for the broader concept of nachträglichkeit.

> ...when a neurotic is led by an anxiety-state to expect the occurrence of some terrible event, he is in fact merely under the influence of a repressed memory (which is seeking to enter consciousness but cannot become conscious) that something which was at that time terrifying did really happen.
>
> (Freud 1937: 268)

This statement illustrates Freud's implicit appreciation not only that the 'terrifying event did really happen' (cf. Riviere's 'worst disasters had already taken place'), but also that the patient's repressed memory is 'seeking to enter consciousness' (cf. Winnicott on: One root of the 'fear of breakdown' is the patient's need to remember, i.e. bring into consciousness).

Therefore, I suggest that the so-called 'negative therapeutic reaction' constitutes the anticipatory phase (in the operation of nachträglichkeit, as set out originally by Freud) because the 'breakdown' in the past is revivified in the present analytic relationship, i.e. the transference. This notion does not negate Freud's formulations that are associated with masochism, unconscious sense of guilt and analysis interminable. But rather it argues against the notion of the death instinct being at the roots of this clinical phenomenon. Instead, following Winnicott's formulations, the negative therapeutic reaction illuminates a deficiency of the early psychic relationship when the baby was subjected to states of madness at the beginning.

From time to time, often related to breaks and/or cancelled sessions, Dr Z would display an intense outburst of paranoia towards me that illustrated a delusionary transference in which there was no distinction between his analyst and his internal archaïc object. This was similar to the work with K., as described in Chapters 3 and 7. The difference was, as I said above, the affect that threatened my sense of self was that I would go mad rather than be murdered. During sessions of this kind, it was a struggle to retain a sense of Self let alone a capacity to think as I was being pulled into mad states of mind. At this time a combination of constructions and interpretations[9] were essential for me to retain an analytic position. If I spoke, whatever I said, I felt I could hold on to my sense of who I was. For example, on one occasion when Dr Z was accusing me of enjoying the fact that he was dependent and that I was just like his mother who needed everybody to dote on her I found myself saying, 'There are times when you speak to me that I feel I don't know what to say because I feel you don't really believe I am like your mother.' I did not think this was an insightful sort of comment, but just to hear myself speaking meant I existed for myself. I think it helped on occasions to bring Dr Z back in the room and reminded him, from his position on the couch, that I was there in the room and was indeed different from his version of his hateful and manipulative mother. Dr Z always felt immensely guilty after such violent outbursts towards me but over time, little by little, I began to see that, at the same time, he felt he was allowed to 'go mad' in the analysis as the psychotic defences gradually diminished. While these states could be described as negative therapeutic reactions my proposal here is that they were phases of 'going mad' akin to 'breaking down', but the difference was that Dr Z had the experience I was a witness who was also experiencing what it was like to be (almost) overwhelmed with a sense of madness and nobody being there who recognised him. Paradoxically, it was on these occasions that I feel I managed somehow to survive, through showing Dr Z I existed and was still with him (at least trying to be with him). When Dr Z terminated treatment, to both his surprise and mine, he felt the pact with his mother (me in the transference) that he was sure he could not tolerate breaking, had indeed been broken and he was allowed to be himself. The themes, although related to Oedipal conflicts, were deeply rooted in the earliest stages when Dr Z had been traumatised as an infant who suffered massive projections from a narcissistic mother, as Magritte's painting depicts in Figure 2.

Summary

Winnicott's theory of madness, as with the whole of Winnicott's theoretical matrix, privileges the facts of the early psychic relationship and, in particular, the mother's powerful role in shaping the infant's psyche. Through drawing on Freud and Riviere, this essay has indicated some of the important influences on Winnicott's conceptualisations. In reference to Faimberg's illuminating observations on Winnicott's implicit use of nachträglichkeit and Freud's proposals on constructions, I have proposed that the 'negative therapeutic reaction' constitutes the anticipatory phase in the operation of nachträglichkeit as advanced by Faimberg. The analyst's reliable holding and interpretation is key to the attempt at least, to psychically survive. In relation to a continuity of psychic *survival-of-the-object*, there is a potential that the patient's phantasy archaïc object will be placed in the past and so liberate the Self to live creatively in the present.

Notes

1 Although Melanie Klein had already been working on the themes in the 1930s (personal communication, R.D. Hinshelwood 2018).
2 At this time Winnicott was probably in analysis with Joan Riviere and it is very likely he would have been present when she gave the paper at a scientific meeting of the British Psychoanalytical Society in 1936.
3 NB that Klein had not yet developed the concept of the 'paranoid-schizoid position' in 1936.
4 Winnicott presented a different paper in October 1965 – 'A Child Psychiatry Case: Description of a Psychotherapeutic Interview' (Archives BPaS).

5 This was the year Winnicott retired from his post as consultant paediatrician (see Chronology in Abram 2013).
6 This indicates further evidence of Joan Riviere's influence on Winnicott in reference to her point about the true and false transference.
7 Cf. Sandler 1983.
8 I first proposed the links concerning Riviere's influence on Winnicott's concept of 'Fear of breakdown' (Abram 2002). Later I found that Haydée Faimberg coincidentally had also made this link (Faimberg 2005: 111).
9 'Interpretation' applies to something that one does to some single element of the material, such as an association or a parapraxis. But it is in a 'construction' when one lays before the subject of the analysis a piece of his early history that he has forgotten… (Freud 1937: 261).

References

Abram, J. (2013) *Donald Winnicott Today* New Library of Psychoanalysis Routledge.

Abram, J. (2021) On Winnicott's concept of trauma Education Section of the IJP.10.1080/00207578.2021.1932079

Faimberg, H. (2007) A plea for a Broader Concept of Nachträglichkeit. *Psychoanal Q* 76(4): 1221–1240.

Faimberg, H. ([1998] 2013) Nachträglichkeit and Winnicott's Fear of Breakdown Chapter 8 in Abram, J. (2013).

Freud, S. (1923) The Ego and the Id SE 19.

Freud, S. (1924) The Economic Problem of Masochism SE 19.

Freud, S. (1937) Constructions in analysis SE 23.

Riviere, J. (1936) A Contribution to the analysis of the negative therapeutic reaction. *Int J Psychoanal* 17: 304–320.

Sandler, J. (1983) Reflections on some relations between psychoanalytic concepts and psychoanalytic practice. *Int J Psychoanal* 64: 35–45.

Strachey, J. (1934) The nature of the therapeutic action of psychoanalysis. *Int J Psychoanal* 15: 127–159.

Winnicott DW (1945) *Primitive emotional development In: Collected papers: Through paediatrics to psycho-analysis*, 1st ed. London: Tavistock.

Winnicott DW ([1947] 1949). Hate in the countertransference. *Int J Psychoanal* 30: 69–74.

Winnicott DW (1952). Anxiety associated with insecurity. In: 1958, 97–100.

Winnicott DW ([1959–1964] 1965) Classification: is there a psychoanalytic contribution to psychiatric classification? In: *Maturational processes and the facilitating environment.* London: Hogarth.

Winnicott DW (1960c). The theory of the parent–infant relationship. *Int J Psychoanal* 41: 585–595.

Winnicott DW (1960d) Ego distortion in terms of true and false self In: 1965: 140–152.

Winnicott DW (1962) Providing for the child in health and crisis. In: 1965: 64–72.

Winnicott DW (1963a) Dependence in infant-care, in child care, and in the psychoanalytic setting. *Int J Psychoanal* 44: 339–344.

Winnicott DW ([1960a] 1963b) The development of the capacity for concern. *Bull Menninger Clin* 27: 167–176 & in Winnicott, 1965a.

Winnicott DW ([1960b] 1965) Ego distortion in terms of true and false self. In: 1965a, 140–52.

Winnicott DW (1965a) *The maturational processes and the facilitating environment: Studies in the theory of emotional development.* London: Hogarth. (International Psycho-analytical Library, No. 64.)

Winnicott DW ([1965] 1989) The Psychology of Madness: A Contribution from Psychoanalysis In: *Psychoanalytic Explorations*, 5119. Cambridge, MA: Harvard UP and Abram 2013 Chapter 1 DWW on DWW.

Winnicott DW (1967). The location of cultural experience. *Int J Psychoanal* 48: 368–372.

Winnicott DW ([1963?] 1974) Fear of breakdown. *Int R Psychoanal* 1: 103–107.

Winnicott DW ([1968] 1989) Postscript: DWW on DWW [1967]. In: Winnicott C, Shepherd R, Davis M, editors. In Winnicott 1989 *Psychoanalytic Explorations*, 569–582. Cambridge, MA: Harvard UP and Abram 2013 Chapter 1 DWW on DWW.

Appendix

The dating of 'Fear of Breakdown' and 'The Psychology of Madness' and why it matters (2018)

What year did Winnicott write 'Fear of Breakdown' and 'The Psychology of Madness' and why does it matter?

The feminine of the human psyche emanates from the mother's womb that is both actual and psychic. The Archive could be thought about as womb-like that contains embryos waiting to be taken into a mind/womb where they will evolve. Archival work is an ineffable experience and, for me, akin to psychoanalytic work. The analyst's silent activity in the session is to wait and to listen. The focus is to listen to the patient and to listen to how it affects the analyst's inner being. There is an implicit inquiry and search that relates to the listening framed by the temporality of the analytic structure. The researcher in the archive is consciously searching for something but does not yet know where the search will lead to. Both activities are an emotional adventure and both analyst and researcher require an open mind. We not only read the papers, correspondence and notes of historical authors and personalities we are interested in, but we touch and smell the paper they wrote on and touched. This experience informs our inner selves at a profound level and it will take time to evolve into an idea or even a concept. It is only in the après coup that we begin to have a notion of what happened in the archive when we first read whatever it may be we read. And as analysts it is the phenomenon of the après coup that leads to elucidation of analytic work with our patients.

Appendix

Following Winnicott's concept of the psyche-in-dwelling-in-the-soma I have recently proposed the notion of an 'indwelling principle' (Abram 2019). This subjective indwelling principle constitutes the abiding presence of the m/Other in each individual psyche 'from which every act derives all its life' (OED). This is one of the ways in which I reflect on archival work. I suggest it has a deep effect on the psyche. How our findings inform each one of us on an intrapsychic level, I suggest, relates to each person's indwelling principle which is at the heart of the feminine in the psyche.

In 2017, Johannes Picht, editor of the well-known German journal *Psyche*, commissioned me to write an article on Winnicott's 'Fear of Breakdown' and its relationship with 'The Psychology of Madness'. I was grateful for this opportunity and it led to the writing of an article that was published in *Psyche* in 2018 and has been revised for Chapter 8 in this collection (see Abram Bibliography).

I had long been quizzical about why 'Fear of Breakdown' was referenced with a question mark, e.g. 1963? In preparing to write that article I took the opportunity to return to the Winnicott archives in my effort to understand why. The following is a short account of my findings and my reasons for wishing to publish these findings in this book.

★ ★ ★

In 1974 when the paper 'Fear of Breakdown' was first published posthumously in the *International Review of Psychoanalysis*, Clare Winnicott wrote a Editorial Note stating that the paper was written 'shortly before Donald Winnicott's death' (Winnicott C. 1974). Since Winnicott died on January 25 1971 the footnote suggests he composed 'Fear of Breakdown' circa 1970. Thomas Ogden, in his article on 'Fear of Breakdown', endorsed Clare Winnicott's footnote and developed his own reasons for concurring with the date (Ogden 2014). But, from my perspective, I believe that 'Fear of Breakdown' was written before 1965 and most likely between 1963 and 1964. Therefore, I do not believe it was Winnicott's final paper. From archival evidence I believe the final paper he was engaged with for the IPA conference in Vienna 1971 was an extension of his preoccupations on the roots of aggression, as I previously demonstrated in Chapter 14 of *Donald Winnicott Today* (Abram 2013).

First of all, let us examine some of the reasons why the dating of its composition is unclear. The Winnicott Trust Editors of *Psychoanalytic Explorations* were Ray Shepherd, a psychoanalyst of the

Appendix

British Psychoanalytical Society, and Madeleine Davis, a philosopher and psychoanalytic psychotherapist. Madeleine Davis was a dedicated Winnicott scholar and it was reputed that she led most of the editing work[1] concerning Winnicott's posthumous publications (on behalf of the Publications Committee).[2] During the course of my archival research I have become acquainted with the handwriting of Madeleine Davis whose comments and amendments to Winnicott's manuscripts are carefully written in a neat hand.

Now, in the main editorial Preface for *Psychoanalytic Explorations*, the editors say that the latter volume is the final book they worked on with Clare Winnicott, who died in 1984. Since it was published in 1989, it is apparent that they probably worked on the manuscript for a further five years after her death. The question is this: when they came to re-publish 'Fear of Breakdown' in this new collection of Winnicott's papers, *Psychoanalytic Explorations*, although they acknowledge in their footnote that it was published in 1974, why do they date it 1963 followed by a question mark? And why do they not refer to Clare Winnicott's Editorial Note of 1974? Was it simply an oversight? Given that Madeleine Davis was reputed to be meticulous in her editing work, this seems unlikely.

A further discrepancy adds to the mystery of the year of composition. When Clare Winnicott published her own clinical paper on the fear of breakdown in the *International Journal of Psychoanalysis* in 1980, in the reference list Winnicott's paper is dated 1970 (rather than 1974 when it was published) (see Clare Winnicott 1980). Does this indicate that 1970 is the year Clare Winnicott believed it had been written because Winnicott was still alive in that year? Later, after Clare Winnicott's death in 1984, Madeleine Davis published a paper on the work of the Publications Committee (by then the Winnicott Trust), which was written in 1985 but not published until 1987, in which she announces that the paper 'Fear of Breakdown' will be included in the forthcoming collection *Psychoanalytic Explorations*. However, she does not refer to its publication of 1970 or 1974 and nor is it in her Reference list (see Davis 1987). It is clear from the editors' footnote to the paper in 1989 that Davis was well aware of the theoretical links between Winnicott's papers 'Fear of breakdown' (1963?), 'Classification' (1964) and 'The psychology of madness' (1965).

Turning again to the Preface of *Psychoanalytic Explorations* written by Madeleine Davis and Ray Shepherd, we learn that before Winnicott died he was planning to compile further new collections of

Appendix

his writings and with that in mind had written two lists. The Editors estimate he compiled these lists in 1968 or 1969. Included in that list is 'The psychology of madness' of 1965. In addition to the two lists, Davis continues, there were two piles of manuscripts 'placed in order'. One of them was 'Fear of Breakdown' and in parenthesis the editors write '(1963?)' (Winnicott 1989: xii).

Despite these discrepancies which create a certain confusion concerning the date of composition of the paper 'Fear of Breakdown', there are three further reasons why I think that the paper was written in 1963 rather than shortly before his death in 1970. I base this on my conceptual and archival research of Winnicott's writings.

1. The manuscript of 'Fear of Breakdown' in the archives is dated 1963. In addition, there are several other writings (and publications) dated 1963 directly related to the specific arguments in the 'Fear of breakdown', as we shall see below.
2. The style of the paper suggests it was written for therapists (rather than his psychoanalytic colleagues). This corroborates that it was prepared with a particular audience in mind as stated on the manuscript, i.e. The Davidson Clinic.
3. Evidence from the archives and other publications indicate that between 1968 and 1970 (the last two years before his death) Winnicott's conceptual preoccupations focused on the theory of aggression and psychic change in psychoanalytic practice.

Let me now elaborate on these three points that highlight the evolution of his concepts.[3]

Archival findings

In the London Winnicott archives the first page of the 'Fear of Breakdown' typescript is headed 'THE DAVIDSON CLINIC, EDINBURGH' – typed and underlined. Handwritten above that, the year date '1963' is written in biro.[4] Below that the heading FEAR OF BREAKDOWN is typed and then slightly below to the right-hand side is Winnicott's address in London. Another handwritten date below the typed address (which could be 1961) is crossed out with the correction '1963'. In addition to the transcript there are two further handwritten notes (in Winnicott's hand), 'On the nature of mental breakdown' dated October 1963 and 'Winnicott's axiom' also dated 1963.

Now let us turn to the publications. Winnicott's paper 'Classification: is there a psychoanalytic contribution to psychiatric classification?', published in the first edition of his 2nd volume of collected papers (Winnicott 1965b), is dated 1959–1964. At the end of the paper, he adds a note: Postscript 1964. This is followed by two further subtitles:

A note on mental breakdown

Some patients have a fear of mental breakdown. It is important for the analyst to keep in mind the following axiom: (1964)

The 'Axiom' (of 1964) is an elaborated version of the 1963 note in the archives. The archive note reads:

> Breakdown has been. The fear of breakdown is the result of the patient's urge to remember a breakdown that was significant. Remembering can only be done by re-experiencing. Remembering implies increasing ego growth which makes for experience which was previously impossible because of ego immaturity.
> (Winnicott Archives, Wellcome Library, London)

Winnicott's style of writing: 'Fear of breakdown' compared with 'The psychology of madness'

In general, there are distinct differences between the papers Winnicott wrote for an audience of mental health practitioners and/or the general public, from those in which he was addressing his colleagues at scientific meetings at home or abroad. The style of writing of 'Fear of breakdown', despite its sophisticated psychoanalytic concept, seems to fall into the category of writings addressed to mental health practitioners – as the manuscript indicates by the heading THE DAVIDSON CLINIC (a Medical Psychotherapy Clinic in Edinburgh).[5] The topic would have probably been quite relevant to the kind of cases the therapists of the clinic would be treating. His audience would have had some training in psychodynamic therapy and there was certainly an interest in Winnicott's work, hence the invitation. The style of the paper is appropriate for this kind of audience. It is quite short and punchy – almost like a PowerPoint with its 15 sub-sections – and re-visits his established early work – Emotional Growth, Early Stages; Absolute Dependence; Primitive Agonies; Psychotic Illness as a Defence. This kind of introductory summary to the main tenets of his work is not a way he would present to his colleagues at a scientific meeting of the BPaS. And while we see he presents his idea as 'new'; it is discernible from a closer reading that the central idea is founded on Freud's original undeveloped theory of temporality – nachträglichkeit (as I comment on in Chapter 8 p.?).

In contrast, 'The Psychology of Madness: A Contribution from Psychoanalysis' has no sub-sections at all. And at the beginning Winnicott does not say this is a 'new' idea but rather that what he has to say, 'may have been said before by Freud or somebody else'; nevertheless, he would like to share his 'latest brainchild' (p. 119). This suggests to me that the new idea in 1963 has continued to evolve in his mind up to the time of writing 'The Psychology of Madness'. When he writes in 1965, however, that 'this might have been said before', he shows an awareness that he may be extending something that Freud (or somebody else) has said or at least started to say. He gave a similar caveat at the beginning of his first seminal paper in 1945:

> I shall not first give an historical survey and show the development of my ideas from the theories of others, because my mind does not work that way. What happens is that I gather this and that, here and there, settle down to clinical experience, form my own theories and then, last of all, interest myself in looking to see where I stole what. Perhaps this is as good a method as any.
> (Winnicott 1945: 145)

However, the apparent undermining of his 'latest brain-child' tends to also indicate his concern about both criticism and scepticism.[6]

Moreover, the tone of the 1965 paper is more considered with all the themes in the fear of breakdown permeating the paper's argumentation. Halfway through he refers back to his 'axiom' in order to amend what he stated previously. This seems to be further evidence that this paper was written after 'Fear of breakdown' and is the paper he wrote for his analytic colleagues at home. It is a mystery why he never presented this paper. Instead, on October 6 1965, he presented a different paper – 'A Child Psychiatry Case: Description of a Psychotherapeutic Interview'. Nevertheless, during 1969 and 1970, his final two years, it is clear from Davis that he had planned to publish this 1965 paper in a new collection perhaps after the publication of the two books Masud Khan was editing – *Playing and Reality* and *Therapeutic Consultations* (which were published later in 1971, a few months after he died). Not only was he busy with clinical, editorial and committee work, but it also seems clear that his final conceptual preoccupations had moved on from 'fear of breakdown' and 'the psychology of madness', as we shall see.

Winnicott's final conceptual preoccupations

It is my view that 'The use of an object', presented to the New York Institute in November 1968, constitutes the core of his conceptual developments and preoccupations towards the end of his life.[7] He believed that 'the recognition of the destructive element in the crude primitive excited idea' was resolved when he wrote 'The use of an object'. I have proposed that he was referring to the core concept in that paper, i.e. *survival-of-the-object*, offering his alternative formulation to Freud's concept of the death instinct (Abram 2013: 308). I have repeated this argument throughout many chapters in this book. However, while Winnicott himself felt he had resolved the problem, at the same time he was frustrated that his New York audience had not apparently understood him. This was demonstrated by the response of his three Discussants. Added to this there had been no time for a general discussion from the audience which is what he was really hoping for from his visit. Soon afterwards, while suffering ill health, he continued to try to formulate his points in a different language in his need to convey the meaning of his conceptual development. This meant he was obliged to address his disagreement with Freud's concept of the death instinct in a more direct way. Interestingly, in one of the papers of 1969 – 'The use of an object in the context of *Moses and Monotheism*' – he began to formulate a further new idea on the role of the father in early psychic development.[8] In Chapters 6 and 7 of this book I elaborate my perspective on Winnicott's work on the early father.

More evidence from the archives strongly indicates that just before his death, between December 1970 and January 1971,[9] Winnicott was preparing a paper for a panel presentation at the IPA Congress to be held in July in Vienna in 1971 – 'The psychoanalytical concept of aggression: theoretical, clinical and applied aspects'. His notes consist of 7 pages that outline a plan for the paper. The first two lines of the notes start: 'I am asking for a kind of revolution in our work. Let us re-examine what we do.'[10] I have previously suggested that these notes strongly suggest that his final preoccupations, just before his death, focused on dissociation, hate, male and female elements, the use of an object and regression (Abram 2012 in Abram 2013).

Judging from the Preface of *Psychoanalytic Explorations* it is apparent that Winnicott felt strongly about his theory of madness and wanted both these papers published. Despite his awareness of having 'stolen' from Freud and others, he was also sure about the originality of his particular approach to psychoanalysis.

Perhaps it will have to remain a mystery as to why Clare Winnicott's Editorial Note of 1974 was by-passed by the Editors of *Psychoanalytic Explorations*. It suggests to me that they did not concur that 'Fear of Breakdown' was written 'shortly before his death'.[11] And despite my investigations, as set out above, each reader will decide where the 'Fear of Breakdown' should be placed chronologically in Winnicott's writings. From my point of view, the evidence in the archives shows that 'Fear of Breakdown' was written in 1963 and 'The Psychology of Madness' in 1965. The wish to publish these findings here is to offer the researcher evidence from the Winnicott Archives that his final preoccupations before he died were on reinforcing his argument that the primary and original relationship took precedence over any notion of the innate factors shaping the psyche.

Notes

1 Personal communication Nina Farhi 1992.
2 This committee was officially re-named the Winnicott Trust just before Clare Winnicott died in 1984 (see Abram 2008).
3 In 1961 Winnicott wrote a 'note' on the time factor (Winnicott ([1961] 1996).
4 I think the handwriting is Clare Winnicott's.
5 In fact, the paper was never presented to the Davidson Clinic. Instead Winnicott gave three lectures at the beginning of August 1964 at The Davidson Clinic Summer School: 'The true and False Self; The Positive Aspect of Antisocial Behaviour with Illustrative Case; Special Talent Helping or Hindering Therapy' (*The Collected Works of DW Winnicott*, Volume 12).
6 Klein and her followers had largely rejected Winnicott's work. Anna Freud and her group were more receptive to some of his ideas, but the majority of her followers did not acknowledge his original contribution to psychoanalytic theory and technique.
7 In January 1968 Winnicott had written to the New York Psychoanalytic Institute offering to give this paper later that year. Might this suggest that he had given up on presenting any 'new brain-child' to his colleagues in London?

8 The development of his proposal in early 1969 of an 'integrate' – the father in mother's mind – is a significant innovative advance to his concept of primary maternal preoccupation. Moreover, this very late work offers further clinical implications as I have attempted to elaborate in Chapter 7 (Abram 2017).
9 Winnicott died on January 25 1971.
10 These words were handwritten by DW Winnicott and are re-produced on the front cover of the paperback version *Donald Winnicott Today* (2013).
11 In her 1987 paper Madeleine Davis refers to disagreements being resolved amicably (Davis 1987).

References

Abram, J. (2008) Donald Woods Winnicott: a brief introduction. *Int J Psychoanal* 89: 1189–1217.

Abram, J. (2012 in 2013) D.W.W's Notes for the Vienna Congress 1971: a consideration of Winnicott's theory of aggression and an interpretation of the clinical implications in Abram, 2013.

Abram, J. (2013) *Donald Winnicott Today*. New Library of Psychoanalysis, Routledge.

Abram, J. (2017) Interpreting and creating the object: a psychoanalytic response to Mannocci's work on 'The Annunciation' Bulletin BPaS.

Abram, J. (2019) On Personalization and the Indwelling Principle EPF Bulletin 73 Panel Presentation with Jasminka Suljagic and Rudi Vermote EPF Annual Conference Madrid, Spain.

Davis, M. (1987) The Writing of D.W. Winnicott. *Int R Psycho-Anal* 14: 491–502.

Ogden, T. (2014) Fear of Breakdown and the unlived life. *Int J Psychoanal* 95 (2): 205–223.

Winnicott, C. (1974) Editorial Note: in Winnicott, D.W. (1974). Fear of Breakdown. Int. R. Psycho-Anal., 1:103–107.

Winnicott, C. (1980) Fear of breakdown: A Clinical Example. *Int J Psychoanal* 61: 351–357.

Winnicott DW (1945) Primitive emotional development. *Int J Psychoanal* 26: 137–143.

Winnicott DW ([1965a] 1989) The psychology of madness in Winnicott, D.W. 1989.

Winnicott DW (1965b) Classification in *The Maturational Processes and the Facilitating Environment: Studies in the Theory of Emotional Development*. London: Hogarth.

Winnicott DW (1989) *Psychoanalytic Explorations*, ed. Clare Winnicott, Ray Shepherd, Madeleine Davis. Cambridge, MA: Harvard University Press.

Afterword

Psychic *survival-of-the-object* in the context of Covid-19 (2020)

The pandemic of 2020 brought the matter of survival to the forefront. Covid-19 is deadly. The fact that this particular virus is more dangerous for those over 65 made a particular impact on many patients in analysis with senior analysts. When analysts stopped working in the consulting room due to the lockdown and 'stay at home' policy the destructive fantasies of damaging the object were confirmed.

In 'The Use of an Object' Winnicott argues that in order to use an object, which he saw as the pinnacle of psychic achievement, the subject has first of all to experience that the object has survived the infant's benign aggression. In analysis the patient, whose original object has not survived, needs to have an opportunity to express maximum destructiveness. The analyst's psychic survival of maximum destructiveness, over time, as the chapters in this book attempt to show, will facilitate the necessary psychic move from object relating to object usage. This will potentially lead to the 'momentous step' that enables the subject to discern that the m/Other has a mind of her own. The corollary to this psychic change is a patient who appears to be in analysis, but does no more than a kind of self-analysis. At the deepest layer of the psyche, they carry a conviction that the object did not survive because of their immense destructive power. The persistence of this conviction makes psychic change impossible.

Afterword

Psychic *survival-of-the-object* contextualises the complexities of the analytic approach. The analyst needs to receive the patient's primal attacks and, essentially, has to retain a position of non-retaliation. This is absolutely key to psychic *survival-of-the-object*. De facto it is the infantile layers of the psyche that are associated with primary needs for the object, rather than the death instinct (Abram 2012). These layers of primitive aggressive needs may test the analyst to their limits of psychic endurance.

When in 1968 Winnicott says that 'these attacks may be very difficult for the analyst to stand…' he adds a footnote:

> When the analyst knows the patient carries a revolver, then, it seems to me, this work cannot be done.
> (Winnicott [1968] 1971: 92)

At first this footnote both intrigued me and made me laugh. On reflection, it was probably because it also made me feel anxious. Now, in the context of the Covid-19 pandemic, it has taken on a poignancy that highlights the deadly seriousness of Winnicott's insight. Let's think about the reality of a patient who is going through a particular phase of negativity in their analysis who one day arrives for their session carrying a revolver. Whether it is loaded or not is irrelevant. Suddenly, the symbolism of the analysing situation is changed irrevocably. How would it be possible for the analyst to remain analytically neutral in the face of an actual threat to their life?

In the context of the pandemic, which started in 2020 and will likely continue into 2021 and even 2022, the ordinary meeting between analyst and analysand has become literally dangerous. For the senior analyst especially, it is as if each patient carries a revolver. And the conscious awareness of this new reality in the consulting room will inevitably cause intense anxieties for both. But the analyst is in charge of the setting. To tell the patient that, from now on, the analysis would have to be conducted online was interpreted by each patient in a different way, depending on the vicissitudes of the transference at that time. It would be odd if the patient did not interpret the analyst's demand for a radical change of setting as having nothing to do with the analyst's fear of what the patient would do to them. The analyst's new rule, as they retreated from the consulting room, was like saying to each patient:

You are no longer allowed to enter my room and stay with me for the duration of the session because you are dangerous to me and could kill me. You make me afraid of spending time with you. I cannot tolerate this level of fear. Stay away until things are safe.

Simultaneously the analyst is saying:

But you can continue to come to the sessions electronically.

The phenomenon of nachträglichkeit is invoked for each patient who lies on the couch mobilising the infantile transference. At this earliest layer – not necessarily psychotic – the couch is the mother's lap or womb and within this layer a sense of helplessness and dependency becomes a normal phenomenon of what it means to be 'in analysis'. Unconscious memories of being fed are induced.

Therefore, to tell the patient that they must only be in contact electronically is equivalent to the mother of a newborn infant retreating from the infant who has become dangerous to her. Instead of holding the infant in her arms while she breastfeeds, she will offer to breastfeed online. Thus, the communication from analyst to patient at this deepest level is changed from one of potential *survival-of-the-object* to one of non survival of the object. The analyst not only withdraws; they tantalise the patient through offering what is impossible to offer, i.e. a remote breastfeed.

The following vignette offers an illustration between one older analyst and his younger patient.

Dr L is a senior analyst, over 65 years of age, and has been working with Mr A for several years in high-frequency analysis. After the winter break, a particular kind of negative transference with strong features of non survival associated with rage and envy had been a prominent feature in the analysis. Mr A felt stuck in his life; despite doing well in his professional and personal life during the years of the analysis he had now come to what he felt was a dead end. His grievance towards his analyst related to fantasies that Dr L was the successful one who had sailed through each stage of his development and was now at the top of his career. Mr A felt he could never achieve this level of success. This layer of the transference resonated with Mr A's version of his parents, who were successful in their careers while always seeming remote and disinterested in Mr A's development. In early adolescence, the patient had made a suicide attempt and after the overdose had phoned his mother who dropped everything and left work to take her son to hospital. Mr A felt he had been lucky to be saved. This fact in his psychic history, while an important layer in the transference, had not yet been worked through. This was one of the reasons Dr L had requested some consultations in order to examine his sense of a countertransference paralysis. Mr A consistently seemed to avoid this trauma in his early adolescent history.

In early March of 2020 the analysis moved online and Mr A, despite understanding the need for this, felt hurt and rejected. When a pending lockdown was announced in the city where he worked Dr L decided, suddenly overnight, to leave the city for his country house, where the danger of contamination was lower. This meant a further sudden change of the setting in the space of 10 days.

These changes of setting occurred several weeks before the usual spring break. The analysis continued online, but Mr A became more and more fragmented and his analyst grew concerned about self-destructive impulses emerging in the transference associated with the unexamined adolescent suicide attempt. The patient felt he was breaking down and he felt the sessions were essential for his mental health. After some further work Dr L decided that he would offer to continue the sessions during the planned two-week break. He felt it was incumbent on him to offer this during such extraordinary circumstances. He was aware that he had left Mr A in the city who was having to continue to work in high risk areas while Dr L had moved to a safe low risk area.

Mr A felt the special 'holiday sessions' to be invaluable. He was grateful to have the space to reflect on his deep anxieties and panic associated with the overwhelming negative transference. Towards the end of the two-week break a national public holiday was pending. Dr L found himself hoping that Mr A would wish to take the day off, but the patient told his analyst that he was counting on the session being available. Dr L agreed but was aware of feeling reluctant in a way he had not felt when he had offered to continue with the sessions during the usual break. At the same time, he felt he could not say no.

In that particular session, when the analyst reluctantly agreed to offer a session on the public holiday, he felt that his patient was like a very young child (around 18 months of age) who was intensely needy and frightened. He needed the object, but this neediness invoked hatred too. In turn, this made him feel terrified. Dr L felt it would be cruel to say no but was struggling with his own sense of hatred and resentment. In the same session Mr A talked in some detail about feeling fraudulent about a situation at work. Dr L wondered aloud whether he also felt fraudulent about expecting the session on the public holiday? The patient said he was starting to feel a bit guilty because he didn't really feel he needed the session as he had done at the beginning of the break. But he was finding it helpful and would like Dr L to be available at a time he was not usually available. The analyst said that perhaps that made him feel special in relation to his analytic siblings? Mr A was not sure, but remembered that he could never ask his mother for any special treatment. Even when he overdosed, he felt his mother had never recognised who he was and what he really needed, despite her taking him to the hospital and therefore saving his life. But when Dr L had offered the sessions during his break it had made a huge difference to his state of mind and he had felt, perhaps for the first time, that he was cared for and seen. He had been in an acute panic and had not been sure how he could continue without the sessions. The offer had made him feel he could really trust his analyst in a way he had not remembered feeling with either parent. Perhaps he also wanted to test his analyst? More discussion ensued about Mr A feeling it was a paradox: his analyst was with him even though he had left him.

Dr L was keen to reflect on this stage of the analysis with his consultant and Continuous Professional Development group asking himself what the Covid-19 situation was doing to his professional boundaries? In over two decades of analytic practice he had never offered to continue sessions with a patient during a break. He was aware of feeling guilty about leaving the city and, escaping as it were, to the countryside. At the same time, he had felt that the move had been essential in order to feel safe enough to continue to work with a sense of equilibrium. His rationale in offering sessions to Mr A during his break was related to the patient's experience of a narcissistically driven mother who craved admiration from all around her. Even in his adult life Mr A felt he was obliged to protect her. Saying 'no' to her demands threatens her. Perhaps the suicide attempt had been related to the rage and unconscious death wish towards his mother played out now towards Dr L in the transference at the point of him moving out of the city and on the point of taking a break.

Winnicott points out the significant distinction between needs and wishes. On further reflection, Dr L noticed how his sense of fear and anxiety was changing in relation to Mr A, who increasingly found a sense of stability over the subsequent weeks after the spring break despite the analysis being online.

When another public holiday was on the horizon Dr L felt he really needed to take this holiday and would tell his patient as usual. To his relief Mr A responded with a slight laugh, 'Okay – I'll give you a break'. Dr L felt irritated by this but, at the same time, saw it as a playful reversing of his analytic authority. Mr A would now be in control of who would leave who. However, there was also a sense of relief that a phase of the work, with its marked negativity and attack, had been endured and the patient also seemed to be conveying that the phase of non survival, at least for the moment, was over. Both analyst and patient could keep each other in mind. Mr A's intrapsychic surviving object had been reinforced as he was able to recover a sense of trust in the Other who could recognise and meet his needs. But the thorny problems related to analysis online were not resolved.

Discussion

There was no doubt that the announcement of the pandemic, quickly followed by lockdown in which large numbers of people were contracting the virus and becoming seriously ill and/or dying, made Dr L feel anxious and afraid for himself and his family. Every one of his patients was around half his age. In continuing to work online with Mr A during the break it could be argued that Dr L was able to show he could psychically survive because he was able to think and reflect in his new setting. But let us examine further the dyadic level of communication to the analysand.

I suggest that the government restrictions constitute the 'law of the father,' so that from the infantile layer in the adult it could feel that the early mother is saying to her infant:

> As long as we don't meet in the same room, I can continue to attend to your needs, and we'll make believe I am breastfeeding you satisfactorily. This is what father forces me to do.

This sets up a situation which, I propose, constitutes non survival of the object at the dyadic level. Despite this, Dr L's experience, which concurs with that of many colleagues, shows that working online proves that effective psychic work continues to take place and perhaps indicates that psychic *survival-of-the-object* functions at the third/

Oedipal level. On the affective level, the analyst demonstrates psychic survival through the ability to continue to think and reflect and to maintain a position of non-retaliation. It also makes a big difference if the online analysis has a substantial ordinary history of analytic work, as indeed it did for Dr L and Mr A. But the different layers of psychic realities always carry psychic resonances in the transferential après coup. The two choices open to analysts as long as the pandemic continues are either staying online or returning to the consulting room but staying two metres apart and preferably wearing a mask.

While both these choices demonstrate a good sense of social responsibility in the face of the reality of the Covid spread, at the same time, they are inevitably conveying a fear of contamination and damage. Once restrictions are lifted because it is then safe to work with the patient in the room then we will return to a normal situation in which, hopefully, there will be a chance to work through this serious rupture of all analytic treatments that is causing collective psychic trauma. But while Covid-19 continues to pose the global threat to life, despite the enormous progress of different vaccines, it means that for all analysts, especially senior analysts, whether working in or out of the consulting room, it is as if each patient in every session arrives to the session carrying a revolver. How possible is it, therefore, to continue the necessary psychic work at the infantile level? No mother can feed her baby online or with a mask two metres apart. Does this mean that the transition from object relating to the use of an object will be compromised at best or impeded at worst? Only time will tell but, at this moment in the pandemic, we cannot yet know. The best we can aim for, therefore, whether in the consulting room wearing a mask or working online, is: 'keeping alive, keeping well, and keeping awake' (Winnicott 1962: 166).

References

Abram, J. ([2012] 2013) D.W.W.'s Notes for the Vienna Congress 1971: a consideration of Winnicott's theory of aggression and an interpretation of its clinical implications in (2013) (ed) Abram J. *Donald Winnicott Today*. New Library of Psychoanalysis Routledge.

Winnicott DW (1962) The aims of psychoanalytical treatment in *Maturational Processes and the Facilitating Environment* (1965) Hogarth Press.

Winnicott DW (1971) The use of an object and relating through identifications in Winnicott DW (1971) *Playing and Reality* Tavistock Publications Ltd.

Abram Bibliography

Books

Abram, J. (1992) *Individual Psychotherapy Trainings: a guide*, London: FAB.
Abram, J. (1996) *The language of Winnicott: A dictionary of Winnicott's use of words*, 1st edn. London: Karnac.
Abram, J. (ed) (2000) *André Green at the Squiggle Foundation*, 1st edn. London & New York: Karnac Books.
Abram J. (2007a) *The language of Winnicott: A dictionary of Winnicott's use of words*, 2nd edn. London: Karnac.
Abram, J. (2013a) (ed) *Donald Winnicott Today*, New Library of Psychoanalysis London: Routledge.
Abram, J. (ed) (2016a) *André Green at the Squiggle Foundation*, 2nd edn. London: Karnac Books.
Abram, J. & Hinshelwood, R.D. (2018) *The Clinical Paradigms of Melanie Klein and Donald Winnicott: comparisons and dialogues*, London: Routledge.

Papers and reviews

Abram, J. (1994) Review of How to Survive as a Psychotherapist by Nina Coltart in Brit. J Psychother 11 (2): 31.
Abram, J. (1998) Squiggles, clowns and Catherine wheels: reflections on Winnicott's concept 'violation of the self' Natureza Humana.
Abram, J. (2003 [1996]) Squiggles, clowns and Catherine wheels: reflections on Winnicott's concept 'violation of the self'. *Le Coq Heron* 173: 2003.
Abram, J. (2005) L'objet qui survit Alcorn D, translator. *J psychanal de l'enfant* 36: 139–74. Paris: Bayard.
Abram, J. (2007b) *L'objet qui ne survit pas: Quelques reflexions sur les racines de la terreur*, Houzel D, translator. 39: 247–70. Paris: Bayard.
Abram, J. (2008) Donald Woods Winnicott: a brief introduction. *Int J Psychoanal* 89: 1189–1217.

Abram, J. (2010a) The Squiggle Game e publication.

Abram, J. (2010b) On desire and female sexuality: some tentative reflections EPF Bulletin 64.

Abram, J. (2011) *Foreword for Deprivation and Delinquency*, London: Routledge Classics.

Abram, J. (2012a) Review of Marion Milner's *On not being able to paint and The hands of the living god*. Int J Psychoanal 93: 1340–1347.

Abram, J. (2012b) André Green, une sorte de Winnicott francais: l'absence et le morceau de chocolat, *Revue Belge de Psychanalyse*, no. 60.

Abram, J. ([2012c] 2013) DWW's Notes for the Vienna Congress: a consideration of Winnicott's theory of aggression and an interpretation of the clinical implications In: 2013.

Abram, J. (2013b) On Winnicott's area of formlessness: the pure female element and the capacity to feel real E.P.F. Basel E.P.F. Bulletin 67.

Abram, J. (2013c) On Winnicott's clinical innovations in the analysis of adults. *Int J Psychoanal* (2012) 93: 1461–1473.

Abram, J. (2014a) De la communication et de la non-communication, recherche d'un objet qui survivra, *Revue Belge de Psychanalyse*, no. 64.

Abram, J. (2014b) Le mirroir inter-analytique: Son rôle dans la reconnaissance des traumas trans-générationnels désavoués (The inter-analytic mirror: its role in recognising disavowed trauma) Revue française de psychanalyse Mai 2014 Tome LXXVIII – 2 (pp. 405–416).

Abram, J. (2015a) André Green a la Fondation Squiggle: Jouer avec Winnicott Revue française de psychoanalyse Juillet 2015 Tome LXXIX – 3 (pp. 846–854).

Abram, J. (2015b) La Mere tentatrice. Réflexions concernant un aspect de la théorie de Winnicott sur le psyché-soma Revue française de psycho-somatique no. 47 (pp. 37–50).

Abram, J. (2015c) Further reflections on Winnicott's last major theoretical achievement: from 'Relating through identifications' to 'The use of an object' Chapter 7 (pp. 111–125) in *Playing and Reality Revisited: a new look at Winnicott's Classic Work* (eds. G. Saragnano and C. Seulin) London: I.P.A. Karnac Books.

Abram, J. (2015d) L'intégré paternel et son rôle dans la situation analytique. *Journal de la psychanalyse de l'enfant*, N° 2, Vol. 5/2015".

Abram, J. (2015e) Affects, mediation and countertransference: some reflections on the contributions of Marjorie Brierley (1893–1984) and their relevance to psychoanalysis today E.P.F. Stockholm E.P.F. Bulletin 69.

Abram, J. (2016b) Sur les innovations cliniques de Winnicott dans le domaine de l'analyse d'adultes Psychanalyse et Psychose 16 (Translation by Alexandre and Zoé Baruch).

Abram, J. (2016c) Creating an object: Commentary on 'The arms of the chimeras' by Béatrice Ithier. *Int J Psychoanal* 97: 489–501.

Abram, J. (2017) Interpreting and creating the object: a psychoanalytic response to Mannocci's work on 'The Annunciation' Bulletin BPaS.

Abram, J. (2018a) Angst vor der Verrücktheit Psyche 4/2018.

Abram, J. (2018b) On psychic conception Bulletin of the EPF 72. Panel presentation On primal repression and the origins of life with Jasminka Suljagic and Rudi Vermote EPF Annual Conference Warsaw, Poland.

Abram, J. (2018c) The inter-analytic mirror Bulletin of the EPF 72 Panel Presentation IPA Working Parties Panel.

Abram, J. (2019a) The surviving object in the context of thirdness and the dead mother complex Parts One and Two – Conference on A Thought and Its Master Istanbul, Turkey.

Abram, J. (2019b) On Personalization and the Indwelling Principle EPF Bulletin 73. Panel Presentation with Jasminka Suljagic and Rudi Vermote EPF Annual Conference Madrid, Spain.

Abram, J. (2019c) Notes on the role of the feminine chez Winnicott Panel Presentation with Kathleen Kelley-Lainé and Roland Havas The role of the feminine in the work of Ferenczi and Winnicott – IPA conference London The Feminine QE2 Event Centre 2019.

Abram, J. (2019d) The Frankenstein Complex: on birth terrors – Annual Conference European Psychoanalytic Conference for University Students, Brussels, Belgium.

Abram, J. (2020) Psychic *survival-of-the-object* in the context of Covid-19 – Conference given to the Swiss Psychoanalytic Society, Zurich; Tel Aviv University; UCL Conference.

Abram, J. On Winnicott's concept of trauma International Journal of Psychoanalysis 102:4 10.1080/00207578.2021.1932079

Abram, J. (2021) The paternal integrate and the 'other of the object': *a certain divergence between Winnicott and Green* (Book Launch of Giocando con Winnicott [Italian translation of André Green at the Squiggle Foundation] Rome, Italy (online February 13, 2021).

Abram, J. (2021) There's no such thing as the infantile I.P.A. Webinar on Holding and Containing with R.D. Hinshelwood.

Index

Page numbers in *italics* indicate figures.

absolute dependence 35
actualised projection 52
adolescence 44–46; and object's survival 125
adults, analysing 94–95; clinical language 95–97; early psychic processes 101–105; late-work clinical examples 106–108; psychoanalytical treatment 98–101; studying other clinical methods 97–98
alienation 59
analyst: function of 129; third in mind of 139–140
analytic paternal integrate 142–143
anger, lack of 43
angoisse blanche 62
'Anxiety Associated with Insecurity' (Winnicott) 13
archaïc phantasy object 140–141
Axiom 156–157

basic split 13–14, *14*
Bion, W.R. 62
birth 62
blank anxiety 53
Bollas, C. 73
Bonaparte, Marie 71
breakdown, fear of 79, 88, 105; axiom for 168
'breakdown, fear of' (Winnicott): archival findings 167–168; dating 164–167; final conceptual preoccupations 170–171; writing style 168–170
British Psychoanalytical Society 11

Campbell, D. 72, 139
Catherine wheel 11, 16, 22
clinical adolescent 125
clinical experience 77, 116, 148, 169
clinical infant 11, 19, 125
clinical vignettes 120
clowns 12
combined love-strife 41
'Communicating and Not Communicating Leading to a Study of Certain Opposites' (Winnicott) 14, 28
compliancy 120
'Concept of a Healthy Individual' 45
constructions, concept of 148
'Constructions in analysis' 105
co-thinking 108
COVID-19, and *survival-of-the-object* 173–179
creative apperception 117–118
cultural experience, location of 36, 156

Danckwardt, J. 87
dead mother complex 33, 53
death instinct 103, 122, 133
deficiency 118, 120, 128, 133, 137, 146, 154, 158, 160
deformation/psychosis 118–119
dependency, stages of 35
depressive position 45, 147–148, 152
depth, manifestation of 34
desire, word 43
destruction 44–46
destruction, object usage and 39
destructive drive 133

183

Index

desultory formlessness 112–113, 120–121, 123
disillusionment 43
Donald Winnicott Today 7, 34, 137, 165
dreams, symbolic value in 120
Dr Z, clinical case of 149–151

early psychic development 27, 34, 37, 102–103, 113, 115, 121, 137, 147, 153–154, 170
early psychic processes 101–105
economic problem of masochism 147
effective thirdness 135–138
ego-coverage 103–104, 127, 136
'Ego Distortion in Terms of True and False Self' (Winnicott) 14, 154
Elizabeth I, Queen 83
environmental-deficiency disease 118, 154
environmental minimum 101, 114
environment–individual set-up 12, 16, 95, 105, 116–117
essential paradox 101
external object 42, 44, 46, 69, 118, 141

Faimberg, Haydée 105
Faith, clinical case of 19–25
false self 19, 154, 157
father, role of 43; as integrate 126–127
female: element distillation 116–117; psychic *survival-of-the-object* 125–126; sexuality 71
fixation point 108
Fonagy, P. 72
formlessness 112–114; adolescence 125–126; in clinical setting 113; creative apperception 117–118; deformation/psychosis 118–119; distilled female element 116–117; identifying 112–114; paternal integrate 128–129; psychic *survival-of-the-object* 125–126; ruthless impulse 121–125; subjective objects 117–118; term 115; three-body relationship 125–126; unintegration 114–116; value in clinical setting 119–121
Frankenstein (Shelley) 59–60
free association 10, 28, 113, 119, 121

Goldman, Dodi 107
Green, André 12, 26, 33–34, 62, 96, 113–114, 126, 132, 134–135

healthy split 14
hilflosigkeit 33
Hinshelwood, R.D. 103
holding 140–141
human nature 34, 95, 103
Human Nature (Winnicott) 34, 118, 122

id-energy 142
immediate effect 106
impingement 54; revivification in analytic setting 105–106
incommunicado self 3, 12, 15, 19; question about 28–29
infants: development of 34; distilled female element 116–117; fear of WOMAN 87–92; formlessness 123; helplessness of 33–34; illusion of omnipotence 36; intrapsychic subjective surviving object 37–39; perceiving destruction 113; primary creativity 35–36; terror 61–62; transitional phenomena 36–37
inherited tendencies 36, 153
integrate, word 133
internal object, term 38
interpretation, mutative 140–141
interpsychic–intrapsychic dynamic 38
inter-related self *18*
intrapsychic subjective surviving object 37–39
intuition of the Negative in Playing and Reality, The (Green) 35
isolate core self 13, 17

Jill, clinical picture of 46–55

Klein, Melanie 34, 62, 71, 97, 102–103, 147, 152; Kleinian theory 12, 35–36, 45; mother 103; on word 'terror' 62
Kohon, G. 89

Lacan J. 34, 134, 136, 148, 157
Language of Winnicott, The 34
'les mots pour le dire' 72
libido 62
life instinct 36
Lisa, clinical picture of 78–87
love-strife drive 133

madness 145–148; in context of theoretical matrix 153–156; Dr Z case 149–151;

184

Index

negative therapeutic reaction 151–153, 159–160; psychology of 146, 152–156; refractory case 151–153
Magritte, René 2
males, and psychic *survival-of-the-object* 125–126
Mary Queen of Scots 83, 85
Me 2, 11, 18, 38, 42, 44, 125–126, 135, 139
Medusa 62
memory, cataloguing 155
'Metapsychological and clinical aspects of regression within the psychoanalytic set-up' (Winnicott) 156
Milner, Marion 11–12, 15–16, 19, 94–95, 114–115; questioning Winnicott 28–29
mother: distilled female element 116–117; suffering of 42
m/Other 4, 6, 34–36, 73, 80–81, 90–91, 98, 102, 106, 115, 119, 123–125, 145, 152, 155, 165, 173
mother–infant dyad 36
mutative interpretation 132, 140–143

nachträglichkeit 5, 7, 28, 105, 142, 145, 148, 155, 175; constructions 157–161
nameless dread 62
negative therapeutic reaction 145–148; 'refractory' case 151–153
New Yorker 11
New York Psychoanalytic Society 132
night terrors 62
non surviving object 59–60; adolescence 44–46; desire 43–44; destruction 44–46; intrapsychic 69–70; intrapsychic subjective surviving object 37–39; parent–infant relationship 35; pictorial representation of xxii; primary creativity 35–36; roots of terror 138–139; transitional phenomena 36–37
Not-me 2, 11, 18, 37–38, 40, 42, 44, 125

object: being found 40; destroying 40; destruction of 16–17, 36–37, 40, 43; other of 126–127, 134, 136; subject relating to 39; survival of 16–19; surviving destruction 40; use of 41–43, 136
obstacles 72, 135, 137
Oedipal phase 135
Oedipus Complex 45, 54, 104, 126, 136–137

Ogden, Thomas 42
omnipotence, illusion of 36, 107, 115, 118
ordinary devotion 112, 118
Other 1
over-intellectualisation 53

parent–infant relationship 3–4, 7, 35, 95, 97–98, 146, 148, 152, 156
paternal integrate 132–135, 137; analytics 142–143; in analytic setting 128–129; conclusions 141–142; holding 140–141; mutative interpretation 140–141; potential thirdness–effective thirdness transition 135–138; roots of terror 138–139
pathological withdrawal 15–16
patient K 59–60, 138
penis envy 106
Perelberg, R. 71
Playing and Reality (Winnicott) 35, 106, 113, 115–116, 119–121, 169
potential thirdness 135–138
primary creativity 35–36
primary dissociation 116
primary maternal preoccupation 15, 36, 38, 40, 42–43, 80, 104, 112, 115, 127, 134, 136, 140
primary narcissism 5, 94, 104, 106, 115, 119
primary signal anxieties 62
primitive agony 53–54, 62, 103, 119, 155, 158
'Primitive Emotional Development' (Winnicott) 43
projections, bundle of 121
projective actualisation 33, 54
psychoanalytic treatment 82, 94, 98–101, 152
'psychology of madness, The' (Winnicott) 153, 167; archival findings 167–168; dating 164–167; final conceptual preoccupations 170–171; writing style 168–170
'Psychoses and Child Care' (Winnicott) 13, 16, 153–154
psychotic anxiety 16

Reeves, Christopher 137
refractory case 147, 151, 153
relative dependence 11, 35
Riviere, Joan 79, 145–148, 151–153, 159
Robin, Christopher 11
Roussillon, R. 104

185

Index

Self 12–16, 115
Self-development, facilitating 121
self-preservation 102
Self-relating 117
self, violation of 10–12; babies 12–16; clinical example 19–25; discussion 25–28; object survival 16–19
Shelley, Mary 59
Shelley, Percy Bysshe 59
Snow White 55
Standard Edition of the Complete Psychological Works of Sigmund Freud 61
Strachey, James 33, 61, 97, 132, 140–143, 148, 152
Stuart, Mary 89
Studies on Hysteria (Freud) 62
subjective objects 117–118
subjective object, term 38
survival-of-the-object: COVID-19, 173–179; defining 1–2; psychic 26, 41, 80, 113–114, 121, 125–126, 128, 137, 161, 174
surviving object 33–35; history of 45; pictorial representation of, xxii; psychoanalytic theories 45
Symington, Neville 73

Target, M. 72
temporality 5, 156–158, 164, 169
terror: as affect 62–63; clinical picture 63–69; intrapsychic non surviving object 69–70; in psychoanalytic theory 61–63; sexuality 61–62; word 61
theoretical first feed 35–36, 45, 102
'Theory of the Parent–Infant Relationship' (Winnicott) 15, 97
thought, freedom of 108

three-body relationship 125–126
total set-up 12
towards independence 35
transference–countertransference dynamic 148
transference–interpretation matrix 108
transitional phenomena 36–37
trauma, revivification in analytic setting 105–106
traumatic repetition 52
Tudor, Elizabeth 89

Ukiyo-e 11, 17, 29, 128, 137
unintegration 15–16, 112, 114–115
'use of an object in the context of *Moses and Monotheism, The*' (Abram) 122
'Use of an Object, The' (Winnicott) 1, 118

Wegner, P. 87
'What Irks?' (Winnicott) 42
'Winnicott and the Two Way Journey' (Milner) 12
Winnicott, Donald: Axiom 156–157; on babies' existence 12–15; clinical innovations 94–108; clinical language of 95–97; cup of tea of 97–98; environmental impingement 13; essential paradox 101; having 'Freud in his bones' 104; late-work clinical examples 106–108; poetry of 10–11; theoretical matrix 34
Wollstonecraft, Mary 59
WOMAN, fear of 71, 77–79; developmental sequence 80; infantile sexuality 87–92; need-wish distinction 80–82; transference 87–92
'work of the negative' (Green) 35